THE ROAD TO

MW01075657

ABNER R. SMALL
AS ADJUTANT, 16TH MAINE VOLUNTEERS

THE ROAD TO
RICHMOND

★ The Civil War Memoirs of Major Abner R. Small
of the Sixteenth Maine Volunteers. Together with the
Diary which he kept when he was a Prisoner of War

WITH AN INTRODUCTION BY EARL J. HESS

FORDHAM UNIVERSITY PRESS
NEW YORK · 2000

© 1939 The Regents of the University of California
© Renewed 1965 by Harold A. Small
Produced by arrangement with the University of California Press
Introduction copyright © 2000 by Fordham University Press

All rights reserved. No part of this publication may be reproduced, stored in a retrieval system, or transmitted in any form or by any means—electronic, mechanical, photocopy, recording, or any other—except for brief quotations in printed reviews, without the prior permission of the publisher.

ISSN 1089-8719
The North's Civil War, No. 13

Library of Congress Cataloging-in-Publication Data

Small, Abner Ralph, 1836–1910.
    The road to Richmond : the Civil War memoirs of Major Abner R. Small of the Sixteenth Maine Volunteers : together with the diary that he kept when he was a prisoner of war / edited by Harold Adams Small ; with an introduction by Earl J. Hess.
        p.   cm. — (The North's Civil War ; no 13)
    Originally published: University of California Press, 1939.
    Includes bibliographical references and index.
    ISBN 0-8232-2013-3 (hc) — ISBN 0-8232-2014-1 (pbk.)
    1. Small, Abner Ralph, 1836–1910.   2. United States. Army. Maine Infantry Regiment, 16th (1861–1865)   3. Small, Abner Ralph, 1836–1910—Diaries.   4. Maine—History—Civil War, 1861–1865—Personal narratives.   5. United States—History—Civil War, 1861–1865—Personal narratives.   6. Maine—History—Civil War, 1861–1865—Regimental histories.   7. United States—History—Civil War, 1861–1865—Regimental histories.   8. Soldiers—Maine—Biography.   9. Prisoners of war—Virginia—Richmond—Diaries.   10. Libby Prison.   I. Small, Harold Adams, 1893–   II. Title.   III. Series.

E511.5 16th S63 2000
973.7'441—dc21   99-087261

Printed in the United States of America
00   01   02   03   04   5   4   3   2   1

TO THE MEMORY OF
MY FATHER

CONTENTS

PAGE

Illustrations ix

Introduction to the 2000 Edition xi

Editor's Preface xix

Beginnings 1

Bull Run and After. 18

Education of a Regiment 35

Fredericksburg 57

Chancellorsville. 80

Gettysburg 98

Service North and South 112

Shoot, Shovel, and March. 135

Libby, Salisbury, Danville 159

Conclusions. 180

Calendars 205

Notes 211

The Diary 249

Notes to The Diary. 297

Index 305

ILLUSTRATIONS

PAGE

ABNER R. SMALL AS ADJUTANT, 16TH MAINE
VOLUNTEERS . . . . *Frontispiece*

REFERENCE MAP . . . . *facing* 32

THE DUNKER CHURCH AT ANTIETAM *facing* 48

A FIELD HOSPITAL . . . . *facing* 120

LEAVING WINTER QUARTERS . . . . *facing* 128

PONTOON BRIDGE, JERICHO MILL . . . *facing* 144

IN THE TRENCHES AT FREDERICKSBURG . *facing* 152
(long erroneously identified as Petersburg)

INTRODUCTION TO THE 2000 EDITION

ABNER R. SMALL's memoir has always been one of my favorite accounts by a Civil War soldier. Born on May 1, 1836, at Gardiner, Maine, he grew up at Mount Vernon, near Augusta, with vivid memories of militia musters that helped impel him to join the Third Maine Infantry at the start of the war. Small was a noncommissioned officer in this regiment, which was led by Oliver Otis Howard, who later rose to command the Eleventh Corps and the Army of the Tennessee. Small was under fire for the first time at First Bull Run, but he did not stay in the Third, which was one of the early regiments that enlisted for three years. A desk assignment as clerk and recruiting officer took him behind the lines from December 1861 to May 1862. Small tried to raise a company for the Sixteenth Maine Infantry but failed to find enough enlistees willing to serve under him. Then he was appointed lieutenant and adjutant of the newly raised regiment.

The Sixteenth Maine saw little action for a long time after its organization. It garrisoned the fortifications of Washington, D.C., for a time and then was transferred to the First Corps of the Army of the Potomac during the Antietam Campaign, but it did not take part in that terrible battle. The regiment participated in its first combat at Fredericksburg on December 13, 1862, when it supported an attack by George G. Meade's division and held a section of the Confederate position on Robert E. Lee's right wing. The penetration was limited and temporary; soon the Maine unit had to retreat. Small was temporarily detached to the brigade staff during the fighting and went back to his regiment after it ended. Five months later, his comrades moved onto the Chancellorsville battlefield on the evening of May 2, but they did not take part in the fierce fighting that decided the battle the next day.

After Chancellorsville, reorganization brought Gabriel R. Paul to command of Small's brigade. The Sixteenth Maine had its greatest day on July 1, 1863, the first day at Gettysburg. Positioned on the extreme right of the First Corps's line, along Mummasburg Road, the regiment fought a magnificent delaying action against overwhelming odds as the Confederates flanked the Union line and drove it in on itself. The regiment fought its way to the left but was trapped by converging Confederate columns from the north and west. Most members of the Sixteenth who were still alive surrendered in the field. They tore their flag into strips to keep it from falling into Confederate hands. Out of about two hundred men who entered the battle that day, only about thirty enlisted men, four line officers, and Adjutant Small escaped the converging enemy columns. The rest of Paul's brigade had escaped earlier and was intact.

Small was once again detailed to the brigade staff on July 2, but the pitiful remnants of the Sixteenth Maine did not take a significant part in the rest of the battle. The brigade rushed to the far Union left that day but missed the action. It also rushed to the center on July 3 to meet Pickett's attack, once again arriving too late to participate. Its bravery and its heavy losses on July 1 had been enough for one campaign.

The Sixteenth Maine participated in the Mine Run Campaign and entered the Fifth Corps when the First Corps was dismantled and its remaining units parceled out to other corps. It was not heavily engaged at the Wilderness but conducted a strong attack at Spotsylvania on May 8, 1864, which took the Granite State men into the abatis fronting the Confederate fortifications, but no farther. A later attack at Spotsylvania also resulted in heavy casualties but no tactical gain. The brigade supported the massive assault by the Second Corps on the Mule Shoe Salient on May 12 but did not take a direct part in it. The

Maine soldiers played a similar role in the North Anna Campaign and at Cold Harbor.

All of this campaigning led to exhaustion, the slow, steady draining of manpower, and a growing sense of frustration among Ulysses S. Grant's men. The Petersburg Campaign seemed to epitomize the frustrated hopes of 1864. Abner Small was captured by Confederates in one of Grant's drives at Petersburg, the Fourth Offensive, in late August of 1864. He was taken on August 18 at the beginning of the Fifth Corps's attempt to effect a lodgment on the Weldon Railroad, one of Lee's most important supply lines from the south. From then until nearly the end of the war, Small had to endure the boredom, disease, and cruelty of imprisonment. He was held at Libby Prison in Richmond for more than a month, then was shipped by train to Salisbury, North Carolina, one of the South's worst prison pens. Fortunately, his stay here was short, for the authorities got wind of a plot by the officers to seize control of the camp and shipped them off to Danville, Virginia.

Conditions there were tolerable until Small was exchanged in February 1865. He found on his return to the Sixteenth Maine that he had been promoted to major during his imprisonment. Assuming command of the regiment on April 29, twenty days after Lee's surrender at Appomattox, Small led it in the Grand Review through the streets of Washington, D.C., on May 23. Col. Charles W. Tilden returned to duty and oversaw the regiment's muster out on June 5.

Small did not let the war or Confederate imprisonment ruin his personal life. He married Julia Maria Fairbanks on April 8, 1865, after his release from prison and before going back into the field to take command of his regiment. He was a businessman after the war and remained very active in veterans' affairs. Small died at Oakland, Maine, on March 12, 1910, at age seventy-three.

Small was known to his comrades as an educated, wise man

with a quiet, even sardonic, manner about him. Respected during and after the war, he nevertheless was reticent. This memoir, published after his death, presents an interesting and valuable insight into his character and into the life of the Union soldier of the Civil War. Small observed everything around him and stored up vivid memories. His description of recruiting the Sixteenth Maine is insightful as to the bureaucratic workings of the manpower mobilization system, including the competition between aspiring officers to nab as many recruits as possible at one another's expense. As well, Small engagingly documents the life of the regiment as it wandered about during the last half of 1862 and always seemed to miss the important battles.

But Small shines at his best when remembering combat. His description of First Bull Run is almost eerie, and his account of Fredericksburg is gripping. Remembering the first day at Gettysburg, Small wrote: "I remember the still trees in the heat, and the bullets whistling over us, and the stone wall bristling with muskets, and the line of our men, sweating and grimy, firing and loading and firing again, and here a man suddenly lying still, and there another rising all bloody and cursing and starting for the surgeon. Lieutenant Deering picked up a musket and fired without first removing the rammer, and the rammer went hurtling away with a crazy whizz that set the boys of his company to laughing. It was strange to hear laughter there, with dead men by."

As this excerpt demonstrates, there is an immediacy and economy of style in Small's writing. His description of helping the Confederate wounded following the repulse of Pickett's Charge on the third day is moving and poignant. Although his battle descriptions tend to pale a bit when dealing with the Overland and the Petersburg Campaigns, Small hit his stride once again when recounting his prison experiences. He vividly recalled the living conditions, the attitudes of his fellow inmates, the difficulty of finding enough food to eat, and the hopelessness that could easily creep up on prisoners. His descriptions of conditions at Salisbury are particularly noteworthy.

Abner Small devoted much of his time and energy to recording the story of his comrades. He authored a history of the regiment that was based on memoirs written by his veteran colleagues and his own newspaper articles. Small also maintained a collection of personal papers, equipment returns, pension papers, and other military records, which are now part of the Abner Small Papers at the Maine Historical Society. He became, in effect, a historian as well as a veteran of the war.

Why the former major of the Sixteenth Maine decided not to publish his memoirs remains a mystery. Perhaps it was because the book was a mixture of fond memories and bitter reflection. Small was unique among Union veterans. While the vast majority of them chose either to assert a positive, even ideologically charged, memory of their war experience, or to ignore the negative aspects of it, Small and a tiny group of like-minded veterans openly voiced their doubts about whether the war experience had had positive effects on their lives. He was too reflective and honest with his feelings to blandly tout a patriotic line that he could no longer hold with automatic surety. Something in his war experience, and it likely was what he saw of the Southern prison system, changed Small a little bit. He did not leave the conflict a bitter man, nor did he discontinue to believe in the government or the cause for which he had fought. But he no longer believed in the romanticized view of war as a glorious history pageant come to life for present generations. "Of course, we laughed at the romance and grumbled at the reality," he wrote of his comrades. Yet Small and his fellow soldiers could not allow their realization of war's dark side to overrule the primary cause for which they had joined the army. The common soldier often found battle disgusting. "He resented it all," Small observed, "and at times his resentment grew into a hatred for those who forced the whirlpool of war—a whirlpool that had so soon engulfed him. He hated his sur-roundings and all that war implied; it was drudgery, it was cruelty; yet he forced himself to resist whatever was inimical to the interests of a hated service. If he had at times any longing to lay down his arms, he carefully concealed it."

Small reserved observations like these for the end of his book, marked "Conclusions." These twenty-four pages of text consti-tute one of the few direct examinations of the nature and worth of war written by a Civil War veteran one will ever find. Few other Northerners spoke so pointedly and thoughtfully about an issue that has haunted each generation ever since the First World War. Small never came to a satisfying conclusion in his own mind about the topic. Speaking again of the generic soldier, Small wrote: "Always in front of him was the enemy, a some-thing which, the more he thought of it, the more he hated; and as likely as not he never quite knew why. He might try to determine the sense of his antagonism that arrayed him in oppo-sition to men like himself. His restlessness would occasionally develop. Then his face would grow into a smile as though carved, as he refilled his cartridge box and his pipe, and rebur-nished his gun. He might have the courage of his convictions, yet behind his bravery there lay something that mystified and repelled him. He didn't know what it was, so inevitably he went to find out. I don't know that he ever got an answer. I didn't."

Comments like this make Small's book unique; no wonder it was a vitally important source when I essayed to write about combat morale in *The Union Soldier in Battle: Enduring the Or-deal of Combat* (Lawrence: University Press of Kansas, 1997). Small's brutal honesty speaks perhaps more readily to modern audiences than to his fellow soldiers, and perhaps that explains why he chose to keep his memoirs private during his lifetime.

In fact, this wonderful book may never have been published but for the efforts of Small's son, Harold A. Small, who was an editor at the University of California Press. The young Small organized the memoirs, carefully edited them, and decided to add his father's prison diary. The entries are curt but still interesting and sardonic. With the addition of a calendar for the Civil War years, a unique find in any book, the memoirs seemed complete.

But, in a sense, they are not. One finishes Small's book wanting to know more about his life after the war. His obscurity befits his character, for Abner Small would not have courted notoriety or fame. He left a gift for his son to edit and for students of the war to cherish. Anyone interested in the campaigns that the Sixteenth Maine participated in, anyone who wants to know more about the life of a typical regiment, anyone who has a need to understand the psychology of the soldier will benefit from a careful reading of Small's carefully crafted sentences. His book reveals more about the inner life of the soldier than the vast majority of other published accounts written by Union veterans, and it is fitting that Small's view of the war will remain in print for some time more to come.

EARL J. HESS
Lincoln Memorial University
Harrogate, Tennessee

EDITOR'S PREFACE

THE PAST *was lived by individuals. If we would know what it was like to live through an experience that is now historic, we shall come nearest to finding out if we read the record set down by a man who did live through it. If he writes well, so much the more enjoyment for us. Even if he writes badly, something will shine through, and we shall see for a moment what he saw and in the sunlight of his day. A novelist may do better? Yes, if he can; but how many Stendhals are there who can put us on the battlefield with young Fabrizio? Nature is not so prodigal of genius as to provide a master hand for each of the world's wars.*

Memoirs of the Civil War are plentiful, and of all degrees of merit. Why have another, good or bad, at this late date? Because if we read only the latest Civil War novel or the latest Civil War history, we may lose as much as we gain. It is true that as time creates a perspective through which we look back upon the past, we are better able to discern the relations of things and to judge men and motives more justly; but the gain in coolness of judgment is likely to be accompanied by a fatal loss in warmth of fellow feeling. The historian, unhappily, may be the first to suffer, and on his pages heroes will stiffen into statues, tides of anger and pride and fierce animosity will congeal as "trends," and pretty soon it will all be reduced to a "complex of forces," and the war—the shots and yells, the blood, the pain, the exultation and despair—will have become a "study." The novelist may suffer equally: however skillful he may be in managing everything else, he will probably fail to give his characters the passions and prejudices of their time; their emotions will be his own.

As the years carry us farther and farther from the Civil War, the more we lose in actual nearness to what was once as near as a trigger to the finger. The only way for us to reach back to it, now, is through a book; and the surest way is through the record set down by a man who was there.

The present memoirist was in the Army of the Potomac. He was in several of that army's great battles, and it is an advantage to his narrative that he was on a part of the field not familiar to us from other accounts: at Fredericksburg, he was in the one successful charge made upon the Confederate position; at Chancellorsville, he made a daring reconnaissance that now helps to fill the gap in the record of what happened on the Union right; at Gettysburg, he was with the regiment that was sacrificed to cover the last withdrawal of troops from Seminary Ridge—a regiment which has never had its full share of honors, because the commanders who would normally have reported the facts were killed or disabled.

Near the latter end of the war he was for six months a prisoner. His prison diary is the actual day-to-day record of what he saw and did and thought, and of what sums of money in debased Confederate currency the members of his mess spent for what articles of food. It shows two things, at least, that ought to be noted by any hardy new commentator on an old controversy: one, that food was available to him who had the money, and the other, that the prisoners were as much galled by the selfishness of many among their own number as by the shortness of the prison rations and the hardness of the prison floors.

When, twenty years after the war, Major Small wrote the official history of the 16th Maine, he referred to himself very little, and then usually in the third person. This was not only right and proper; it was also characteristic of the man. He feared the loquacity of the old soldier. He rarely spoke of the war, unless to remark that it had given him bad dreams, and the only occasions when he "fought it over again" were when he entertained old comrades. They urged him to write about his experiences, and in his last years he did so, composing—upon a basis of sketches that he had used, years earlier, in writing the regimental history, and others that he had sent, earlier still, to newspapers—chapters that might some day be arranged in one continuous narrative. The arrangement as made by me does no violence to his facts and opinions. The voice that speaks from the page is his.

The illustrations depicting Civil War scenes are from photographs taken at the time. Two of these, which show, respectively, a corner of the Antietam battlefield and the pontoon bridge over which the 5th Corps crossed at Jericho Mill, illustrate actual passages in Major Small's narrative. The others, of wounded in a field hospital, wagons rolling out of camp, and veteran soldiers ready to move, are typical of certain aspects of life in the Army of the Potomac; what troops or localities are represented in them, I do not know, nor does it matter.

For assistance in verifying names and other particulars, and for supplying information which I have used in the Notes, I wish to acknowledge my indebtedness to Lieutenant-Colonel Donald B. Sanger, Signal Corps, U.S. Army, Lieutenant-Colonel J. M. Scammell, N.G.U.S., Dr. Douglas S. Freeman, of Richmond, Virginia, Professor Herbert C. Libby, of Colby College, Waterville, Maine, Mr. H. G. Butler, of Berkeley, California, and the librarians and staffs of the Maine State Library and the Library of the University of California.

Two years ago, I had the pleasure of editing a Civil War journal by a Confederate—Joseph LeConte's account of his adventures in the backwash of Sherman's march through Georgia and the Carolinas. It seemed to me that the record set down by a man as alert, intelligent, and self-possessed as was Professor LeConte would be a valuable contribution to our knowledge of what it was like to live through such an experience as his, and to our mental picture of the collapsing Confederacy. It now seems to me that in presenting my father's memoirs I am in a manner evening up the score: here is a Northern book to put beside that Southern one. We may learn from both, if we will.

HAROLD A. SMALL

Editor of the University of California Press

THE ROAD TO RICHMOND

BEGINNINGS

The war resumes, again to my sense your shapes,
And again the advance of the armies.
—WALT WHITMAN, *Leaves of Grass,*
Songs of Parting, "Ashes of Soldiers"

MY FIRST recollection of war is of the 'forties, when my father took me to a militia muster. That was not war? Mars on a holiday in the country, whooping and spitting powder and rum, was enough for a small boy.

Readfield Corner was the rendezvous; the rum kegs in the corner grocery there were exhaustless. Fresh sand was strewn in the store, that morning. Boots crunching in the sand, the clink of glasses, the hearty voices—do I hear them yet? Or sniff again the warm and spicy air? Or see my father turn with dignity and grace to acknowledge a greeting?

"Abner, your health, sir! You bring a recruity?"

"This is my son, sir; perhaps a soldier, some day."

We went outside, and passed the cider vendors crying their wares from hemlock booths, and walked down a crowded lane to the muster field. Against a board fence by the field a Vienna farmer backed his cart, to deal out strong apple-juice at two cents a glass. Two boys from Mount Vernon found an auger, tapped the barrel through the fence, and offered cider at one cent a glass. Their first customers had the impudence to go outside the fence and accuse the old farmer of selling drinks above the market price. In five minutes not a boy was to be seen anywhere within half a mile.

All eyes, I watched the militiamen coming to the field. Some had music, and I beat time to their drums and puckered my lips to whistle like a fife. I looked up at my father and discovered that the show amused him, though he controlled his smile. The dress and equipments of the heroes were anything but uniform; here we would see martial glory from head·to foot, and there an old cocked hat and a bare sword. Now and then a musket was shot off resoundingly. Horses tethered to fences round about smelled powder and snorted, flourishing their tails. Dogs trotted under foot, and their yelping mingled harmoniously with the sounds of confused preparation for a sham Indian fight.

There was to be a barbecue after the fight, and already the odor of roasting ox was in the air. It made me hungry. I had eight cents in clean money in my trousers pocket. The jingle reminded me that I could buy gingerbread. In a moment, I was all stomach; I lost interest in militia and artificial Indians and the promise of seeing the governor in his stovepipe hat. The gingerbread vendor came, and I was happy. I bought three sheets, and tucked one under each arm and the other into my mouth as far as I could, and sauntered down among the white warriors. The red warriors were in the woods beyond, painting their faces to suit their fancy and swigging firewater from the corner store.

Anything might happen now, and I should enjoy it; but the general had not yet come, and without him there could be no battle. An important little somebody from Gardiner, with a hat too large for him, and a sword too long, was making frantic efforts to separate officers from men,—persisting, apparently, in the hope of finding privates enough to form a line for the reception of the commander-in-chief. There was no guidance in dress or adornment; a preponderance of hat and ancient lace was not a reliable indication of rank. The laciest figure on the scene was a mere captain from Mount Vernon, gorgeous in a red flannel coat with yellow facings and brass buttons, gilt braid swarming on his sleeves and down the seams of his pantaloons, big spurs projecting murderously from his heels, and on his head a Bona-partist hat with an astonishing eruption of red and white feath-ers. He was a tired farmer when at home; here, he surpassed my gaudiest imaginings of Marshal Murat. In his fiery steed cov-ered with trappings, no one would have recognized the old grey mare which yesterday was hauling manure with the captain for driver. Animals as well as men developed unthought-of qualities on parade.

Wild whooping shook from the trees and sent chills down my back. I was glad that some of the militiamen had actually fought Indians. A few of the older boys crept to the edge of the woods and threw green apples among the wigwams. This brought forth an Indian fearsome in war paint; he had only had time to decorate half his face; the painted half looked like the devil, the other half like old Shaver of Readfield. The venturesome boys came running back to camp, yelling: "Injuns! They're goin' to scalp us!" I almost hoped to see it done; but just then someone shouted: "The gineral's comin'! Make way for the gineral! Fall in!" There was a mad rush for a sight of the hero. One sheet of my gingerbread was trampled in the mud. General Batchelder rode through the crowd with a show of genuine authority. He got his troops into position, more or less; but, in spite of discipline and the earnest endeavors of the captains and file closers, first the right of the army, then the left, and finally the entire rear rank melted away and formed a sort of skirmish line from the roasting ox to the corner grocery, and called for drinks. Not all this faction returned.

Then suddenly the whizz of an arrow gave warning of the grand event. There was a terrifying succession of whoops and yells; the entire tribe of Indians made a wild charge on the ranks of white heroes; arrows flew, muskets banged, and the four-pounder opened fire with a boom that sent skittish horses to the rear and civilians to the cover of walls and fences. The general rode courageously in front of the cannon and was unhorsed with his face full of powder. The dead and wounded were seen crawling rapidly towards the roasting ox, and discipline was at an end. Captains bawled and waved their swords, but the ranks broke and fled in a wild race for the barbecue, where fallen heroes were carving the choice cuts and devouring them with relish.

Colonels, privates, and Indians crowded into a hand-to-hand and hand-to-mouth struggle. Blood flowed from the ox and ran down the faces of the masticators.

In a pursy old sachem in red petticoat and moccasins I recognized a neighbor. He was on his dignity and ignored the little fellow that ran errands for him in private life. The captain in the red flannel coat was likewise puffed up with consequence. He drove me off with his sword. I retaliated by calling him "Bonaparte" and "Corporal." The second title clung to him, and he never forgave me.

Thenceforth I cherished an antipathy to the title of corporal, notwithstanding the honor conferred upon it by the little Corsican. When I was grown in years, and of a mind to fight for the Union, and Captain Hesseltine offered me a corporal's warrant, I at first spurned the offer. It seemed an affront. I told a comrade, Frank Haskell, that I had decided to refuse the honor.

"Smalley," he said, "don't be a fool. Take it, and creep up!"

I took it, and in course of time crept up.

II

WHEN the rebels fired on Fort Sumter, their shells traveled remarkable distances; one flew north and exploded under me. I landed in the ranks of the 3d Maine. Two companies for this regiment, G and H, were recruited at Waterville, a city of lovely elms, a college, and a good deal of profitable industry and patriotism; and there, the first possible day, I joined Company G. Henry Fairbanks and I went from the West Village together, and signed the papers in the office of Joshua Nye. Our minds were made up; we needed no persuading; and I am sure it was the same with our comrades from the little town: George Benson left his anvil, Jim Ricker his plow, Frank Pullen his school books, Will Wyman his paint pot hanging to the ladder.

One morning, in obedience to orders, we formed in line on Elm Street in front of the Hanscom Block; and after prelimi-

naries of "Eyes—right!" and "Mark time!" our captain shouted,
"Right—face! Forwa-a-a-a-rd—march!" The long file ahead of
me rose and fell, bobbing like a string of corks in rough water.
Between six-foot Bill Copp, away up at the right of the line,
and away down at the tail end myself, barely five feet four and
a half, there was a ridiculous contrast. The pace changed to quick
time, and the long legs of Corporal Copp took longer strides;
quick time at the head of the file became double quick at the
rear, and a run for me. When the tallest man on the right entered Hathaway's hedge gateway, the eighth corporal was far
down the street, pawing air, his pride and consequence painfully disturbed. He heard a bystander inquire "what that little
fellow was," and he burned to shout a hot reply, but he could
only mutter curses and hurry on.

We were making, by invitation, a raid on the products of
a shirt factory. Manufacturers were patriotic, and some, with
eyes to future government contracts, were fairly generous with
timely gifts. A shirtmaker of Waterville, governed perhaps by
the higher motive, gave a woolen shirt to each member of the
two companies.

Corporal Copp and others were standing in Hathaway's
doorway, arrayed in picturesque grey, when the eighth corporal,
sweating and swearing, entered the gate. Chadwick was there,
too, and how he had got there so early, when he was hardly
taller than I, was a mystery. I learned later that he had straggled
and cut across lots.

Frank Haskell and I went in together. Somehow we were
not noticed until Company G was formed in line again, when
we were conspicuous by our lack of grey shirts. As Hathaway
looked at us, presumably considering whether it would pay to
open another dozen and fit us, Captain Hesseltine, in the tone
of command that was still new to him, desired to know of me
the duties of a corporal. "To keep up behind and take what's
left," I replied; and the truth was made manifest on the instant,

as Hathaway handed over to Frank and me the only two shirts that had failed to fit other members of the company. There was no man big enough to fill them out.

Frank and I were fantastic in those shirts. We didn't wonder that our comrades laughed at us, while the town dudes quizzed us, and the college boys all smiled their peculiar smile. Sergeant Lowe, who never lost a chance to remind me of my subordinate position and inches, advised me to "have my best girl take a tuck in the flaps." I hated him for saying that; but otherwise I didn't much mind. Hathaway's grey shirts, except in size, were uniform. We thought we were beginning to be soldiers.

We were as green as the new grass under foot and the leafy elms arching overhead. So were our officers. Their pretenses of assurance didn't deceive us; we knew that privately they bound wet towels around their heads and absorbed their military knowledge from books. Captain Hesseltine, especially, was a studious young man; if I remember rightly, he had not yet completed his course in Waterville College. He was earnest and capable, and soon won our respect; never our affection. Our first lieutenant, Nat Hanscom, looked wiser than a faculty and forbade any challenge of his wisdom; he was touchy and reserved, like a singed cat. Our second lieutenant, Will Hatch, was a favorite with us. He was friendly, though firm in discipline; conscientious in doing his duty, but contemptuous of fuss and show. All three did their best with us; yet we made ridiculous mistakes, and we laughed in spite of the scowling and scolding of our first superiors. We all smiled complacently to think how easily we were gaining glory. Boarding at the Continental House, going home every third day, and sitting up Sunday nights with our sweethearts and talking about war, was fun.

One day in May, the two companies were ordered to march on the West Village. The distance was hardly more than five miles, and the road ran through a pleasant woodland with occasional farms; yet the way seemed very long. Our dandies learned that tight boots and college slippers were not for campaigning; vanity and ease were punished. We marched grandly through the village, and felt equal to anything; but just as we got to the foot of the lake a thunderstorm burst suddenly upon us, and we bolted for cover in Deacon Hitchins' barn. We chaffed and sang. Lieutenant Day, of Company H, piped "The Sword of Bunker Hill," and we heard the high, shrill notes above the most outrageous thunder. The storm rumbled away, and we moved to the woodsheds of the railroad, where the ladies of the West Village set out a picnic for us. They showered bouquets upon us. They flattered us with titles of rank, none below that of captain; we were all captains then, except the eighth corporal, whose importance was less obvious than his shirt.

Another day, we marched to "escort and protect" the 2d Maine a little of its way from Bangor to the front; the railroad bridge over the Kennebec at Kendall's Mills, above Waterville, had been damaged by fire, and the 2d was obliged to march over the County bridge to trains on the west side. We were proud of the regiment we honored; it was smartly uniformed and fully armed and equipped. I envied those stalwart fellows as they marched by. I noticed how proud and handsome the officers were, two lieutenants in particular. If I had been told then that we three were to become the officers highest in command of a regiment not yet existing, and that we should be comrades-in-arms and lifelong friends, I should not have dared believe my fortune. If they saw the little corporal at all, I doubt they counted him among the possibilities of the future. I was far from robust. Indeed, I was in precarious health, and extremely sensitive to the assurances of my comrades that I should never reach the front.

III

Soon the Waterville companies went to Augusta, and I was there, a few miles nearer to the front, and creeping up. I was now fourth corporal of Company G, though my warrant, dated

May 20th, merely proclaimed that I was a corporal and absolved me from all errors committed prior to that date by sealing my rank and title as from the day of my enlistment; yet I seemed no nearer to martial glory, and certainly I was no farther away from Sergeant Lowe, whose musket would accidentally persist in scraping my knuckles every time we performed a right wheel.

The entire regiment was now in camp on the State Grounds, a sort of park, green with trees and rough grass. I remember the scent of lilacs there at dusk. Below us ran the silvery Kennebec River, and above us rose the old State House, its cupola burnished by the morning sun. We had new white tents. We were clothed in new grey uniforms, and equipped and armed; our guns were Springfield smooth-bore, muzzle-loading muskets, fitted with the common bayonet. We were drilled under the direction of Sergeant Edwin Burt, of Augusta, who had served in the regular army; or, if he hadn't, we certainly were under the impression that he had. He was assisted by a fellow townsman, Frank Pierce, who had attended a military academy.

My lot was cast among a mess of sixteen quartered in a Sibley tent, a large cloth cone surmounted by a cape that was raised up for air. By night we slept on our backs, our legs pointing to the pole in the center, and by day, when we were not drilling or chatting with numerous visitors, we squatted on the tent floor and formulated precise opinions of our military superiors. Officers were not gods to us; they were studied most critically and their capacities were closely measured.

We were organized for active service as a regiment May 28th. The mode of organization required the selection of the field officers by the captains and subalterns; and the colonel, lieutenant-colonel, and major were elected accordingly. Some of us lesser fry were certain that we could have named better choices.

Our colonel, Oliver O. Howard, of Leeds, was a graduate of the United States Military Academy, and pious. His first command had been the Kennebec Arsenal, across the river from where we were now in camp. He had served as an ordnance officer on garrison duty in Florida, where he had got converted, and since then had been a mathematics instructor at West Point. Resigning his commission of first lieutenant in the regular establishment, he came hurriedly from the Point to his regimental command, arriving in Augusta May 29th, the day after his formal election to the colonelcy.

I remember him distinctly as we first had sight of him the next day, when Governor Washburn, who had just received him in the State House, brought him over to us. Blaine came with them. The governor, a most energetic man, was short of stature, and in order to make himself seen and heard he mounted an up-ended half-hogshead. He started to speak. We interrupted him with cheers. He said a few flattering words about our new colonel, and then called Howard up beside him. We saw a pale young man, taller than the governor, and slender, with earnest eyes, a high forehead, and a profusion of flowing moustache and beard. Howard talked down to us ("My men—") with the tone and manner of an itinerant preacher. He told us all about himself and his little family and the Ten Commandments.

Our lieutenant-colonel was Isaac Tucker, of Gardiner. Before Howard was elected, Tucker was first choice for colonel. He was easygoing; everyone called him "Uncle"; and it was supposed that he would give the boys a good time with a minimum of discipline. He never got the chance. Our major, Henry Staples, of Augusta, was more favored in our regard; he was a handsome man and possessed of a remarkably winning address; but I shall speak of him later, for he, and not Tucker, was to be our colonel after Howard.

We knew nothing of our future, of course. At that time, we all thought we were going to Fort McHenry at Baltimore; perhaps no farther. There might not be a war, after all. But if there was to be one, I was solemnly prepared for it. Late in May I went down to Gardiner to see my grandfather, General Plumer, who was very old and ill and near death, and his last words to me were: "Be a man and distinguish yourself." I felt sad at leaving him, and full of determination to do my whole duty.

Tuesday, June 4th, we were mustered into the national service by Captain Thomas Hight, of the 2d United States Dragoons. The ceremony half turned into a funeral. Our colors were lowered and there was read to us an order from the governor honoring the memory of Stephen A. Douglas, who had died the day before.

Early the next morning we broke camp. This was not so simple as it sounds; Colonel Howard's order for breaking camp was intricate and showy. I seem to recall that the formalities were abbreviated, or we should not have got away that day.

Trains awaited us near the river, one for our baggage and horses, and one for officers and men. A crowd gathered and pressed down to the tracks. At camp little family groups drew aside with their soldiers for the last good-byes. There was a warning blast of whistles, a shouting of commands. We marched down to the cars. The band of the regiment began to play. The cars moved. There was a last waving of handkerchiefs and flags, a confusion in my blurring eyes. We rounded the southward curve, and were gone.

Everywhere in the first part of our journey, friendly folk turned out to cheer us. At Brunswick the faculty and students of Bowdoin College swelled the welcoming crowd; there were Bowdoin boys among our officers and in the ranks. At Portland a greater throng greeted us, and pretty girls came offering us flowers and good things to eat; but we couldn't stop to enjoy this hospitality. We went on to Boston. A smartly drilled and uniformed company (I don't recall what soldiery they were) escorted us through jostling streets to Boston Common, where Governor Andrew came out from the State House and gave us welcome. We had a plentiful supper at long tables under the trees. Then we marched to another station and took trains to

Fall River, where we went aboard a steamer, the *Bay State,* which carried us down Long Island Sound to New York. I rode in style; Chaplain Church kindly shared his stateroom with me.

The second day of our journey was stormy; we went ashore at New York in a downpour of rain. A committee of an association called the Sons of Maine met us at the pier and guided our march up Broadway to the White Street Arsenal, where a handsome national color was presented to us. Colonel Howard, making a pious speech of acceptance, fell off the limber that he was using for a pulpit, and almost swore. After the speechmaking, the rank and file of the regiment ate at the arsenal, the officers at the Astor House. Then we marched to a pier and went by steamer to South Amboy, and again took trains. We stopped at Camden and were ferried across the Delaware to Philadelphia, and there we had a welcome late supper at the Cooper Shop.

The third day, on our preparing to pass through Baltimore, where we should have to march from one railroad station to another, we were reminded to keep handy the ten rounds of ball cartridges that had been issued to each man. When we arrived and filed out of the cars, a curious and menacing crowd watched us form in line and obey a loudly voiced order to load our muskets. Baltimore was hostile. We knew how the 6th Massachusetts had been assaulted there. We were ready for trouble, expected it, almost hoped for it; but our march in the rebellious city was uneventful. We steamed on to Washington without adventure, and arrived in the evening of Friday, June 7th.

We were not received with glad acclaim. It could hardly be said that we were received at all. Our quartermaster, guided by an officer from General Mansfield, led us to a bowling-alley and contiguous saloons and said that we were to sleep there. After the hospitalities of unmenaced Northern cities, this seemed inadequate; but there was nothing we could do about it except grumble. We rolled up our coats for pillows and went to sleep on the hard floors.

Colonel Howard surprised us, the next morning, by taking us to Willard's Hotel for breakfast. That made us feel better. Then, after some delay, we marched out Pennsylvania Avenue to Fourteenth Street and out Fourteenth Street about two miles to Meridian Hill. It was stifling hot and sultry, and many of our men, as yet unaccustomed to carrying weight, dropped out for rest. As we neared the hill, we marched into a terrific thunderstorm. Howard, in his great religious narrative of himself and the war, recounts an incident in this wise:

"About the time the rain set in one poor fellow left the ranks and undertook to get over a fence; he pulled his loaded musket after him with the muzzle towards him. As the hammer struck a rail or stone an explosion followed, inflicting upon him a desperate, disabling wound..."

My vivid recollection of the incident does not agree with the Howard version. A soldier near me, while securing arms, accidentally shot off his musket into the legs of the man next ahead. Colonel Howard then ordered all guns to be discharged into the air, and an indiscriminate firing followed, some of the balls flying into the tents of the 2d Maine on the hill. He omits to mention this.

Apparently, Colonel Howard had forgotten that the muskets were loaded. The charges ought to have been drawn, or the guns ought to have been shot off properly in the open without endangering anything or anyone. It was providential that no one had been shot the night before, when each man had put his gun somewhere before lying down to sleep. The men in the bowling-alley, where I was, had stood their guns against the walls, or laid them down in the conduits, or piled them in the corners.

In spite of the fusillade, the 2d Maine boys took us in, dried our clothes, and gave us a warm supper. Next day, the weather cleared; we set up our tents and made our beds of straw. Again we thought we were beginning to be soldiers. We were in camp, and drill and discipline became our only portion.

We began to be conscious of the immensity of icy space between the officers and the rank and file. Friendly neighbors in
civilian life, one spreading manure and the other cleaning fish,
were now immeasurably apart. The fourth corporal of Company
G was deep down in the glacial crevasse. He was occasionally
corporal of the guard. This tended to increase his chest measure
and conceit, but it failed to raise his perpendicular and official
consequence above the lowest notch in the ice.

Creeping up seemed almost improbable.

IV

As soon as I had a chance, I obtained a pass from Colonel
Howard and went down to see the sights. I found that Washington was not really a city. The vast and showy public buildings were surrounded by mere scattered huddles of dingy brick
houses and small shops. I saw few sightly homes. The White
House attracted me; but that was a home, or ought to be treated
like one, I thought, and I spared myself the impudent pleasure
of intruding upon the President. I headed for the Capitol and
walked easterly along Pennsylvania Avenue, a tedious thorough-
fare lined with barrooms and other places of business and half-
heartedly furbished with dusty green trees in whitewashed
palings. The saloons were driving a roaring trade, and the sidewalks were noisy with promenading soldiers. The crowd thinned
away near Capitol Hill; I went up almost alone to explore the
huge edifice. The size of the building and its promise of mag-
nificence impressed me, though it was not completed; where the
dome was to rise, there was scaffolding and ropes and cranes, and
the ground beyond the east front was tumbled with cut stone.

From camp we could see the Capitol, and the stump of the
Washington Monument, and beyond that the Long Bridge over
the Potomac, and perhaps we could discern, away down the
other side of the river, the steeples of Alexandria. Somewhere
beyond that farther shore were the rebels in arms. Their pickets

had been on the heights across the water, in sight from Washington, hardly two weeks before we had come to the city. Union
troops were there now.

While we were encamped on Meridian Hill, we were developed into parade soldiery of the regulation pattern by a lieutenant, fresh from West Point, who appeared to take an exquisitely
painful pleasure in the development. In his eyes we were a different species of vertebrate from that evolved at the Academy;
an inferior species, not capable of standing fully erect; a species
grown all awry and possessing neither comeliness nor sense. It
didn't seem to occur to him that his laced figure, his crammed
education, and all his other military attributes were the product
and property of the government, which lent him for our use.
He put us through our paces with a competence only equaled
by his contempt for us. He might easily have won our esteem;
but, as it was, we soon cared less for him than for the indifferent
bread and bacon that were dealt out to us as rations.

We were in this camp of instruction almost a month, and
improved much in soldierly appearance. July 3d we gave up the
grey regimentals that we had worn from home, and received
new uniforms: loose blue flannel blouses, looser light-blue pantaloons, and baggy forage caps; not a fit in the lot. July 4th we
heard bells ringing, cannon booming, and other sounds of rev-
elry in the city, but few of us joined in the celebration; Colonel
Howard was no longer generous with passes.

Saturday, July 6th, we rose early and broke camp, and after
some delay we marched, with our colors flying and our band
playing, down from the hill and through the city to a dock, and
aboard a steamer that carried us down the river to Alexandria.
As we marched through Alexandria we noticed how gloomy
the town was, many of its dingy brick homes and shops deserted. The sentiment there was for the rebels. With arms at
the carry we tramped past a bearded and scowling officer, who
took our measure with a sharp eye; this was Colonel Heintzel-

man, of the regulars, who was about to command a division of the volunteer army. We went a mile or more beyond the town and made camp on the farther side of Shooter's Hill. Above us, on the hill, was Fort Ellsworth. Beyond us, the farm fields that scattered away into patches and forests of pine and scrub oak were in the country of the rebels. We were at the front, if the raw troops and raw scars of new earthworks on the sacred soil of Virginia might be said to constitute a front. We began to feel more important.

Colonel Howard felt more important, and showed it, because he was made a brigade commander. The day after we crossed to Alexandria, he was directed to select three regiments to be brigaded with ours and to fetch them over. He brought to the Virginia side of the river, on succeeding days, the 4th Maine, the 5th Maine, and the 2d Vermont; and these regiments and ours, together, became the 3d Brigade of Heintzelman's division of McDowell's army. Colonel Howard now heading a brigade, and Lieutenant-Colonel Tucker being absent on detached duty, the command of the 3d Maine was taken over temporarily by Major Staples. He felt more important, I suppose. As for me, I was now a sergeant. My warrant, dated June 27th, secured me in my new rank as from June 4th.

We stayed only a few days at Shooter's Hill. Friday, July 12th, we moved farther out; Colonel Howard established brigade headquarters at Bush Hill, on the farm of a Mrs. Scott, about four miles west from Alexandria and just south of the Orange & Alexandria Railroad, and his four regiments encamped near by and posted their picket lines beyond. We guarded the left front of the Union line. We endangered rebel garden truck and fowls; and why not, when our rations weren't always fit to eat?

"About this time," says Howard, "there was much camp criticism of McDowell. . . . The accusers said that he had too much tenderness towards the enemy's property. . . . This conduct did not, however, proceed, as charged, from Southern sympathy.

McDowell and his associates wished to prevent the demoralization of the soldiers, for to take property *ad libitum* would soon overturn all order and leave no basis for rightdoing."

He exhibits as a "specimen of the prevailing restriction" a brief communication which he received from division headquarters. This was a note advising him that the bearer, one R. F. Roberts, a farmer, was complaining that soldiers of the 4th and 5th Maine had stolen some potatoes. "The general commanding wishes you to investigate the matter and put a stop at once to all such proceedings. If the men can be identified, punish them severely." The general commanding seems not to have been disturbed about the possible "demoralization" of the foragers.

Can Howard have been unaware that the "prevailing restriction" was intended chiefly to prevent wanton destruction of valuable property? Within the territory occupied by his brigade there was committed a deplorable act of vandalism which he does not mention. The sacking of Commodore French Forrest's home, Clermont, was inexcusable. Costly mirrors in the parlor walls were cracked and smashed; bookcase doors were wrenched from their hinges, and fine volumes were tumbled out under foot; curios, collected from foreign lands, were thrown helter-skelter; cupids with broken wings, busts with broken heads, and tables with crushed and splintered marble tops and broken legs, were strewn crazily on the floors. As an orderly reporting to Colonel Howard, I saw all this and more.

From the yard, near the front door, I picked up a folded sheet of paper covered with handwriting; my eyes caught the name of John Brown. It was the end of a letter, completed on December 2d, 1859, the day the abolitionist was hanged. The commodore had written to his son:

"Your mother is extremely alarmed about the execution of Brown today. She apprehends difficulty, and all I can say to compose her nerves is ineffectual; she conjures up every violent course of the abolitionists, and is preparing to spend a day or two with your Uncle Charley at the Navy Yard, where she thinks there is safety. I shall remain at home. My presence here is all-important. I am busily engaged getting out my corn, and making ready for a good crop of grain the coming year; my wheat is up and looks promising....

"December 2d. This is the day of the execution of that outlaw and miscreant, John Brown. It would have been much more to the credit of Virginia if all these fanatics of Harper's Ferry notoriety had been tried one day and hanged the next. The excitement which now prevails would then have been avoided, and while justice was meted out to them, the laws would have been vindicated and a terror would have fallen upon all his friends and sympathizers."

Doubtless, old Commodore Forrest was of the same opinion still. He had left the service of the United States for that of Virginia, and at the time I picked up the letter he had become a captain in the rebel navy and was in command at the Norfolk Navy Yard. He was an enemy of ours; but that did not excuse the damaging of his home. The place to inflict damage upon our enemies was the battlefield; and near Manassas, twenty miles to the west of us, the rebel General Beauregard and his army were preparing, as we were, for a fight.

We knew from the massing of opposed armies that a crisis was near; yet our situation appeared, just then, more like a celebration. Flags were flying, bands playing; there was a great deal of stir and jingle and parade. Once, I stood near the carriage of General Scott, the antiquated general-in-chief of the national forces. He was a grim old giant, gorgeously appareled, surrounded by a glittering staff, and apparently equal to the mild occasion. It was plain that this infirm old man, riding on a softly cushioned carriage seat, couldn't be in the fighting; yet the mere living presence of the ancient hero seemed to foretoken victory. We all knew Scott from history. We only knew of McDowell that he commanded us, under Scott.

BULL RUN AND AFTER

No more words; try it with your swords!
Try it with the arms of your bravest and your best!
—FRANKLIN LUSHINGTON, "No More Words!"

POLITICS and popular emotion forced our first battle. We were not ready for it except in good intentions; we were not an army except in name; yet we were started hopefully against the enemy. Our brigade left camp at Bush Hill on Tuesday, July 16th.

We made our way westwards along the old Fairfax road, south of the railroad, and managed to progress about eight or nine miles. It was a worn and lazy land that we passed through, roughly forested and scattered sparsely with tired farms. The sun was blazing, the dust rose and hung about us in smothering clouds, and the deceptive woods gave us no shade. There was a good deal of straggling. Late in the day there were halts, and we discovered the chief cause of them when we got to Accotink Run. Men of the brigade ahead of ours were crossing in single file on a log. They had stopped to take off their shoes in order to walk the log more securely, but in spite of that advantage some lost their balance and fell with a splash into the shallow water; amusing, but slow going. Colonel Howard gave orders for us to close up and ford the stream. This saved us an hour or so in getting on, and already it was evening. We bivouacked after nightfall near Pohick Run.

Wednesday morning we marched only three or four miles to the vicinity of Elzey's farm, and in the afternoon we moved about three miles farther and bivouacked on a hillside near Sangster's Station. The outposts of the enemy were falling back westerly, abandoning a few scattered breastworks and some soldiers of their picket lines. Hardly a musket shot was fired; but our commanders were fearful of masked batteries, and proceeded as timidly as old maids eating shad in the dark.

General McDowell had imposed the warning that it would "not be pardonable in any commander to come upon a battery or breastwork without a knowledge of its position." He had given orders for "advance guards with vedettes well in front and flankers and vigilance," to guard against any possible surprise. Long before this, newspaper correspondents had written columns of balderdash that had filled the army with fears of masked batteries. I doubt there was a soldier in our regiment who hadn't already written home tall tales of concealed rifle-pits, mined roads and bridges, and masked batteries, which had no existence except in the ink pots of the penny-a-line journalists. All the advancing columns were now searching for hidden perils and finding none.

Our division spent a day in hunting for nothing. It was not until late Thursday afternoon that we crossed the railroad and went on, perhaps four miles, into the old Braddock road and the vicinity of Centreville. We looked for a town; but Centreville was half a dozen houses at a crossroads.

Our stomachs were our chief concern through the next two days, while we stayed near Centreville. Rations for three days had been issued to us before we had left camp, but these had been eaten up, or thrown away because the haversacks were burdensome, and we were hungry; we hadn't seen the supply trains, and began to doubt their existence; and because we were green soldiers we didn't yet know how to forage expertly for ourselves. Friday we managed to raid some farms, and then the supply trains came, and Saturday we got enough to eat.

Before dawn of Sunday, July 21st, we were roused out of our sleep and made ready for a march to battle. We gulped down a hasty breakfast of hardtack and coffee, and were under arms and in line by half-past two; and then we had to wait until six o'clock before we could move a step. The divisions ahead of ours were very slow in making their way over a single road, the Warrenton turnpike, in the direction of Bull Run. The leading brigade was encumbered with a cannon that weighed three tons, a monster as spectacular and burdensome as a mock dragon at the head of a Chinese parade. Perhaps it was intended to frighten away the evil spirit of masked batteries. It threatened to stop our advance. Haltingly behind it Tyler's division moved away, then Hunter's, then Heintzelman's. Our brigade brought up the rear.

Soon after sunrise, and while we were waiting to move, the first sound of battle broke the quiet of the Bull Run countryside. Away on the turnpike the dragon gun had settled on its haunches and roared. There was no reply from the enemy. We had hardly begun to move when it roared again, a little farther away. Again there was no reply.

We marched through Centreville and down a slope, and went inching westwards along the turnpike through open country under a hot sun. The columns ahead of us crowded the pike; we halted and closed up, halted and closed up. About a mile beyond the hamlet we crossed a rickety wooden bridge over a small stream in a ravine, and a little way beyond that we turned to the right into a narrow track that led into a patch of woods. General McDowell was there, giving orders. He was a big, muscular man, with a look of solid strength about him, but his chunky face was half tired, half worried. Presently, he rode away by the forest track, where the other brigades of our division were moving off slowly among the trees. Our brigade was left behind in reserve.

We stayed in that woods road four mortal hours, longer hours than I had ever known. The battle was begun within our hearing but beyond our sight. It was stifling hot; not a breath of air was stirring. Our flags hung limp. I think it was while we were waiting in this place that we knelt and repeated the Lord's Prayer. The long suspense fretted us. Our nerves jumped.

Shortly after noon a mounted officer came dashing out of the woods and drew rein where Colonel Howard was fidgeting. There was a sudden stir, a shouting of orders, and we started up the forest track. We marched through the woods and came to an open flat, where Lieutenant Burt met us and told our commander that we were to hurry. We went on at the double quick, but a mile of this was all that we could do; the heat and the fretting of our long wait had weakened us; men dropped, exhausted and fainting, by the wayside. Another mile, and another, we hurried on at quick time; this meant double quick at the rear, and we lost other stragglers. Men still on their feet and pressing forward threw away their blankets, their haversacks, their coats, even their canteens. When we got to Bull Run at Sudley's Ford, many stopped to drink; scooped up muddy water in their hands, their hats, their shoes; drank too much; were lost to service for that day. Not half the brigade, nor half the regiment, crossed the run.

Beyond the stream, we went up through a scattering of trees and came out into cleared lands. We passed an improvised hospital near Sudley Church. I can see today, as I saw then, the dead and hurt men lying limp on the ground. Up the road from ahead of us came ambulances filled with wounded. Farther away there were rattles of musketry and the quick and heavy thuddings of artillery. Puffs of white smoke and straggling clouds of dust rose wavering into the still air. There was the battle, and we were coming to it late; it must have been near three o'clock, by then.

We hurried on, down the road and off obliquely to our right through the fields. When at last we neared the scene of battle, broken regiments and scattering stragglers were drifting back. We pushed on across the Warrenton turnpike, splashed through the muddy shallows of Young's Branch, and turned to our left in a ravine; and there, under cover of the trees and bushes that screened its farther slope, we caught our breath and wondered for the last time, confusedly, what it was going to be like to face fire. The brigade was now formed in two lines, the 4th Maine and 2d Vermont regiments ahead, the 5th and 3d Maine behind. Up through the trees Colonel Howard led the forward line, out of our sight; and we that were left waiting had a last anxious quarter-hour. We felt that our numbers were very few, and we wanted company.

Where were the brigades that we had come to support? We didn't know that they had been flung, regiment by regiment, up the slope, in vain efforts to support or bring off the guns of two batteries. Those guns had been lost and recovered and lost again, and back and forth over the field where they stood unlimbered, the gunners lying dead around them, the battle had been hardest fought. Colonel Howard, going up with his first line, met an officer "with his face all covered with blood, on a horse that had been shot through the nose." This was the only officer surviving, not disabled, of one of the lost batteries. He was bringing off a caisson, and this was to give rise to a rumor, afterwards, that our brigade was sent up in support of a battery that was leaving the field.

Some cavalrymen, pelting for the rear, broke the ranks of the 5th Maine, and carried away some of the wreckage in their blundering flight. From off to the right a rebel battery opened fire, and the survivors of the unhappy 5th suffered more damage and disorder, a ball striking their flank.

Colonel Howard came back for his second line, and up we scrambled. The next thing we knew, we were in the field on the hill and facing the enemy. I can only recall that we stood there and blazed away. There was a wild uproar of shouting and firing. The faces near me were inhuman. From somewhere across the field a battery pounded us; in the hot, still air the smoke of the cannon clung to the ground before it lifted; and through the smoke, straight ahead of us, flashed and crackled the rebel musketry. We didn't see our foes; they were obscured in smoke and trees. We felt that our lines were needlessly exposed, and weak without cannon to return blow for blow. David Bates, one of my close comrades, was smashed by a solid shot; and what reply could we make to that? We wavered, and rallied, and fired blindly; and men fell writhing, and others melted from sight; and we saw the glitter of bayonets coming against our flank; and we heard the order to retire. It was the turn of the tide.

II

THE spent waves drew back by the way they had come up; from the hill and the hollow below it, disordered soldiery streamed across the fields. There was no stopping the ebb. Not far from where the battle was begun in the morning, General McDowell made desperate efforts to form a new line, a battalion of regulars moved up, and a battery made ready to fire; but these attempts at encouraging a rally were unavailing.

What was left of our brigade fell back at first together, in some disorder but in no great hurry. We were so tired that we couldn't have left the field as fast as we had come to it. Men near me were plodding heavily and panting. Their faces were all sweat and grime, their eyes red from dust, their lips black with the powder of cartridges bitten off in the fight. They were dirty and weary and angry. So was I. We made our way off the field as we would, without order or discipline.

I don't know where we went back across Bull Run. It was not by the ford that we had crossed before. It must have been nearer to the stone bridge, where the Warrenton turnpike led straight back to Centreville, for it was on the pike that the panic started when a rebel battery fired on a mass of stragglers there, and I remember that as we took to the woods we heard an uproar on the highway.

We lost our organization in the woods, and some of us nearly lost our heads. Every now and then some man would take his gun by the barrel and mash the stock against a tree. I caught the notion of spoiling my musket, too, and discarding it, but just then Baxter Crowell, a musician of Company H, came to my side and said: "Keep going. Give me your gun for a rest." He insisted on carrying it till we got to Centreville.

All the way to Centreville, on the turnpike, were strewn guns and equipments, overturned supply-wagons, abandoned ambulances, and wounded men. Stragglers filled the road, and mingled with the soldiers were spectators of the battle; all sheep.

I picked up an elegant and elaborately mounted haversack. It was locked, but I had no hesitancy about forcing it open, for I was desperately hungry. I found in it, besides food, a treasury of toilet articles adorned with gold and silver. It must have belonged to an officer of rank and wealth. The presence of a big bologna sausage and a jar of sauerkraut indicated that its former possessor was a German. Surely, no Yankee would have thrown away the flask of Bourbon that I found at the bottom. I didn't admire bologna, and I had no use for the whiskey at the moment; I satisfied myself with plenty that better suited my hunger.

I don't know what became of that haversack. I had it when we got to Centreville. Colonel Howard was there, and the brigade gathered, except the dead and missing, and we moved on as dusk was falling. I took my prize along, though I had no notion of what I should do with it.

We lay on our arms, that night, at Fairfax Court House. I felt happy that I was alive, and that I had my precious gun safe under me; I remember feeling for it as I went to sleep. In the morning it was gone, and so was the haversack. I grieved at the loss and felt humiliated as I took my place in line at roll-call, though as a soldier without a gun I was not an exception; no, not by many. It disgusted and hurt me to think that there was a man in the regiment so mean that he would save his reputation at the expense of a comrade. I noticed that Sergeant Lowe had a musket with a stock like a blazed tree. A knife had cut away the initials of my name, which I had put there just before starting for the battle. I claimed the gun, but I couldn't prove that it was mine; I was laughed at and abused.

We marched wearily towards our old camp. As we neared Bush Hill, a drizzling rain began to fall, and we were glad to find that cars had been sent out to take us into Alexandria. A great number of stragglers, fagged out, hungry, and footsore, were pouring on into Washington; but some regiments, even some brigades, had hung pretty well together, and these, ours among them, were stopped on the Virginia side of the river. We spent that rainy night in empty houses in the rebel town.

I never was in a gloomier place than that was, the next morning. Everything seemed at odd ends. Yet somewhere there must have been a steadying hand in affairs, for our brigade was ordered back at once to camp near Bush Hill and set to guarding the approaches to Alexandria. Our regiment moved out that day. So did the 4th Maine, I think; the others two or three days later. The 5th Maine had lost or discarded so many of its tents, blankets, and other necessaries, that it was unable to camp until fitted out again. We all suffered from shortage of supplies. In discomfort of body and mind we guarded empty roads; no enemy came.

Soon we learned that General Scott had sent for General McClellan, who had won some little victories in western Virginia, and that McClellan was now in command of all the Union forces in and near Washington. McDowell was continued for a while in nominal command of the troops on the Virginia side of the river, but we saw little of him and less of his army. Almost all his troops were three-months volunteers, and already they were being disbanded as their terms of service expired. Regiments to serve for three years came rapidly to replace them. The regiments of our brigade had been mustered for three-years service; we stayed at the front.

Colonel Howard, reporting our part in the Bull Run battle, recorded a brigade loss of fifty killed, more than a hundred wounded, and a large and uncertain number missing. Few of the killed were of my regiment; yet, turning that over in my mind, I couldn't decide that numbers affected the first shock of seeing death in battle. One man or a thousand, the dead were dead.

Our losses would have been much heavier if the enemy had been able and ready to fall upon the retreating army of McDowell, but there had been no pursuit worth mentioning. Neither was any attempt made against Washington. Only the outposts of the enemy came near, throwing up breastworks on Munson's Hill, and Mason's, and flaunting the rebel flag within view from Washington.

Along the heights of the Virginia shore, and all around Washington, the Union forces began to build a strong system of fortifications. Within that rising circle of defense General McClellan began to create his Army of the Potomac. We couldn't see our future as he saw it; we held on rather miserably, lacking confidence in many of our officers and refusing to take for granted the proficiency of more distant superiors. We had been led to defeat, not victory, and our lack of success rankled.

III

"ALL was quiet along the Potomac." Was it? I heard a grumbling that was loud and continuous and sometimes ominous. Colonel Howard was conspicuous in his efforts to restore order and spirit in his command, yet with others less energetic and determined he suffered in the prevailing unpopularity of our commanders.

Our hospital was about the only regimental institution that was not a target for complaints. Under the able direction of Surgeon Palmer and the ministrations of Mrs. Sampson, the nurse, it was probably as good as any other hospital among the troops; it was better, certainly, than some others that I visited. Both before and after the Bull Run battle, it was at Clermont. I spent much of my spare time there, and I think I grew old then at the sight of suffering.

The first man we lost by disease was George Blaisdell, of Company I. Diphtheria made short work of him; he died July 28th. Frank Pullen, of my company, was stricken also, and only the most devoted nursing saved him. Having a personal interest in him, I did all I could to encourage him to cling to life. At the height of the disease, and when it was supposed that he was dying, I sat on his cot and for hours held his head raised in my arms. The surgeon came and suggested that Frank was dead. I was just going to lay him down when he sprang forward, seized a basin of water from the foot of the cot, and dashed it over his face. His throat cleared with a sudden violent discharge; and from that moment he rallied. He was a genial fellow. All his comrades liked him, and rejoiced at his deliverance.

Our hospital was far preferable to the hospitals in Alexandria, where some of our boys were taken, never to return. I visited one of these places, and in the attic, or whatever you would call a room close under a hospital roof, I found Jim Ricker, of my company. He was under the supposed care of a German woman, a slatternly old hag, who was unable to speak or comprehend a single word of English. By all appearances she was unfit to care for either sick or well. My pleadings with the surgeon in charge for permission to send in a nurse, or to give my help in any way, or to have anything done that money would pay for, were unheeded by the arrogant Jack-in-office; and my comrade died. It did not seem a soldier's death.

When soldiers died in hospitals at that time, it was possible to have the bodies embalmed and sent home. We desired these services for the body of Jim Ricker, but no one of us, nor a score of us together, had money enough to meet the cost, which had to be paid totally in advance. Frank Pullen and I applied to several officers and found them all short of cash. Finally we went to Captain Hesseltine; he gave us his gold watch to pawn, trusting us to repay the loan, and we raised the money. Red tape was more difficult to manage. I think it was three days that the casket lay unsheltered on one of Alexandria's straggling wharves before we could obtain transportation of the body to Maine. Meanwhile, a telegram had been sent to the father of our dead comrade, telling him how Jim was returning, and several times, as I learned afterwards, the grieving man went with a hearse to the home railway-station for the body of his son, and went empty away.

"All was quiet along the Potomac." We were drawn in from our outlying position and set to work on fortifications, our numbers being divided so that on six days of the week we took turns at digging and drilling, and on the seventh all rested. One Sunday, at early dawn, Companies G and H were called into line and told that they were to make an excursion to Mount Vernon, once the plantation of George Washington. I was delighted, thinking how I should take it all in and write home a description of the place where the "Father of His Country" had lived.

Mount Vernon was only a few miles distant from us, down the riverside from Alexandria. Like other estates in that part of Virginia, it was possibly endangered by the near presence of armies, but there was, I think, an understanding that it should be treated as neutral ground and left undisturbed. General Scott, who revered the memory of Washington, issued an order saying: "Should the operations of the war take the United States troops in that direction, the general-in-chief does not doubt that each and every man will approach with due reverence and leave uninjured not only the tombs, but also the house, the grove, and walks which were so loved by the best and greatest of men." We didn't doubt that the enemy shared these sentiments. Nevertheless, we were cautioned to keep our visiting column closed up and to guard against any possible surprise.

Preceded by a line of skirmishers and protected by others on our flanks, we make a quick and vigilant march. We had to be quick, both going and returning, in order to be back in camp by "Taps," if not earlier. On our way down we halted only once, at a crossroads in the woods, to make sure of our way and to discover masked batteries if any should be there.

The Mount Vernon mansion was easily recognized; many of us had seen it pictured in woodcuts. For the moment satisfied to find the exterior as represented, I left the interior to explore last. I went down to the rotting wharf on the Potomac, and all over the unkempt grounds, to the gloomy tombs, and through the empty stables; but when I sought to enter the house I was barred out by an armed guard, who said that only commissioned officers were permitted to enter. I turned away in disgust, though not before catching sight of the key to the Bastille, hung over a door in the hall.

Why should I have been denied Mount Vernon's interior? It was no Holy of Holies. A man with shoulder straps was no better entitled than any other citizen of the United States to enter the home of a common father. Captain Hesseltine's exact description of the rooms where Washington received his guests had no interest for me. I have never since thought of Mount Vernon except to recall that it was the home of a stiff aristocrat, who was human enough, occasionally, to swig rum and swear.

I had more interest in the wonderland that met our sight as we neared camp on our return. It was almost nine o'clock and quite dark. As we made a turning, we saw ahead of us a multitude of illuminated tents apparently suspended in the air, and just at that moment "Taps" was sounded, the bugle notes floating through the stillness, and suddenly every light disappeared and all was darkness.

"All was quiet along the Potomac." Occasionally there were slight skirmishes with outposts of the enemy. In one of these, a mild affair occurring near Bailey's Crossroads, Companies G and H took part. The rebels in front of us were behind an earthwork on a height. While our skirmishers were being deployed towards the height, we lay in a small patch of woods and nervously awaited developments. We were startled, all of a sudden, by the discharge of a musket; Michael McFadden, of Company G, had shot himself, not very seriously.

There was a more spectacular comedy in this affair. Some of our boys went into an old building across the road and carried

out a section of stovepipe. They also found a forward pair of
wagon wheels. By turning the wagon tongue rearwards for a
trail and mounting the pipe between the wheels, they made a
fair imitation of a fieldpiece. They rushed it into the open, and
with loud cheers pointed it towards the enemy.

The rebels rose to the challenge of the strange and sudden
gun, promptly opening fire on it with a real piece of artillery.
After the first solid shot had come bounding over, our boys
abandoned their mock fieldpiece and joined us in watching the
enemy blaze away at it for several minutes. The rebel marks-
manship may have been good; I don't remember. At any rate,
their bombardment of our stovepipe made good sport for us.

IV

IN THE long interval between the retreat from Bull Run and the
spontaneous settling of the army into winter quarters, our regiment was occupied in doing picket duty, building fortifications,
and drilling, drilling, drilling. We shifted camp several times,
to our benefit; with each move we got rid of bad rations, helped
ourselves to fresh garden truck, enjoyed a change of scene, and
collected rumors for the refreshment of our conversation. Camp
talk was our diversion, and everything that was rumored as
about to happen, besides everything that actually did happen,
was furiously debated.

Not long after the battle, our brigade was broken up and
Colonel Howard was returned to the command of the regiment.
In the new organization later effected, the 3d and 4th Maine
were brigaded with the 38th and 40th New York and the brigade was placed under the command of Colonel John Sedgwick,
a regular army officer, who was promoted brigadier-general of
volunteers. Our first impressions of Sedgwick were not happy.
I have heard that a smile occasionally invaded his scrubby beard,
but I never saw one there. His official manner sent chills down
the backs of the rank and file. He was an old bachelor with

oddities; addicted to practical jokes and endless games of soli-
taire; rather careless of his personal appearance, and habitually
crowning his rough head, when not on parade, with a hat that
looked like a small beehive of straw.

Colonel Howard was promoted like Sedgwick, but for a while
he was without a command, and when he did get a new brigade
he got none of the regiments that he had led at Bull Run. He
left us with expressions of regret; his, not ours. He issued a farewell order specially composed for the occasion, doing us the
honor of acknowledging that he "owed much of worldly notice
and position" to the regiment, and doing his successor the favor
of calling down upon him the blessing and guidance of Heaven.
He cherished, he said, a firm conviction that the enemy would
ultimately be conquered; nevertheless, he advised us to appeal
daily for help from on high. Howard had set us a brave example
in battle and otherwise had led us ably enough, but his vanity
and cold piety had wearied and repelled us.

Major Staples became our colonel and assumed the command.
He promised well in his new rank and station; his judgment in
military matters was good, his conclusions rapidly and correctly
formed; but, unfortunately for him and the regiment, he was
not always equal to the necessity of refusing the requests of his
associates, who presumed too much upon his yielding disposi-
tion and their old acquaintance with him. When I served as clerk
at regimental headquarters, I couldn't help seeing how things
went, nor noting with surprise and regret how the colonel chafed
under the offensive arrogance of subordinates, yet gave way to
blustering petitioners when he should have dismissed them with
a reprimand. He ought to have had a regiment of strangers; he
might then have asserted himself and at the same time have
won devotion by his kindliness. He was always kindly to me.

Other changes in our roster of officers did not affect my fortunes or my personal and unimportant opinions. I merely saw
them occur. Some followed in the line of promotion. Some were

forced; volunteer officers were ordered into the presence of military boards of examination, which determined (often, I suspect, having predetermined) their fitness to command, and many incompetents were dismissed or compelled to resign.

Governor Washburn came to make a personal inquiry into the condition of the Maine regiments and to satisfy himself that he was doing everything in his power to serve their needs. He brought with him a new chaplain for our regiment, the Reverend Henry Leonard, a zealous and cheery henchman of the Lord. Our first chaplain, the Reverend Andrew Church, had resigned. His going was our loss. His theology was of the practical kind that prompted him to go often from camp to Washington, usually on foot, through the mud and rain or the dust and heat, to get franked envelopes, letter paper, and other gratuities for the men. Some of his own letters home, which found their way into the newspapers, may not have been judicious; but if this were so, he was by no means the only offender. His conduct among the troops was exemplary. His courteous attitude towards everyone, regardless of differences in military rank, was truly Christian. He was happily unlike a certain godly officer, who caused to be hung in tents in the absence of their proper occupants large placards demanding, "Have you prayed this morning?" Pious impudence!

Captain Hesseltine of Company G, my company, was discharged to become the major of a new regiment, the 13th Maine, then being raised by Neal Dow. I almost went to that regiment, myself. From Howard the pious to Dow the prohibitionist! I shudder now at the thought of my narrow escape. I had a letter from Colonel Dow, who wrote that he had appointed me sergeant-major of his regiment and that I was to report at once at its rendezvous in Augusta.

Colonel Staples promised me a lieutenancy in the 3d Maine. I appreciated that, but an offer in hand seemed better than a promise, and I insisted upon his approval of the transfer desired

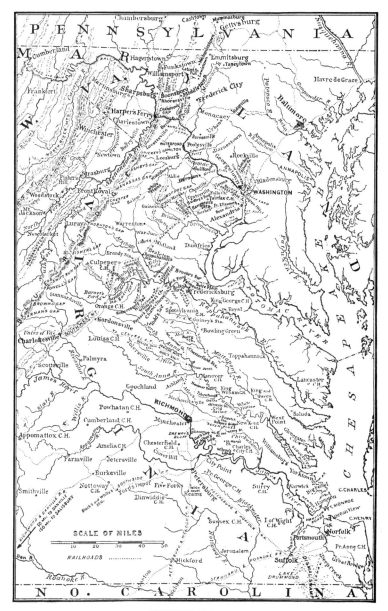

REFERENCE MAP

by Colonel Dow. I obtained this in proper form, and with the precious document clutched in my fist I hurried round by the road to brigade headquarters to get the necessary indorsement from General Sedgwick. The reception I had was more than chilly; it was glacial. My transfer was refused. The general dismissed me like breaking off an icicle, then called me back and in a kinder tone informed me that he was disapproving the transfer at the earnest request of Colonel Staples. The colonel, as soon as I had left his quarters, had gone rapidly across a field and through some bushes and talked with General Sedgwick while I was going round by the road. When I returned, my face must have shown how I felt, for the colonel put an arm around my shoulders and sought to comfort me. He explained his contradictory acts by saying that he had a liking for me and couldn't spare me. I forgave him, and was reconciled for a while.

Winter shut down, and our regiment, like many others, went into winter quarters by whatever expedients could be devised for keeping warm. There was drill to keep us busy, but no prospect of field service until spring. The winter roads were impassable to armies. The rebels had long since withdrawn their outposts; their flag had disappeared from our horizon. Under these conditions I found army life empty and monotonous, and wished greatly for a holiday at home.

Before long, my hopes revived as I learned that Colonel Staples was going to name a detail for recruiting service in Maine. I lost no time about securing the good offices of Mrs. Sampson and Mrs. Staples; and did I get a place on that detail? So much for the influence of the sex on a newly married man. Colonel Staples had only recently married a girl from home. He could refuse her nothing. I went to Maine, a happy soldier.

With the other members of the detail, I reported, on arriving at Augusta, to Major John Gardiner, late of the 2d United States Dragoons and now, representing the Federal government, superintendent of the recruiting service in Maine. Major Gardiner had been an officer of the regular army for more than twenty years and was somewhat frosty in appearance and manner; an able, brisk, impatient man. His office in the State House was for business only, and the business transacted there was done without waste of time. It was a pleasure to me to serve under his direction. He was friendly to me and assisted me in creeping up; I was not with him long before he made me sergeant-major of the post.

EDUCATION OF A REGIMENT

Through summer's heat, and winter's cold;
Through pain, disaster, and defeat ...
—GEORGE HENRY BOKER, "Upon the
Hill before Centreville"

ONE MORNING late in May, as I was laying out the work on my desk, Major Gardiner said to me, suddenly and rather shortly, "Sergeant-Major, the governor wishes to see you at once." What could that mean? While I was yet staring blankly in surprise, he added, "I've recommended you for a commission."

I lost no time in reaching the governor's room; took the stairs three at a leap. I gave my name to the orderly, but before I could state my business the governor swung round in his chair and said to me:

"We're to raise a new regiment. I want recruiting officers. I want them now. I'll give you authority to raise Company B, and when you've raised it I'll commission you captain. When can you go?"

"This afternoon, sir."

"Report to the adjutant-general for your papers."

Thunder! I felt as if fired from a cannon. I flew straight to the adjutant-general's office and found his chief clerk, Charles Partridge, laying out the papers. Authority in hand, I went back to Major Gardiner and thanked him. All that he said in reply was, "Make good my promises to the governor."

So I was to raise a company for the 16th Maine? I tried. That first afternoon, I went to Vienna and got one recruit. His name was Henry Dexter. A few years before, my brother Emilus had saved him from drowning, and now he confused me with Emilus to my advantage. I promised him a sergeant's warrant and had his name in a few moments. Vienna gave me no other recruits. I went to Mount Vernon. There I secured one more, Thomas Hopkins; I promised to make him either clerk or orderly.

Recruiting was a discouraging business. I called up all the eloquence of my ancestors, if they had any; I pleaded, cried, swore, and prayed, yet only two patriots were enrolled to my credit. I lacked sixty-two for a captain's commission. I went to Readfield Corner, the old rendezvous of the militia, and painted the town red with patriotic posters ornamented with pictures of model soldiery. There I enrolled one minor, whose father led him home by the ear and threatened to make a dead hero of me if he should find me in town by Saturday night. I was saved when Friday night's mail brought me an informal note from the regiment's colonel-to-be:

Augusta, Maine,
June 5th, 1862.

Abner R. Small,
Dear Sir:

I have appointed you Adjutant of the 16th Regiment. Please report here at once.

Yours very truly,
A. W. WILDES,
Col., 16th Reg't, M.V.

I reported at once, and discovered the reason for the change in my fortunes. Charles Hutchins, of Augusta, had been recruiting successfully and had asked Governor Washburn for the captaincy of Company B, the company that I was failing to raise. I soon satisfied all concerned that I would make a better adjutant than captain, which simplified matters. In Room No. 9, off the rotunda of the State House, I began in earnest my work in the organization of the regiment, and as I was, for the time being, the only commissioned officer with authority, I had my hands full.

At first, recruits were rushed in daily, especially by the enterprising Hutchins and by Daniel Marston, of Phillips, who were rivals for the post of honor, the captaincy of the color company. I kept, to the exact minute, a record of all recruits received, and every morning at nine o'clock I reported to the governor the progress made. As the rivalry between Hutchins and Marston became almost bitter, I had all I could do to keep my temper and keep the record straight as well.

There came a day of reckoning, when the governor had the rivals in his office and went over the figures with them. Although my tabulation showed conclusively that Hutchins was the winner, Governor Washburn allowed himself to be persuaded that I had favored Hutchins over Marston. He got angry and sent for me. As soon as I entered the room, I saw what was up. Marston had a sickly smile, Hutchins a red face, and the governor was like a fighting cock, spurring both the captains-to-be with language that astonished me. He turned on me as I entered and let fly at me, too, refusing to hear a word of explanation. Then he ordered us all to leave the room. My star seemed to have fallen. I almost wished that I was a fourth corporal again.

The next morning, as I was crossing the rotunda, I saw the governor standing in talk with Blaine, Stevens, Farwell and, I think, Lot Morrill. He saw me, and, breaking off his talk, said:

"Adjutant Small, I owe you an apology. You were right and I was wrong. I beg your pardon."

This from him, and in the presence of such distinguished men! It was so unexpected that I was overwhelmed with confusion. I can't recall how I replied; I only know that just then I thought Governor Washburn a greater man than ever. My star shot up again.

From every part of the state, recruits came forward slowly in June. The governor was nervously impatient at the apparent want of spirit. July 4th, he issued a proclamation, calling upon the people to make a "prompt and hearty response to this new demand upon their patriotism," and, a few days later, the adjutant-general published an order, reminding all "citizen soldiers" that they had "a country to save" and that they could give "most efficient aid in this holy and patriotic work." These and other appeals were printed in full by all the loyal press of the state, with editorial comment full of patriotic ardor; they were read from pulpits; they were posted on barns and crossroads fences. They brought to us many good men. There also came to us, to be shaken off as soon as possible, some misfits.

One morning, I found at the door of No. 9 two anxious civilians of decided mould. Patriotism oozed from every pore, and found utterance in voices heavy with war thunder and poor whiskey. They could hardly wait for the opening of the door, and were lounging against the jambs, and growling, "This gov'munt can't be so hard up for trupes, or the boss would be around airlier in the mornin'."

I scrutinized them closely. One was cocky, but he must have been at least forty years old. The other appeared to be of any age from twenty to eighty; stripped of his clothing and the mysteries of hair dye, he would have presented a type of the Resurrection. The regulation inquiries developed what was what, and the afternoon train took the young man with his swagger, and the ancient with his war paint, back to where they had come from. Visions of large bounties and an early discharge on a comfortable pension had vanished in their new determination to aid the cause by "votin' agin the war."

Governor Washburn's appeal awoke a spirit of patriotism in the breast of a young man away in Piscataquis County. He came to camp towering above all his comrades, and, Apollo-like, he was the personification of manly beauty. His curled hair betokened neatness; his step, confidence; and a new-born scowl and close mouth denoted firmness and courage. He bristled all over with fight, and was spoiling for a scrimmage. We picked that man out for a model soldier, and a successful competitor in the race for shoulder straps. We waited upon him graciously, for his superiority impressed us. We were flattered by his order to carry a valise and two large trunks to his quarters.

There is nothing like the stern realities of war as exemplified in rations of hardtack, bacon, and salt pork, for the development of an I-want-to-go-home feeling. Only five days, and there came into No. 9 our model soldier, demanding a discharge. Major Gardiner reminded him of the terms of his enlistment, and told him that he was for three years at the option of the government.

"But don't you never discharge a man?"

"Only for disability."

For a moment he stood silent; then, drawing down the corners of his mouth and planting both hands over his bowels, he fetched a fearful groan and fled to the surgeon. Five minutes later, our model soldier came bounding back into the office and shouted, "I can't go! I'm *busted!*"

Notwithstanding an order that none but able-bodied men should be received, some invalids crept into our ranks; a future embarrassment to us. There were others essentially timid. They put on uniforms, hung a sword or bayonet on one side, a pistol on the other; and hung tales of heroism on the other sides, and in various places pinned artificial records of campaigns.

II

ONE DAY, as I was busied in camp at guard mounting, I noticed watching me a handsome young man, who was evidently an officer although he was not in full uniform. He sported a white beaver hat, which was very becoming, and carried himself with the dignity of a senator. As I went on with my duty, and he watched, the authority and consequence that I had been accumulating were rapidly unsettled. A feeling came over me that he was my military superior. And so he was. He introduced himself as the new regiment's major and requested me to show him through the camp. "Farnham, late of the 2d Maine," he said he was; and suddenly I remembered that I had seen him once before, when I had stood in the ranks of a company of raw recruits by a dusty roadside and watched him going gayly by.

Another day, an officer in the uniform of a captain came briskly into No. 9 and informed me that his name was Tilden, that he was the new regiment's lieutenant-colonel, and that I was to take my orders from him; and as I looked into his bold face I saw that he was the other of the two officers, lieutenants then, whom I had so admired and envied, that day in May of the year before. In the absence of Colonel Wildes he proceeded to finish what I had so pridefully begun, the organization of the regiment.

Shorn of my authority, I could only watch, wait, and obey orders. It was months before I came to know Colonel Tilden. It took time to learn from him that a man could be both brave and gentle, severe yet just. I respected him, and later admired him, and yet later came to be friends with him and was honored by it; and with Major Farnham, too, and was thus twice honored. All the regiment respected these two officers, and trusted them, from the start.

If I have less to say of Colonel Wildes, it is because he was never long in service with the regiment. Wildes had a warm heart and a winning manner that gained him many friends; but he was beginning to feel his years, his health was not of the best, and we all knew, and he realized, that he was not equal to the demands of active field service. He had been superintending the transportation of Maine troops to the front, and doing it well, being much experienced in railroad affairs. We regretted that he was induced to quit this work and go to the front as a regimental commander.

We were organized, at last, with a full complement of officers and nine hundred and sixty men, and on Thursday, August 14th, the regiment was mustered into the national service by Major Gardiner. Of the field and staff officers besides Tilden, Farnham, and myself, only Quartermaster Tucker had seen service; this was the Tucker that had been lieutenant-colonel of the 3d Maine. Of our thirty line officers, only four had smelled powder, and few of our rank and file knew what it would mean to face fire. Yet, fresh from civil life though most of us were, we had a realizing sense of the situation. The first year of the war had shown the cruel necessity of further sacrifice. Exactly how much our offering of ourselves was owing to patriotism, how much to ardor kindled by tall tales of heroism, and how much to large bounties and prospective pensions, I make no attempt to say. I know we realized that some of us would not come back alive, and perhaps not dead.

None of us had a gluttonous appetite for a scrimmage or a morbid desire to fill the last ditch; but when, on the afternoon of Sunday, August 17th, we were told that the regiment was ordered to the front, we raised cheer after cheer. Every order published was greeted with cheers and tigers. Monday we got rid of surplus baggage, packing up and sending home the temporary conveniences of the camp; this didn't seem to leave us much to get along with. Tuesday we departed. We left Augusta quietly, neither expecting nor receiving any marked expressions of profound gratitude or wild expectancy to cheer us on our way to war. Our journey to the front was nearly the same as I had made with the 3d Maine: by rail to Boston, to Fall River; by steamer to Jersey City; by rail again to Newark, to Philadelphia, to Baltimore, to Washington. We arrived in the national capital in the evening of Thursday, August 21st.

Under orders from General Casey, whose duty it was to receive new regiments and assign them to provisional brigades, we marched out of Washington the next day, crossing the Long Bridge over the Potomac and tramping another mile or more in the sultry heat to our first camp on the sacred soil. Sunday, we were ordered to report to General Whipple, who commanded some of the forts and troops west of the river; we moved our camp to the vicinity of Fort Tillinghast, and were brigaded with heavy artillery troops (the 1st Massachusetts and 1st Wisconsin) that manned the defenses. Monday, three companies of our regiment were detailed for instruction as artillerists in Forts Tillinghast, Cass, and Woodbury, and details from other companies were set to work digging a line of rifle pits between Forts Wood-bury and De Kalb. It was not to our liking, as infantry, to be turned into gunners and ditch diggers, but in the exigencies of war our preferences were not consulted.

Washington was supposedly in danger. Somewhere beyond the western haze, Pope's army was stumbling into a fight; and past our camp and away to battle marched some of McClellan's unhappy troops, just back from their unfortunate Peninsular campaign. We were not much troubled by rumors of dissension and disaster, confusion out of sight being out of mind; what disturbed our nerves was the bang and rattle of the "Long Roll" beaten at dead of night. We heard it at half-past two in the morning of Thursday, August 28th, drumming us out of our sleep and into readiness for action. Within ten minutes we were in line of battle. We stood with weapons in hand till sunrise, and saw no enemy. The reason for this untimely call to arms we didn't know, as we hadn't been taken into the confidence of the commanding general; it may have been that he merely wished to learn how quickly we could turn out, but more likely he feared a rebel cavalry dash. Poor Pope was in for a whipping, and Washington was jumpy.

Friday, we heard a distant mutter of cannonading; the second Bull Run battle was being fought. Saturday, the battle was continued, and the defensive activities of our regiment were amplified. Companies H and K were assigned to picket duty. Companies E and I were sent farther out to watch for the enemy, and near Falls Church they captured a lost black pig, several hens, and some leaf tobacco. These companies, having solved the mysteries beyond our lines and returned to camp with choice things to eat, were for days the envy of companies less fortunate; their rations of hardtack and salt horse were flanked with chicken and roast pig.

Tuesday, September 2d, Pope and his army retired to the defenses of Washington, defeated, humiliated, and discouraged.

The attitude of the troops that tramped past us was one of mortification and rage, tempered slightly with disgust. The column passing with its ragged banners, and the long ambulance train with its awful freight of torn and battered humanity, burdened us with a crushing sense of the business we were engaged in; yet there were jokes at the expense of Pope and the reversal of his fortunes. I can see Ike Thompson now as I saw him then, standing with a backward tilt, blanket thrown gracefully across his shoulders, hat shoved forward, one eye closed and the other brightly cocked at Pope and his staff as they rode wearily by. As they passed from sight, like a funeral procession, Ike assumed a tragic attitude and declaimed, with the wild melancholy of a mourner with his second bottle:

"Great God! What could you expect of a man who will persist in wearing his shirt wrong end up!"

Pope wore a huge stand-up dickey.

That same day, General McClellan was placed in command of "the fortifications and of all the troops for the defense of the capital." No one, except envious rivals, then held his failures against him. A glory of great expectations encompassed him with a superficial brilliancy. Troops cheered themselves hoarse at sight of him. Our regiment, like many others, hailed him extravagantly as a savior.

We were now completely relieved from our artistry in dirt. With the exception of the color company, which was to perform guard duty at division headquarters at Arlington, all the companies not previously detached as artillerists were ordered distributed for instruction in the chain of forts. Colonel Tilden was placed in command of Fort Corcoran, guarding the approach to the Aqueduct Bridge, and two companies were sent with him to that fort; two others were sent to Fort Albany, west of the Long Bridge, and one to Fort Craig, and one to Fort De Kalb.

We got instruction, but no action. The rebels didn't move against Washington. The next we were to hear of them, they had marched rapidly northwards and crossed the Potomac at the fords above Leesburg, attempting an invasion of Maryland.

III

OUR first departure on campaign was unexpected by us, and sudden. Orders came at eleven o'clock Saturday night, September 6th, for our scattered regiment to assemble at Fort Tillinghast. By four o'clock Sunday morning we were all at that place and every man was supplied with rations for two days and forty rounds of ammunition. We were to proceed with all possible dispatch to Leesboro, ten miles north of Washington, and to report for duty with the right wing of McClellan's army. Since we were to hurry, we were ordered to go in light marching order; the tents, knapsacks, and overcoats of the men and the trunks of the company officers were to be left behind under the charge of our quartermaster. There was some grumbling at this, but in our greenness we expected that they would follow us in a few days, as a matter of course, or that we should return to them. At half-past four we started, crossing the Aqueduct Bridge over the Potomac to Georgetown and marching away on unfamiliar roads. We bivouacked, that night, under the stars and pines on the country estate of the Blairs at Silver Spring.

Monday we marched a few miles farther and halted near Leesboro. Our presence was formally reported, and we were assigned to Hartsuff's brigade of Ricketts' division, Hooker's corps, the other regiments in the brigade being the 12th and 13th Massachusetts, the 83d New York—or 9th Regiment (Militia), as they preferred to call themselves—and the 11th Pennsylvania. The rapid marching was continued, with short halts, and Thursday the regiment went into camp near the town of Ridgeville, on the Baltimore & Ohio Railroad. Saturday we were detached from the brigade as railroad guard. We were to stay a while at Ridgeville. The officers had their tents, but the men had to shelter themselves as best they could with makeshifts.

Ridgeville was a town of rebellious tendency. Its inhabitants, though few and lazy, defended with stubborn watchfulness their vegetable gardens and haystacks, and demanded six cents a canteen for water from their wells. They had received with open doors and regaled with the fatted calf the rebel officers who had stopped there a few days before, but they had no welcome for Yankees. Only the loyal people of the vicinity visited our camp and brought us baskets of luxuries and words of encouragement.

One afternoon a young lady of striking face and figure watched our parade with absorbing interest, taking in every detail of the movements and the camp. When parade was dismissed, she mounted a beautiful horse and rode away; but soon she returned, and approaching Major Farnham she unlimbered her batteries of eyes and voice and invited him to tea. I happened to be standing within close range, and she said to me, "May I expect you, too?"; but from her tone I could only take this to mean that I was to go along as a sort of chaperon to the major. Possibly Maryland etiquette demanded it. She almost utterly ignored my presence as she rode home absorbed in the major, the handsome fellow. Like a squire I rode in the rear, and like a squire I offered at the end of the ride to unsaddle her horse. The offer was scornfully refused. She said that she was perfectly capable of caring for her mount. I almost expected that she would care for mine, too, she looked so doubtful of me.

Impressed as I was by her grand air, I was astonished at finding that her home was a mean little house, which apparently had never been painted or even whitewashed. We mounted a ramshackle porch and followed our lovely guide through a door that opened straight into the living-room, where the young miss introduced us with charming grace to an elderly woman of evident refinement. Tea was served in a small room adjoining, which had two windows and a slide that was opened for ventilation.

Being ignored, indeed scarcely spoken to, I improved the opportunity to drink in along with my tea every detail of the scene. I have never lost the remembrance of it. The house and its furnishings were primitive, such as only the poorer folk of New England own, but the table, with its spotless damask and elegant appointments, upheld some of the tastiest food that I have ever eaten, and the service was faultless. The only part of the conversation that I recall was the young lady's avowing that "their family was reckoned the handsomest in the county" and that her sister was the "belle of Frederick City."

Our hostesses of this occasion excepted, our observation was that there was a lack of womanly delicacy in the feminine chivalry of Maryland. There was a coarseness, an absence of the nicety of manners that we had expected to find in one of the oldest states in the Union. As for the young men, they looked and bore themselves like the greenest rustics, and exhibited a reckless indifference to dress and deportment, as well as to any opinion that we might form of Maryland youth.

Our opinion of ourselves as a regiment, at that time, was depressingly short of the military ideal. We were fairly well drilled in the manual of arms, and were able to perform creditable evolutions of squad and company, and doubtless could have got through a gap in a fence without breaking ranks; but we were not ready to meet the requirements of a battle except in resolution. We realized this, and dwelt constantly upon the thought of what we should have to do and how we should do it when called into action. The advance of McClellan's army, and the certainty of a battle, kept us in anxious expectation of orders to move.

Colonel Wildes, unwilling to command under these circumstances, and painfully conscious of his own deficiency, resigned, and Lieutenant-Colonel Tilden assumed the direction of the regiment. Wednesday, September 17th, the expected battle then raging some thirty miles to the westward, we were ordered to the field. We broke camp and marched. When we halted at Frederick City, I kept an eye out for the belle of that place, but somehow failed to descry so unmistakable a beauty. We pressed on, crossed the hazy Catoctin range, the lovely valley of Middletown, and the South Mountain ridge beyond. Friday we bivouacked near the battlefield. Our presence was formally reported, and I heard General Williams say that our regiment, as yet a raw one, should not have been sent from the defenses of Washington. Our promptness in marching under orders that had originated in error was acknowledged, however, with warm approval.

We learned that the rebel army had gone back over the Potomac the previous night. The invasion of Maryland had failed. The battle that we had missed was the battle of the Antietam. Many of our officers and men were disappointed that we had not been in the fight; they feared that the reputation of the regiment must suffer. I felt no deep regret when I went over the field. The dead were still there. They lay in windrows, in some places almost entire companies together. The sunken road southeast of the Dunker Church was heaped with grey corpses, rebels no more. The cornfield north of the church was strewn with blue. The church itself, a plain, small building, was battered terribly; solid shot had gone through it, and thousands of bullets had pitted its brick walls. From a knoll near by I counted two hundred dirty and bloated bodies, blue and grey together. If I had looked where all the fighting had been, I should have counted twenty times as many.

Saturday our regiment crossed the battlefield and went into camp near Sharpsburg, there rejoining the brigade, which was now commanded by Colonel Coulter of the 11th Pennsylvania; General Hartsuff, its former commander, had been severely wounded in the battle. Coulter was a big, quick man, vigorous, impatient, and often violent in speech and action. We felt an immediate liking for him.

We changed camp several times, finally settling down near the river and about three miles west of the town. An incident occurring there gave rise to a story that grew to fabulous proportions, multiplying converts to Christianity and the Baptist persuasion, until it bore to our Northern homes the glad tidings that entire regiments had enlisted in the army of the Lord. The way it began was this. Our chaplain, the Reverend George Bullen, baptized in the chill autumnal waters of the Potomac two men of our regiment, who had confessed their faith before they had left home. A few days later, Chaplain Bullen paid his respects to Colonel Coulter at brigade headquarters; and, declining as superfluous the customary social appetizer of old Bourbon, he told the colonel all about the baptisms. He dwelt upon the probable good effects, both godly and military; the men, he felt sure, would be the more amenable to orders and discipline; he had not omitted, he said, to remind them that they should render unto Caesar. Now it happened that Colonel Coulter, though commanding the brigade, was jealously attentive to the growing reputation of his regiment. He interrupted suddenly:

"How many men did you say you dipped, Chaplain?"

"I baptized two, Colonel."

"Orderly!" The colonel's tone was peremptory. "Tell my adjutant to detail a sergeant to take a man from each company down to the river and baptize them in the Methodist persuasion. I can't allow any damned Baptist to supplant my authority, either spiritual or temporal."

IV

McCLELLAN did not pursue the enemy after the Antietam battle, but kept the army near Sharpsburg to refresh and refit it. Our regiment was overlooked. The property that we had left behind, as ordered, was not sent to us; neither were other supplies issued. Our men, with nothing but their blankets and the clothing they stood in, were suffering for lack of their tents, overcoats, and the knapsacks that held their extra wear. Many were already ripened for the hospital by exposure to the chill of night after the heat of fast marching. Our bivouacs had been bad for us. Our camping without tents was worse. We were bitterly

THE DUNKER CHURCH AT ANTIETAM

chagrined, besides, to see others well supplied while we were neglected. Some of our sister regiments, fully clothed and blanketed and tented, were secure against the weather, and apparently were proudly amused at the sufferings of their neighbors, who by day wore blankets and at night withdrew to rude shelters contrived from fence rails, cornstalks, and boughs. They called us the "Blanket Brigade," insulted us, mocked us, and pretended to avoid our loathsome and contaminating presence.

Our men could hardly bear this shameful neglect, this contempt of their needs by commissioned Jacks-in-office, this callous ridicule of their plight by soldiers no better than themselves. They sank into despondency and uncleanly ways, and sickness, and despair. The rapid decline from fastidious neatness to filthiness of condition and habits changed some of them beyond recognition. I remember a college graduate, a royal good fellow, who was only brought to himself by the free use of a corn broom and brook water.

Our medical staff did their best to help the ailing, but with no proper housing for the sick in camp, and with a short supply of medicines, they were unable to do much. They sent the worst sufferers to the division hospital at Smoketown, and there in a little field beside the road were buried some of those unfortunates, eternal accusers of neglect and red tape.

Our rank and file may have accused their nearest commanders of negligence and incompetence and cursed them as the authors of much misery. If they did, they were mistaken. I know that at regimental headquarters the officers suffered at the suffering of the men. They did their best to set matters right. In spite of repeated rebuffs and delays, they persistently applied for the return of our supplies. The orders and requests, which are still somewhere officially on file, preserve the unhappy record.

Colonel Wildes was induced to recall his resignation, at the suggestion of superior officers, and was restored to the command. He did not, however, stay with us long; his health was so much impaired that he was obliged to take a leave of absence. Lieutenant-Colonel Tilden again assumed the direction of the regiment, and carried on the campaign of official correspondence for the return of our supplies, while Colonel Wildes reported our plight to the authorities at home and sought to gain for us what assistance he could from that direction. Our quartermaster still being absent, supposedly guarding our property where it was useless to us, Lieutenant Lowell was detailed acting quartermaster; he was not envied for that.

Our regiment mustered on parade less than half its proper strength, and made a sorry showing when, on Thursday, October 2d, the corps, now commanded by Reynolds, was reviewed by McClellan and President Lincoln. Just where we took up our position in line, a rail fence was found to be much in the way of the mounted officers directing us. Colonel Coulter, after jumping it several times, turned to my clerk, Dwight Maxfield, who was wearing a Burnside blouse, and said to him sharply:

"Here, Chaplain, make yourself useful and tear down this 'rip-gut' fence!"

"Beg pardon, Colonel," said Max, "but I'm not one of that useful class. I'm only an adjutant's clerk."

"Good God! I took you for a chaplain. Where are they?"

"That group on the knoll," said Max, pointing, "are spoiling for the chance."

The colonel spurred to the group on the knoll.

"Pull down that fence!"

"But, Colonel, we are chaplains!"

"I don't care a god damn. Double quick! By God, you'll do something to earn your salaries as long as I command this brigade!"

The chaplains took down the fence.

We had a view of our highest commanders. The debonair McClellan always made a fine appearance, on foot or on horseback; when mounted, he was a king. The tall and lanky Lincoln was an odd figure on a horse, and the odder for wearing a stove-pipe hat that increased his height and angularity; yet he bore himself with a dignity that somehow made McClellan's urbane distinction less important. Our corps commander, Reynolds, was alertness personified.

Next day, our brigade was reviewed by General Taylor, for-merly colonel of the 72d New York, and five days later this of-ficer assumed the command of the brigade, succeeding Colonel Coulter, who was returned to his regiment. Taylor was sympa-thetic to our needs and approved and forwarded our requests for the return of our supplies, as Coulter had done; to no avail.

Our men now lacked food as well as shelter and clothing. Sutlers reaped a rich harvest among them, for they were willing to pay any price demanded for shirts and something to eat. There was a flurry of hope when cases of hardtack were distributed, but faint cheers were turned to curses and wry jokes when it was seen that the cases were marked "Yorktown," which meant that the crackers had been through the Peninsular campaign of the year before. I learned then by demonstration why "worm castles" was the popular name for hardtack.

Foraging was forbidden; but it was generally practiced, and many a choice fowl, an occasional lamb, and any amount of garden truck mysteriously satisfied the hunger of our troops. The cornfields on our flanks were gleaned to the surface for man and beast. I saw men bring in ears of corn, pick up sardine tins in the rear of brigade headquarters, and with a nail convert the tins into graters, and on the graters rub the corn until enough was prepared for a genuine Maine hasty pudding; and as they rubbed, I heard them humming to the tune of "John Brown's Body":

      "Worms eat hearty in the commissary stores
        While we go starving on."

One day the entire camp was roused suddenly by loud explo-sions near the river, and a commotion was visible at brigade headquarters until the racket was explained. The chief forager of our regiment, one Tibbetts, had returned from a raid on some Maryland hen-yard and kitchen with a large frying-pan and a brace of fowl. He had improvised a fireplace by the riverside, dressed the fowl nicely, put them in the pan, and set them over a smart blaze. Then he had gone to cadge seasoning. He returned just in time to see mixed fragments of chicken and iron go shooting into the trees; in building his fireplace he had mistakenly used some unexploded shells. We saw him rushing into the woods as if a shell were chasing him. Scared? Not at all; he was starting for more supplies.

Occasionally a sly gift from Tibbetts would find its way to our headquarters table, to our pleasure, and no questions asked. Market prices current as paid by officers to sutlers were two dollars a bushel for potatoes, forty cents a pound for butter, eleven cents for sugar, and ten cents a quart for milk. Good food was a luxury. Officers might pay for it, but privates could not afford it unless they foraged and got it for nothing. The army food was scanty and bad. The issuing of full rations of good quality, October 20th, was noted in my diary as a rare occurrence.

We had been more than a month near Sharpsburg when, on Tuesday, October 21st, we received marching orders. We were to go the next day; but when the next day came, it rained, and the orders were cancelled. Then we hoped that we should stay a while longer, for at last we had permission to send for our much needed supplies, and Captain Ayer was sent to Washington, where they were now stored, to get them. On Saturday, however, we received marching orders again, and at four o'clock Sunday morning we broke camp and started away. We marched in a downpour of rain through Sharpsburg, and all day eastwards over roads deep with mud, through Rhorersville, to Crampton's Gap in the South Mountain ridge. After dark we halted in the road nearly an hour, waiting for troops ahead of us to move on, and then we took to the woods for shelter, on the west side of a bleak hill. The regiment passed a dismal night in a furious storm of rain and wind. We left Captain Williams sick in a house at Rhorersville; we never saw him again.

Two days later we reached the village of Berlin, under a hill on the north bank of the Potomac. Berlin was on the line of the Baltimore & Ohio Railroad and was just then a depot for supplies. Shelter tents and shoes were issued, and were thankfully received, but there were neither shoes nor tents for all our men. Late Thursday afternoon we crossed a long pontoon bridge from Berlin to the Virginia side of the Potomac. As we crossed, we saw at our left the tall stone piers of the railroad bridge, standing strangely empty; the bridge and tracks had been wrecked by rebel cavalrymen early in the war. Our rank and file were cautioned to break step while crossing, since the cadence of marching would rack a pontoon bridge to pieces. No bands were permitted to play.

Our advance southwards into Virginia was cold, hard, wearisome going; the Loudoun valley was harsh at that season, the roads were muddy, and our marches and bivouacs were miserable. Wednesday, November 5th, as we halted to let a wagon train pass, McClellan rode by, and a great wave of cheering swept with him into our hearing, and was loud with the shouts of our men, and swept away down the road. Our regiment went on after that with livelier spirit; so great was his power over the rank and file.

When we were halted near Salem to bivouac, that night, we were close by the home of a rebel colonel. Before the usual order to guard property was published, some of our boys discovered supplies; there was a rush for the outbuildings, boards were ripped off, and out poured corn and potatoes in abundance. Orders, threats, even leveled muskets, couldn't stop that raid. Hunger knew no discipline. The buildings were ransacked, and there was brought to light not only food but also boxes of ammunition and hogsheads of salt stored for the rebels.

Friday, we reached Warrenton in a blinding snowstorm; while we were on the march, water froze in canteens. Saturday was another day of hard marching, made doubly long when a stupid guide led us miles out of our way, and at one o'clock in the morning of Sunday, November 9th, in a storm of snow and hail, we got to Rappahannock Station. There were rebel pickets on the western bank of the Rappahannock River, and our brigade was pushed forward in support of the advance guard of cavalry under General Bayard, which was picketing the eastern bank near the station. After daylight we retired out of musket range into a patch of woods, and built fires and made coffee, and wondered whether we were going to camp or fight.

Our men were cheerful and plucky, ready for anything, although they numbered fewer than two hundred for duty; dirty, half-fed, half-clothed, and some of them sheltered only by the blue heaven, and the clouds, above the blanket of snow. Their persistent good spirits and hardihood deserved respect; yet the jeering name of "Blanket Brigade" still clung to the regiment, and hurt us more than hunger or cold or pain. Ridicule was the one thing that we could not learn to endure.

Later that day, we camped. The next morning, our colonel received from General Bayard a present of half a slaughtered sheep and hung it on a tree in front of his tent. Hungry eyes measured the number of mouthfuls it would make, and mouths watered until only the gambrels of that carcass remained; I recall that headquarters had little of it. Captain Waldron, arguing that where half a sheep had come from there must be another half, went for more, and somehow, after being at first bluffed off, he succeeded in drawing a fat mutton. The arrival of this new supply set the regiment wild. Foraging talents were duly exercised, and in a few short hours there rose from the neighborhood of every company the delicious odors of baked lamb, boiled sheep, and roast mutton. It was simply extraordinary how versatile our camp cooks were.

Lieutenant Chapman, who was then a corporal and a forager, credits four members of his company with the capture of a brood of chickens and two hives of honey. He says: "The funny part of this incident was that the foragers with their plunder came suddenly upon General Taylor and his staff at a bend of the road in the midst of a dense wood. The general took in the situation at a glance, and with grim humor faced to the front with his staff and guard and allowed the boys to 'pass in review' in single file without breaking their formation. Not a word was said nor a salute given by anyone in either party, but the marauders saw as they glanced up hastily, filing by, that the face of the brigade commander was stern, and visions of the guardhouse rose vividly in their minds. As they hurried towards camp, an orderly followed, who went to the colonel with instructions from the general to send the chickens and honey to the division hospital for the use of the sick. The honey was disposed of, however, before the order reached the boys." Blankets and boughs here and there hid suspicious-looking boxes, with busy bees buzzing around; and a sweet, satisfied look crept over the entire command.

There was a sequel to this, concluding quite to my taste. We had reported so many of our men sick that the division commander, then General Gibbon, ordered the condition of the regiment to be investigated. His medical director, Surgeon Nordquist, came to make an inquiry on the day after the honey turned up missing. Surgeon Nordquist insulted us and at the same time gave us unwilling praise.

"Diss retchiment are poor soltchers," he told our colonel, "but dey are tamn goot foratchers."

Calling me into his presence, he added:

"Atshutant, py Godt, your men will all pe deadt pefore night unless you take dose honeys dose tamn tiefs got! You shust take de names of dose men and send to me, or I'll report you to de sheneral."

"All right, Surgeon," I said, "your order shall be obeyed." I raised my voice. "Boys, I'm going for paper, and when I come back I shall expect to be told the name of every man that stole honey."

So the names were demanded in obedience to orders, but, as I expected and desired, I failed to find out who "dose tamn tiefs" were. When I returned to my quarters, I passed some men who smiled at me stickily as they courteously touched their hats, and in my tent I found about ten pounds of as delicious honey as Virginia could afford.

FREDERICKSBURG

Listen! Again the shrill-lipped bugles blow
Where the swift currents of the river flow
Past Fredericksburg ...
  —THOMAS BAILEY ALDRICH, "Fredericksburg"

BURNSIDE was now in command of the army, superseding McClellan. Tuesday, November 11th, the orders were formally read to us and were not happily received. We had already heard disquieting reports of the change. Under other circumstances it might have been welcomed by some of us, who were troubled at seeing that McClellan did not get on as successfully as he should have done; but now we were in the midst of a campaign, and we knew that the men would fight better for "Little Mac" than for any other commander. He still possessed their confidence and their devotion. Burnside was liked because he was in no way suspect, but it was not certain that he would win victories. We could only hope that he would do well.

Our nearer concern at that time was our condition as a regiment. Sufficient shelter was supplied, but our men were still so short of proper clothing that some of our companies were decently excused from duty. Our sick list was frightful. The commission ordered by General Gibbon to investigate us exonerated our officers from all blame, but this was cold comfort; we couldn't clothe our men with reports and red tape.

We learned that Captain Ayer had obtained our supplies at Washington and sent them to Hagerstown, the nearest point by rail to our camp near Sharpsburg. They had arrived there the day after we had marched away. Our quartermaster had then gone from Washington to have the property forwarded to us, but the post quartermaster at Hagerstown had refused transportation. Almost despairingly we sent Lieutenant Lowell to fetch the supplies. He was hardly gone before we moved again. Our regiment was transferred from Taylor's brigade to Duryée's, which now became Root's, the other regiments in this brigade, under its new commander, being the 94th, 104th, and 105th New York, and the 107th Pennsylvania. On Sunday, November 16th, we joined them at Bealeton, not far up the line from Rappahannock Station, and four days later we marched with them southeastwards over muddy roads to Brooke's Station on the Richmond & Potomac Railroad, a few miles north of Fredericksburg. We camped at Brooke's Station on Monday, November 24th.

Thanksgiving Day came, and we wondered what we had to be thankful for; and then Lieutenant Lowell arrived with the long-withheld overcoats and knapsacks. How happy our men were! The overcoats gave them warmth and respectability, and the knapsacks yielded up their stores of extra wear and their little conveniences and keepsakes brought from home: needles and thread, letter paper, Testaments, tintype pictures of loved ones, and various odds and ends cherished as reminders of life without war. The regiment was reconciled to the poverty of the countryside, which offered to our foragers not so much as a hen to make a Thanksgiving dinner. Salt horse, hardtack, and black coffee were given other and more savory names for the occasion, and were eaten and drunk with good cheer.

Despondency gave place to buoyancy of spirits. Food, clothing, and shelter set us up again. Regimental and company drills were done daily and done well. December 3d there was brigade drill and our regiment was complimented by Colonel Root; we had regained a decent appearance on parade. There was a darker side to our condition; our absent sick were many, we knew that not all would return, and we lost some of our present sick. In this first week in December three deaths occurred in camp; three times the remains of a soldier were borne to a grave soon to be grown over with bushes and forgotten. Those burials of men from the ranks are among the saddest that I recall. The slow march of the escort, with arms reversed, muffled drum, and pierc-

ing fife; the volleys crashing over the grave; the lively tune and
the march in quick time back to camp: soon over, long remembered. We tried not to think of it, then.

Forewarnings of action came to us, in orders directing us to
send our surplus baggage and our disabled sick to the rear; and
then, in the morning of Thursday, December 11th, came the
order for battle. I had expected it, had even wished for it, almost
prayed for it, yet I felt a grey pallor creep over my face as I took
in the full meaning of the paper indorsed "Official" by our brigade commander. Was it true that our brigade, our regiment,
were ordered to prepare for immediate action? And was I to go?

I shook myself to know if I were truly awake to the meaning
of that brief and simple order. I went to the door of my tent
and looked out into the winter dawn. It ought to have been
gloomy; but no, the morning sun was bright, and birds were
astir and singing, as the breeze bore back to me the sounds of
the mounted orderly hurrying to other regiments with copies of
the order. I saw a group of our men joking and laughing, and
suddenly I felt sick at heart. I turned back into my tent. There
was my desk all open for the business of the hour: morning reports to be consolidated, memoranda of details to be made, papers to be indorsed, orders to be copied, routine work laid out
for the day. There hung my sword and sash for evening parade—
a parade that would never be held. I heard the melodious voice
of black Ben singing "Jordan Water, Rise Over Me," and someone whistling "Home, Sweet Home." No, it could not be true;
yet there lay the order, and again I read, "Headquarters, Army
of the Potomac . . . prepare for immediate action." Yes, it was
true; and I was once more alive to my present duty, and hastened
to Colonel Tilden, who ordered copies dispatched to the company commanders for their information and signatures.

After that, the quietness of the camp was oppressive for about
five minutes. Then I heard a lone, loud yell, and then from all
the men a wild whooping, and then cheer after cheer. Then

there was almost a silence, and down the wind came the notes of a bugle at corps headquarters. Before the last note died away, the call was repeated by the division bugler, and again repeated yet nearer at brigade headquarters, and then it was sounded, clear and full, in the street outside my tent. It was the "General," the warning to pack up. I watched our boys cheerfully dismantle their homes, and separate and fold up their portable canvas houses; choose from their little treasures what lay nearest to their hearts, and destroy what remained "for want of transportation"; pack their loads and make ready to march.

"Fall in, Sixteenth!"

I mounted my horse and took my place; the bugle sounded the advance, commands were shouted, and the column started away; and just then an orderly came riding and handed to Colonel Tilden an order appointing me acting aide to the brigade commander. I was not happy to leave the regiment, yet I was proud and glad to try my new duty. Riding ahead, I reported to Colonel Root. He was a young man of striking appearance, with bold features and manner; rather imperious now, reining his impatient horse.

We rode to the low heights above the eastern bank of the Rappahannock, a mile or more downstream from opposite the town of Fredericksburg; the brigade, following, halted in a small grove of trees, and stacked arms; and there we stayed all day. Our short march had been part of a general movement of Reynolds' corps, which was to cover the crossing of Smith's corps over the river. The laying of the pontoon bridges was not completed, however, until afternoon; and Smith's corps went over late in the day only to come back again, except one brigade, because the rebels had interfered with the building of other bridges across the river at the town, and the crossing of Sumner's grand division there had been delayed.

We loafed and waited for orders. A squadron of cavalry swept by us like a whirlwind. Section after section of artillery wheeled into position along the heights on our right, commanding the river and the town. Regiment after regiment of infantry massed in readiness to cross. Late in the forenoon there was a vast thunder of cannonading as all the Union guns that could be brought to bear were turned on Fredericksburg. Rebel sharpshooters were firing from cover on the western shore, discouraging the work of Union pontoniers, and the bombardment was meant to crush and scatter the annoying riflemen. Chimneys toppled, bricks and timbers flew, and great gaps opened in the walls of buildings by the river, yet the rebels kept up their fire; they were only driven out when Union troops, using pontoons for boats, crossed over and cleared the way for more, so that the town was taken. By nightfall both Sumner's and Franklin's grand divisions had a foothold on the farther shore. So far, success; and we slept on it well enough.

Early the next morning our brigade was up and under arms, and we moved to the riverside, ready to go over; but Reynolds' corps had to wait for Smith's to cross first. There was a dense fog, darkened by smoke from the now burning town, and the troops and batteries that went ahead of us over the bridges were lost to sight. As we waited, a jaunty-looking soldier, with his gun across his shoulders, and over each end of it a long arm dangling, and his cap ornamented with some kind of animal's tail, wandered up and asked:

"Say, can any you fellers tell right nigh whereabouts be the Hunner 'n Thutty-Six?"

"The 136th what?" asked Colonel Root.

"Pennsylvania, you damn fool!"

Colonel Root closed the Testament that he was reading, and laughed. The only unmilitary order that I ever heard him give was spoken soon afterwards, when he said with a smile:

"Fall in, you fellers!"

It was then about noon. We crossed, and then went to the left perhaps a mile, and halted behind and within supporting distance of Taylor's and Lyle's brigades, which were deployed at right angles to the river. We were a little beyond Mansfield, the stone mansion of one Bernard, a rebel civilian. In a stand of trees to the landward side of Mansfield, General Franklin set up his headquarters. Burnside came over the river in person and, with Franklin, rode the lines.

Presently the fog began to clear away, and about four o'clock our brigade moved forward a little and changed front to the right, conforming to a similar movement of the first and second lines of our division. At this time Meade's division moved to our left and Doubleday's formed in rear of Meade's. Now, extending a mile to the north and a mile to the south of Mansfield, all the troops of Franklin's grand division were ranged in long lines, Smith's corps on the right and Reynolds' on the left, about half a mile from the river and roughly parallel to it, and bending at the left extremity to the shore.

Hidden from sight in the woods that covered a low, broken ridge in front of us, hardly a mile away, were the rebels awaiting us. We knew that they were there, for random shots came over from their batteries. On the plain, from the cover of hedges and ditches, puffs of blue smoke and the crack of muskets revealed their line of skirmishers, and ours; but there was no battle that short afternoon. The winter day was soon spent; the hills became grey shadows; the winter sun went down beyond them. A mist rose up from the river and spread its dim folds until it covered all the plain, and hid from sight the hills and fields, regiments and batteries, horses and men; and under that chill blanket we lay down on the frozen ground and slept, and dreamed.

II

WHEN I awoke, it was very early and I was shuddering with cold. A wind was stirring, and I heard an incessant murmur from leafless trees that I could not see; the fog obscured everything but sound. The darkness paled to a watery grey, bugles quavered huskily, and the vast bivouac roused for the day of battle. Men stretched their stiffened limbs and swore, horses neighed, mules brayed their hay call; voices shouted and replied; there was a great dim stir, but I could see only the hazy forms of my associates of the brigade staff, chilled and shivering like myself, stamping on the sere winter grass and swinging their arms to get warm. There was nothing in the world so important, just then, as coffee. We took it scalding hot. Then we smoked and waited.

After a while, the fog began to thin, the Union lines were here and there revealed, and rebel batteries began to fire. Union batteries replied. Bugles blared, and our division began to move; Taylor's brigade tramped away, then Lyle's; then our turn came.

We felt our way to the left perhaps a quarter of a mile, then changed direction to the right and came upon a ravine. The slopes of the ravine were thickly covered with bushes; we had to wait while our pioneers cleared the way. Shells were bursting over us, and jagged fragments of iron hit some of our men; my regiment was receiving its baptism of fire; these were the first hot sprinkling drops.

We crossed the ravine and a rise of ground beyond it and came to a road, the Bowling Green turnpike. There was a ditch on each side of the road, and outside of each ditch the displaced earth was heaped up in an embankment. Fences were down, and the ditches were bridged for the passage of artillery. Beyond the road was a plowed field, now trampled into mud, the winter stubble crushed into it by hoofs of straining horses and heavy wheels of cannon and the slogging feet of hundreds of men. Out in the open field was Taylor's brigade, and nearer was Lyle's, the men lying flat in the mud and protected by a slight rise of ground from the fire of rebel skirmishers. Close on the left of Lyle's brigade was Hall's battery, which must have come up in a hurry; the horses were steaming, the guns were spattered, and the wheels had gathered great sticky rims of mud. There was mud everywhere, mud on everything; the boots of our men were clogged with it; my horse was bothered by it, and stumbled, and for a moment I forgot other and more serious dangers in a vision of how I should look if I should take a sudden header into the muck.

The regiments of our brigade went into position as supports: two were deployed in support of Hall's battery and the left of the brigades in the field, and three, mine included, were formed to the right and rear of the guns. The men were ordered to lie down, some in the field and others in the protection of the sunken road. Mounted officers became more conspicuous. General Gibbon rode up and spoke to Colonel Root, and I admired the handsomely dressed and mounted figure of our division commander, and his soldierly bearing.

We stayed there through hours that seemed eternities, all the while under fire from rebel guns. A spent ball came rolling along the pike. Men moved aside and watched it, mentally measuring its force; and then an unwise foot was thrust out to stop it, the iron ball rolled on, and the groaning victim was carried to the rear. Another spent ball struck a man of my regiment in the back and killed him. Shells burst and flung down spatters of pain; here a man clapped a hand to his bleeding face and cursed, and there another squirmed deeper into the mud and cried, unnerved.

By eleven o'clock the fog had lifted and the sun shone brightly on the plain. We could make out rebel flags in our front, where along the farther edge of the field there ran a line of railroad on a slight embankment; this handy breastwork was lined deep with our foes. Behind them was a short bare slope, rising to the wooded ridge, and up the slope beyond our right was a cluster of sharp flashes and clouds of smoke where a massed battery was firing rapidly. To the left of our front, a spur of woods came across the railroad into the field. To the left, farther away, we could see Meade's division pushing ahead. The Union batteries were set to pounding their opponents, and through more than an hour all the artillery of both sides flashed and thundered. Over our heads roared shells from heavy guns behind us, some of them on the far side of the river. Close by, Hall's pieces were blazing away; and I was proud to know that some of the gunners were men previously detached from my regiment.

I observed an example of coolness under fire. Captain Hall, sitting his superb horse as calmly as if on parade, was watching closely the work of his battery. Now and then he shouted a remark to Colonels Root and Tilden, who reined their mounts near by, and they shouted replies. Interrupting the conversation, a solid shot came hurtling between the captain and the colonels and hit with a mighty thud a caisson of the battery, smashing it and exploding the magazine in a howling ball of flame. Captain Hall looked annoyed. He got down deliberately from his horse, walked over to one of his guns, and sighted it; raised his hand, and an iron missile sped for the mark; a crash and a roar, and in the midst of a rebel battery there was a sudden upheaval of bursting shells, wheels, splinters, and human flesh. The captain returned to his horse, mounted, and went on with the interrupted talk.

By one o'clock the most annoying of the rebel guns were silenced, or driven off, or as severely damaged as our well served artillery could manage. Meade's division pressed forward again, and presently Taylor's brigade advanced in our front, and then Lyle's, and our batteries were limbered up and whipped ahead, almost across the field. There was a great burst of musketry. The brigades in advance were close to the rebel line, and hotly engaged, and apparently were stopped in their tracks. Then came the order for our brigade to carry with the bayonet the position of the enemy.

Our men rose up quickly and formed for the attack. Knapsacks were dropped in the mud. There was a clash and ring of steel as bayonets were fixed, then the tread of hurrying feet, and over the muddy furrows and ditches our steady onrush swept into the storm of battle. We passed through broken regiments of Taylor's and Lyle's brigades, now retiring to the rear in confusion, and some of our men went down, and a part of our first line slackened its pace and opened fire.

Colonel Root rode forward, shouting encouragement, and so did General Taylor, who still had in hand two regiments of his brigade, the 97th New York and the 88th Pennsylvania. Of Lyle's brigade one regiment, the 12th Massachusetts, was holding its ground. These regiments joined with ours in a charge.

Our lines ran forward with a shout. Men were hit and fell sprawling. Their comrades bent to the storm and went on, slogging through the mire, which now was spattered by solid shot and swept by a stinging rain of bullets. Deep ditches, suddenly appearing under our feet, were taken at a leap. Nothing could stop us. Over the railroad embankment we swept, and drove the rebels off. The fighting was savage. Bayonets and clubbed muskets overbore the defenders; many were killed, and prisoners and colors were taken and sent to the rear; the survivors were driven up the slope and into the trees.

Our brigade commander, seeing the charge succeed, rode rapidly back to find General Gibbon and ask for supporting troops and further orders. He left to his aides and the regimental commanders the duty of disentangling our lines and encouraging the men to hold the ground gained. We had our work cut out for us. The rush had been so impetuous that our right was much disordered; men of the second line had crowded up with the first, and the regiments of Taylor's and Lyle's brigades that had joined with ours were mixed with both our right and our left. We got them into the best positions we could, and directed a vigorous fire against the enemy intrenched in the woods in our front.

Colonel Root now returned with instructions to press forward; but our foes had rallied in superior force and were holding their ground with obstinacy and fury; the woods were crowding with black muzzles, and a murderous fire swept our line. Again he rode back to ask support from the division commander. He also applied to Colonel Lyle, entreating him to return with his men, but he could not, he says, persuade him to do so. General Gibbon was wounded and left the field, and the command of the division passed to General Taylor, who directed Colonel Root to withdraw the brigade from the woods if this should be necessary to save it from destruction.

We were holding on, but our grip began to loosen. The regiment farthest on our left had noticed the rebels pushing down through the wooded spur, and that regiment began to give ground. The others in succession, from left to right, did likewise, and my own regiment had no alternative but to follow. The Maine regiment had gone farthest ahead, and stayed there, and was willing to try another charge, but without support it could neither advance nor stand. Colonel Root perforce gave the order to retire.

As we drew back reluctantly, the rebels followed, in defiance of the batteries protecting our flanks, and swept us again with musketry, and their batteries caught us in the open; shells burst close upon us, and solid shot plunged into our ranks and knocked men, bleeding and senseless, into the mud to die. Yells of victory, cries of defeat, curses and groans, accompanied our hapless return. Hall's battery opened fire on the rebels emerging from the spur and smashed them with case-shot and canister; men and colors went down. The gunners kept on firing until we had passed them, and then, their caissons empty, brought off their pieces with no time to spare. So many horses were killed at one piece, when the attempt was made to limber it up, that the gun was left on the field. Birney's division, of Stoneman's corps, came up as we retired, and drove the rebels back to the woods; men of my old regiment, the 3d Maine, recovered the lost gun, and Captain Hall went out and brought it off and with it the harness of all the dead horses.

Our brigade was halted at the Bowling Green turnpike, faced about, and formed in line of battle, and one regiment was deployed as skirmishers; but there was no more fighting for us. I felt a strange exaltation. I had passed unscathed through the Valley of the Shadow, and was no longer a slave to the fear that at first had nearly overpowered me. I was horribly glad to be alive and unhurt. What mattered it if men around me had fallen, and shrieked in agony, pleaded for succor, cried and prayed and cursed! I was safe; dead, at that moment, to all human sympathy.

Waiting, I went to the nearest field hospital, where wounded men were lying on the ground awaiting their turns at further mutilation by the surgeons. I saw an endless procession of agony from the ambulances to the hospital, an endless procession of death from the hospital to the burial ditch. Four men walked past me, each holding a corner of an army blanket; it was full of arms and legs, and a dark red spatter dripped from its sagging folds. Here lay a man whose blood was yet pulsing though the top of his head was shot away. There another looked sadly at his shattered feet and cursed. I hurried back to my post.

Just before sunset the rebels again for a short time opened fire with all their artillery. Perhaps they thought of attacking, but if they did they must have changed their minds when the Union guns replied. The firing dwindled, ceased. The darkness fell. Colonel Root sent out parties to recover the arms, equipments, and ammunition of our fallen, as far as this could be done without inviting more death and wounds.

We lay on our arms till dead of night, and then were moved perhaps a mile to the left, and at dawn our brigade was deployed in line of battle facing south. We were a little below Smithfield, the mansion of one Forbes. Behind us were deployed Lyle's brigade and Taylor's, which latter was now Leonard's. Our division was in support to Doubleday's, on the extreme left of the army.

All that day and the following night and the next day, we stayed under arms, expecting to fight again, but the battle was not resumed. Actually, there had been two battles, and we knew that both had been lost. Sumner's grand division had failed, though trying manfully, to reach the heights in its front at Fredericksburg, as Franklin's had failed to carry the ridge below the town. The Army of the Potomac had suffered a dreadful repulse. The rebels held to their position, and their batteries kept up a spiteful fire; we had to change position several times to keep away from their shells. The suspense of the two days of waiting was harder on our nerves than the fighting on the day of battle.

We all felt a very great relief when at last night neared again and we were allowed to have fires. Their cheer, their warmth, and the homely task of cooking food, were good restoratives. The brain resumed its equipoise, reason returned, opinion roused and found expression under the stimulus of coffee. Criticism ran wild. Officers were praised without stint and damned without mercy.

I went down the line of my regiment, fewer than half its men surviving, weary and dirty, their clothes torn and muddy, knapsacks rent, canteens battered, hands and faces daubed with muck and splotched with powder. There were pale faces and faces flushed, anxious and expectant faces, many that I had scanned three days before; the same, yet changed. There was something in the expression, the attitude of those men, that awed me. An uprush of emotion blinded and choked me as I turned away.

Darkness deepened, and the bivouac fires made little red glows on the plain as far as the eye could reach. A rainy wind came over and made them wink and waver, and other tiny lights went joggling towards the ridge, where stretcher bearers with lanterns were searching for life among the dead. Under a flag of truce, Colonel Root and a party including myself rode back to where our brigade had fought, to look for any wounded of ours that might have been left there. Through the courtesy of the officer commanding the rebel pickets we were enabled to make a search almost as far as the woods. We found only a scattering of dead. The corpses that lay farthest forward had been stripped white; the rebels must have needed clothes.

Night closed in, and a gusty wind and pelting rain swept over the scene of battle, and under cover of the turbulent dark we obeyed orders to make ready in silence to move. Then we marched unmolested back to the pontoon bridges that we had crossed three days before, and back across the bridges, muffled now, to the east side of the river. The whole army was spirited away. The field was left to the enemy and the storm.

III

SOON after we went back over the Rappahannock, I returned to duty with my regiment. What tales I heard of death and glory! Captain Hutchins, commanding the company that might have been mine, had been killed in the charge. I remembered that he had been sick with a fever, and now I was told that when he went forward with his men he was so weak that he could hardly keep up, and gloomy with an apprehension that he was marked for death in the battle; yet he had insisted upon doing his full duty. His body, brought off the field when the regiment retired, was found twice pierced with bullets, in the head and near the heart. Lieutenant Herrick also had been killed while leading a company. Captain Ayer and Lieutenant Edwards, both severely wounded, had fallen into the hands of the enemy; we were never to see them again. How many of our men were dead was not certainly known; the list would be long.

I wondered then, and I wonder now equally, at the mystery of bravery. It seemed to me, as I saw men facing death at Fredericksburg, that they were heroes or cowards in spite of themselves. In the charge I saw one soldier falter repeatedly, bowing as if before a hurricane. He would gather himself together, gain his place in the ranks, and again drop behind. Once or twice he fell to his knees, and at last he sank to the ground, still gripping his musket and bowing his head. I lifted him to his feet and said, "Coward!" It was cruel, it was wicked; but I failed to notice his almost agonized effort to command himself. I repeated the bitter word, "Coward!" His pale, distorted face flamed. He flung at me, "You lie!" Yet he didn't move; he couldn't; his legs would not obey him. I left him there in the mud. Soon after the battle he came to me with tears in his eyes and said, "Adjutant, pardon me, I couldn't go on; but I'm not a coward." Pardon him! I asked his forgiveness.

Another man was determined on going ahead. His trouble was in getting started. He was a nervous, excitable man, and while we waited under fire before going into action he found it impossible to keep still and wormed his way up and down the ditch where he lay. When he heard the sharp command to fall in, he was away from his place in the ranks, and began dodging wildly up and down to find it again. Great beads of sweat broke out on his face, and his eyes were staring; he was ridiculous and pitiable; but when at last he found his place he kept it without faltering.

In Company F was a soldier named Oliver Crediford, a large man, of great physical strength. A fellow soldier named Levi Barker fell wounded, and Crediford picked up Barker and started for the rear.

"Crediford!" his captain shouted. "Come back into the ranks! Leave that man where he is!"

"Cap'n," he shouted back, "you must think I'm a damn fool to let Barker die here on the field."

He kept on going and was seen no more in the battle. If he kept his head to save his skin, I suspect he was the only man that did. A few may have found themselves out of the fight, but how they had managed to turn up missing, I doubt they knew. The many went forward, and the officers and men that made the charge won for the regiment such praise as green troops rarely receive after their first battle.

General Gibbon, commanding the division, wrote in his official report: "I desire to call special attention to the services of Brigadier-General Taylor, Colonel A. R. Root, 94th New York, and to the gallantry and steadiness under fire of the following-named regiments: 12th Massachusetts, Colonel Bates; 97th New York, Colonel Wheelock; 88th Pennsylvania, Major Griffith; and 16th Maine, Lieutenant-Colonel Tilden. The last-named regiment, although for the first time under fire, gave an example of gallantry and steadiness worthy the imitation of some of the older regiments. . . . Hall's battery was under the severest fire, and was served with its usual efficiency and gallantry."

Colonel Root, commanding the brigade, wrote: "I am happy in being able to bear testimony to the gallant manner in which the regimental commanders took their men into action, and I deem it a duty no less than a pleasure to make especial mention of the 16th Maine, Lieutenant-Colonel Tilden commanding. This regiment is a new one, and here fought its first battle, and I felt some apprehension lest the terrible fire from the enemy's concealed rifle pits would be too severe a trial for its men; but the gallant manner in which this regiment charged the enemy's position excited my surprise and admiration, and reflected the highest honor upon its officers and soldiers. . . . Previous to the battle thirty-eight men of this regiment had volunteered to do duty with Hall's battery, and their conduct is represented by Captain Hall to have been creditable in the highest degree."

The past was redeemed. The voice of insult and reproach was forever silenced. The regiments which had hitherto ignored our claim to respect joined heartily when the 2d Division raised three cheers and a tiger for the 16th Maine.

IV

AFTER the battle of Fredericksburg the army went into camp scatteringly in the broken country between the Rappahannock and Potomac rivers. The camp of my regiment was at first about midway of this country and seven or eight miles east of Fredericksburg, on the estate of one James Taliaferro. No doubt this incorrigible rebel was in communication with the enemy and gave us away at every opportunity. Captain Waldron, officer of the picket, believed so, and Major Farnham and I did, too; yet the major and I called on him frequently, for we found his conversation peculiarly entertaining.

Old Taliaferro, like a shabby sunflower, lived in habitual adoration of the source of his name: he would talk all day of the glory of his family; and, while he talked, his sadly crossed eyes would wander at random, seeking recognition of his title as a faithful though seedy exemplar of the F.F.V. I dare say his pretensions were well grounded. At any rate, his garrulity was enjoyable. Major Farnham would brace him up to descant upon wealth and respectability, and we could only admire the insistence with which he would turn the conversation from lucre to the pet illusion of his old age.

War was fast reducing his little wealth of slaves and produce. In the near presence of opposing armies he feared the worst, and in a last effort to keep a remnant of his riches he began to make a show of loyalty both ways; daytimes, with us, he shed tears for the Old Flag, and at night he hung out the rag of rebellion to encourage the Southern Cause. His shuttlecock life was a curse to him. The rebels ran off his livestock and the Yanks acquired his niggers.

His spacious, rambling house fronted towards the Rappahannock, and commanded a wide view of picturesque woodlands, and fields of pasture and tillage divided here and there by thrifty cedar hedges. He would stand with us by his front gate, revolve his hand in a graceful circle, and bid us gaze upon some distant loveliness. From the direction of his eyes I never could tell whether he meant to indicate the Union camp, whence came his sugar and coffee supplies, or the rebel camp over the river, where his son, he said, was a flower of chivalry. It didn't matter; the view was pleasing, even in winter, if one looked anywhere away from the Taliaferro walls. There was a strange incongruity, an unhappy mixture of pride and want, of beauty and ugliness, in the home of this sad aristocrat.

The mansion had no particular design or shape; it appeared to have grown haphazard as the family had prospered and multiplied. The best room, or parlor, was in the main part of the house, and the dining-room was in another part, and the way between was a brick walk out of doors, which gave the dinner guest a chance to shake off the odors of pork and cabbage before settling down to talk and toddies by the fireside. The parlor wore a shabby splendor. Its walls were hung with portraits of Taliaferros and other eminent Southerners, in gilt frames, the haughtiest Taliaferro staring down from over the mantel. The huge brass firedogs, of old kept bright by slave hands, had lost their luster. A dusty look marred the beauty of everything. The piano, lacking tune, had a venomous sound as Miss Betty mashed an accompaniment to "The Bonnie Blue Flag" and "Dixie." Miss Sally, about to sing for us, said mockingly:

"We always reckon to play these yer to Union soldiers. When our troops pay us a vist we play and sing 'The Star Spangled Banner' and 'Yankee Doodle' over and over again."

They played and sang, and charmed away our memory of the standoffish airs they had assumed when we had introduced ourselves. They professed an intense hatred of Northerners and gave us to understand that, although Southern hospitality obliged them to treat us politely when we were their guests, they would not recognize us socially outside their doors. We said nothing to that; but I read in Major Farnham's face a determination to put it to the test if an opportunity should offer, and I hoped to be with him and take my part in the snubbing.

Not many days afterwards, when he and I were returning from a ride to corps headquarters, I noticed him putting away his pipe, straightening up in his saddle, and assuming his most intense dignity. I straightened up, too, and for a moment I wondered what was coming. Then I heard a crazy rattle and shuffle, and around a bend in the road came a ramshackle turnout drawn by a flabby horse and a bony mule hitched together. The driver was an ancient Uncle Tom. Two feminine figures were sitting primly behind him; and, sure enough, they were the Taliaferro girls. We drew aside and raised our hats and smilingly awaited recognition and perhaps a pleasant word. Alas for our hopes! They went past as if the roadside were empty. Yet the next time we called at the Taliaferro house, with the usual gifts of sugar and coffee, we were graciously received. The old man solved the social problem with one eye on the packages and the other on the girls. Miss Betty and Miss Sally played and sang.

I have always felt grateful to the house for the shelter it afforded to my brother Emilus, who lay ill in one of its rooms for weeks. The only personal attention he received was from a negress, one of the few slaves that stayed by the Taliaferro family. She seemed to be the only person capable of doing anything, until she lost her life; she was accidentally shot dead when a gun fell to the floor and went off as she was moving a piece of furniture in a room just over the one where Emilus lay. The presence of my brother in the house was forced, or I should have expressed more gratitude when I paid the exorbitant price demanded for use of the room.

While he was there, and I was visiting him as often as I could, the regiment moved a mile or more northwards and went into winter quarters near Fletcher's Chapel. No orders for winter quarters came down from on high. We merely interpreted the state of affairs and prepared accordingly. It was January 3d when the change of camp was made. Two days later Colonel Wildes, who was still out of health, paid a visit to the regiment and at dress parade made known his intention of resigning his commission, and bade farewell to the command. The next day he left us for good.

The ground for our winter home was a gorge with a brook of good water running down the middle. Quite a grove of trees had to be felled, which were all utilized for houses and firewood. The men built log pens with a hearth at one end, and made flues of small sticks plastered with mud; then they fastened their tents over the pens, and set their fires going, and so had rooms that were high enough to stand in and fairly warm. Headquarters was established on a side hill, into which we dug for the foundation. At the back we made a neat fireplace; above it we built a chimney surmounted by a pork or lard barrel; and I remember that the barrel, when dry, often took fire and illuminated the entire camp.

Max and I built generously, and inside our finished house, in the warmth of a roaring blaze, we set up bedsteads, and overlaid them with pine boughs for mattresses, and covered the boughs with blankets for counterpanes. How proudly and fondly we gazed upon those beds! We had slept on the ground, between knolls, to keep from rolling down hill, in all kinds of weather, and now we were to have a heavenly rest secure above the sacred soil. We longed for night and measured with impatience the going down of the sun. Even the silvery voice of black Ben, announcing that tea was ready, failed to move us from rapt contemplation of those beds. Just as the sun began hiding itself, there came darkly into view a horse, then an ambulance, and in the ambulance two women, visitors.

"Oh, Lord of Hosts!" I groaned.

"Oh, hell!" said Max.

We slept on the ground, or tried to; we lay in the cold frosts, beneath the stars, shivering under one poor blanket, and near enough to our ravished house to hear the visitors exclaim:

"What splendid beds these soldiers have!"

"How romantic it must be to sleep on boughs!"

Those women robbed us of our rest; they ate, for supper and breakfast, supplies that had cost us five dollars, and some things from home that we could not replace; and they left us nothing, hardly an acknowledgment of our courtesy. They rather conveyed an impression that it was they who had favored us. What they had come for, God only knows. Max said, later, that they did leave a cheap Testament and a calico blouse, and that Ben embellished the blouse with red tape and wore it as an undress uniform until the starch was out, when he used it for a dishcloth.

Monday, January 12th, we received orders to have on hand cooked rations for five days. We took this to mean that Burnside was going to try another campaign. There were no cheers. We had lost all confidence in the man behind the whiskers. Yet, if he were to try at all, now was the time; the weather had been splendid, the roads were passable, and the enemy, still on the other side of the Rappahannock, could not prevent Burnside from starting as he pleased.

Wednesday all surplus baggage and camp furnishings were ordered disposed of, which meant "destroyed for want of transportation," as we were to move the next day. This doomed all our furniture, the tables and chairs and desks made out of barrels and boxes, all our handy aids to housekeeping, and all the things the men had fashioned to while away the time. Dice, chessmen, checkers, and playing-boards abounded in every company, and the owners found it hard to part with them. One man in Company C dug a grave, piled in his little treasures, and read service over them, preaching a sermon from Hosea, twelfth chapter, first verse: "Ephraim feedeth upon wind, and followeth after the east wind . . ." Then a storm came, the order to march was countermanded, and camp duties were resumed.

Tuesday, January 20th, we received orders at nine o'clock to pack and be ready to march at noon. Acquired, improvised, and stolen housekeeping utensils were again "destroyed for want of transportation," and at noon we marched, in a miserable cold rain. The men were cheerful enough, though asking if they were to try another Fredericksburg. The line officers had no answer;

they swore most horribly. We of the field and staff were only reconciled to the prospect when we saw the forager Tibbetts disappearing over the hill and Ike Thompson heaving in sight with four canteens; the early departure of Tibbetts meant a probable good dinner, and the canteens meant plenty of whiskey in the meantime.

We marched towards Falmouth, and beyond, and went on northwesterly not far from the Rappahannock till nine o'clock at night. Our march was made over roads that were beaten into quagmires by the passage of artillery, or over soggy fields and swampy meadows, or through dripping woods. The rain fell now in a slow, exasperating drizzle, and now in drenching torrents. The day went out in water. The night was a black flood. In the storm and darkness regiments and brigades blundered apart, companies went astray, and divisions were in hopeless confusion. Regardless of orders or discipline, the men bivouacked wherever they could. Some, I know, tried a sandy flat beside a little brook. Before morning the brook became a stream that swept away their shelter tents and knapsacks. They warmed themselves with curses.

Wednesday we marched about three miles farther. I don't know where we had come to; it was said that we were near Banks's Ford. Wherever it was, we stayed there stuck in the mud. Supposedly, Burnside had intended us to move around the flank of the enemy. Why didn't we move? I saw a part of the answer; in a field near my regiment was a battery, stuck so hard that its floundering horses could scarcely move a single gun.

That attempt at a campaign, remembered now only as the "Mud March," was a failure. Thursday we started slogging back, and Friday we returned to our old camping ground near Fletcher's Chapel. We felt that we were to stay a while, refitted our shelters accordingly, made new furniture, and resumed housekeeping as if we had never left off. The man in Company C who had buried his valuables congratulated himself; he had fixed a neat headboard to mark their resting-place, and guided by this he opened up the grave and resurrected the numerous corpses without ceremony.

Camp duties and diversions were recommenced, and there was much talk of a change in the command of the army. The change was soon made; by orders read to us on Tuesday, January 27th, Burnside was superseded by Hooker. The rank and file were pleased, but the officers were not all of one opinion; some felt that we should be less gratified to be commanded by Hooker than happy to be rid of Burnside.

CHANCELLORSVILLE

Over their graves, the pine-cones fall,
And the whippoorwill chants his spectre-call ...
—GEORGE PARSONS LATHROP, "Keenan's Charge"

HOOKER took command of an unhappy army, defeated, despondent, ravaged by desertion, unpaid, and stuck in the mud without hope of moving before spring. I recall that when I went home on leave, February 7th, I was troubled at what I must tell my friends. Yet I knew that my regiment, for one, was reliable; that our officers and men, with few exceptions, were dependable in duty and steadfast in devotion; and why shouldn't I believe that all the army was a multiplication of our strength as of our weakness?

Matters had already begun to mend when I returned, February 22d; a new spirit was beginning to show itself, reflected from the vigor and confidence of the new army commander. Wise measures were taken to check the evil of desertion and to satisfy the wants of the men: furloughs were granted generously; new clothing was supplied, of better quality than the old; rations were increased, and fresh bread was issued. The troops were inspected frequently and drilled as often and as thoroughly as the weather would permit.

Changes were made in organization and officers. Our division was now under the command of General Robinson, formerly a brigade commander in the 3d corps; Gibbon was absent, recovering from his wound, and Taylor, who had succeeded Gibbon on the field at Fredericksburg, had resigned. General Robinson was an officer of long experience in the regular service, and was rather fierce in appearance and manner. In a much bearded army he was the hairiest general I ever saw. Colonel Root was continued in command of the brigade. In the regiment, well deserved promotions made Colonel Tilden, Lieutenant-Colonel

Farnham, and Major Leavitt the names and titles above mine on the roster of the field and staff. Under these able officers, untiring in effort and unrelaxing in discipline, we survived a difficult situation.

Winter wore away in crazy weather. I had returned to the army to find it almost hidden under snow. That day being Washington's Birthday, salutes were fired, the cannon roaring defiance at the storm, but the fall of snow was so heavy that other observances of the occasion were omitted. March 4th brought more snow and a savage wind. The huts of our men were nearly all stripped of their canvas roofs, chimneys were blown down, and books, papers, and clothing were scattered in all directions; our camp had the appearance of a laundry drying-yard. March 15th brought a thunderstorm and hail, disrupting a regimental inspection. March 28th was wild with wind, and bitter cold. A bleak New England winter could hardly have been more trying than that season in the Sunny South.

General orders and circulars now swarmed as thick as snowflakes, all indicating active service in the near future, and the regiment welcomed the prospect of a change. We would gladly be quit of our life in winter quarters and the wearisome and endless round of dull camp duties. We kept an eye on the skies and roads and prayed for clear weather and dry ground.

Thursday, April 2d, Hooker reviewed the division. Our regiment was early on the ground, and we watched with enjoyment the pageant of blue and steel and scarlet as the brigades and batteries took their places. The trimly clad men with their burnished guns, the proudly mounted and gayly uniformed officers, the brilliant standards fluttering in the breeze and the measured tramp of veterans marching to the crash of bands, the evident satisfaction of Hooker and the conscious power plainly shown in his handsome but rather too rosy face, all combined to excite our hopes and ambitions. Despondency and doubt had given way to pride and confidence.

President Lincoln came to the army and visited the camps and reviewed the various corps; Thursday, April 9th, he reviewed our corps at Belle Plain. Our regiment never looked better than when it marched for that review. The "Blanket Brigade" had vanished forever; we were spruce and soldierly, without fuss; no pipeclay about us, not so much as a paper collar. On our way to Belle Plain we halted at a crossroads, and the men of a sister regiment went past, flaunting a stunning toilet, and turned their heads as far as they could in their paper dickeys and eyed us with their old scorn and shouted their ancient jeers:

"Hello, 'Roostooks; where's your blankets?"

"Get away! Pick off them lice!"

"Had your bath yet?"

Not a yip from a Sixteener; our colonel stared along the column, his eyes commanding every man, and his look was obeyed. In silence we moved on, marching in the footsteps of the offending regiment. The sun was hot, and presently a discarded dickey was seen by the roadside. A man of ours hooted derisively, and was not rebuked. Another dickey was seen, then another, and then a few more, and then a continuous litter, and a roar of jeers and laughter broke from our delighted men. They speared those wilted collars with bayonets, and when we got to the plain they made a pile of them and set above it a board with the inscription:

"Sacred to the memory of Bay State pride."

Collars lost their importance as marks of distinction when, a few days later, orders were read announcing that corps badges were to be worn by all the army. The badge for our corps was a sphere, red or white or blue to distinguish the three divisions in the corps, white for our division.

Everything was ready for the campaign. Wednesday, April 15th, we thought we were to move, but a rainstorm came and we stayed in shelter. The next Wednesday, though it rained again, we broke camp and marched about half a mile; to harden us, our humorists said. The regiment was in good spirits. All that we needed was a good band. Our principal musician, John Shea, had organized a band while we had been in winter quarters, and now a set of instruments came, a present from the officers. There was a grand discord of tuning up, and practice was started, but contrary to the usage of the best tradition we went to battle before the band began to play.

II

Tuesday, April 28th, we broke camp at noon and started in rain towards the Rappahannock. We had somewhat lost our high spirits. We had been expecting a distinguished though unnamed visitor from Maine, and as the cheers of a sister regiment had hailed the appearance of somebody from another state—was it Governor Parker, of New Jersey?—our rank and file, in defense of local pride, had talked loudly about our coming man; but he hadn't come.

A few miles from camp we were halted in a field full of stumps, where we received the announcement that General Robinson and his staff had gone to fetch our distinguished visitor. They soon came back at a mad gallop, and in their midst on a plunging colt clung Somebody with a stovepipe hat mashed down over his left ear, his trousers hitched up to his knees, and his coattails flying. We were ready to cheer, but as the cavalcade brought up suddenly in front of the regiment and landed His Excellency Governor Coburn astride the neck of his wild horse, the cheer exploded weakly in something resembling laughter. Colonel Tilden advanced with bared head and gave his hand to His Excellency, inviting him to dismount. The governor said, "I guess I will get off." After shaking hands with some of the rank and file, and asking them "what they had to eat," he turned to Colonel Tilden, saying, "Colonel, you keep a rooster, don't ye? I keep a private rooster myself, and I want all my colonels to keep one." By this time the faces of the entire regiment were distorted by a conflict between respect and disgust, and relief was as plainly expressed when the incident was closed abruptly by General Robinson's order to resume the march. A remarkably quiet and inoffensive body of men proceeded to pick its way through a wilderness of stumps, in a silence broken only by one audacious mocking cockcrow from the throat of some wag.

We made a short march, and bivouacked for the night near White Oak Church, and the next afternoon we came to the river about three miles below Fredericksburg. All our corps was centered there, and Sedgwick's near by, upstream, and Sickles' in reserve. Pontoon bridges had been laid, and Wadsworth's division was on the farther shore; Brooks's division of Sedgwick's corps had gone over at our old crossing; the rebel outposts had been driven in, and now there was some firing by skirmishers on the plain, and rebel batteries were throwing shells from the farther heights. Were we going to try another battle on the scene of our repulse? Must there be another Fredericksburg? Our men appeared not to care; they played poker and chased rabbits as if a campaign were an outing. We stayed in bivouac to the end of that day and through the night.

Thursday was Fast Day, proclaimed by the President. I don't recall that any of us indulged in fancy humiliations. We had a holiday that we hadn't expected; no marching, no fighting; we loafed happily in the spring sunshine under the green trees. A congratulatory order from Hooker was read:

"With heartfelt satisfaction the commanding general announces to the army that the operations of the last three days have determined that our enemy must either ingloriously fly, or come out from behind his defenses and give us battle on our own ground, where certain destruction awaits him."

We hoped that all this was true. We were glad to know, at any rate, that a large part of the army had marched unopposed northwestwards, crossed the Rappahannock and the Rapidan, and was now in a position to flank the rebels and force them out of their intrenched lines.

Preparatory to the general slaughter soon expected, the chaplains of our brigade proposed to hold divine service. Accordingly, about four o'clock in the afternoon, the brigade was formed in a hollow square, the chaplains gathered in the center, and the holy work was begun. All was quiet across the river as the innocent twelve-hundred-dollar shepherds expounded to their lambs the cause of God and the glorious Republic. They were eloquent in their appeals to patriotism, and pictured in glowing colors the glory that would crown the dead and the blazons of promotion that would decorate the surviving heroes. They besought us all to stand firm, to be brave; God being our shield, we had nothing to fear.

Whoosh! Suddenly interrupting, there came a great rushing sound. Crash! A great crackling and bursting rent the air. The explosions of shells, the screams of horses, and the shouted commands of officers were almost drowned out by the yells and laughter of the men as the brave chaplains, hatless and bookless, their coattails streaming in the wind, fled madly to the rear over stone walls and hedges and ditches, followed by gleefully shouted counsel:

"Stand firm; put your trust in the Lord!"

"Come back and earn your twelve hundred dollars!"

The scare was soon over, but no persuasion could induce those chaplains to come back and confess their surrender to the weakness of the flesh. I wouldn't say that they were other than good Christian men trying to discharge their duties under peculiarly trying circumstances; I would only suggest that there was a practical deficiency in their training for the field. The danger was real enough. A few men of our brigade were wounded, and a few among other troops near by were killed.

The fire increasing, our brigade was withdrawn by order of the division commander to the cover of hedges and ditches bordering the riverside road. We remained there under fire through that night and all the next day. There was no fighting, only the cannonading. The troops on the farther side of the Rappahannock did not advance, nor did the rebels move down against them from the heights; and on our side of the river, Sickles' corps marched away northwesterly to where Hooker had gone. Our quiet May Day was celebrated with a ration of spirits all round.

Saturday, May 2d, our corps was ordered up the river. Under the fire of rebel batteries across the Rappahannock, we marched past Fredericksburg and pressed on for United States Ford. The march was rapid and exhausting; twenty miles under a hot sun, with few and brief halts. We reached the ford near the latter end of day, crossed a pontoon bridge over the flowing water, halted, and fell out to rest, perhaps to bivouac.

Our halt was short. Orders came for us to hurry on, and we set off by a rough road as night was falling. We passed a brick house, where artillery was parked in a field, and about a mile from the ford we marched into woods. Before we had gone far, our column began to come upon stragglers hurrying towards the ford. One regiment of our brigade, the 94th New York, was deployed to drive them back. They came on more thickly, and we heard their vague shouts of disaster; a fight was raging in the forest, and Howard's corps had been routed in panic. The confusion slowed us as we pushed ahead. After a while we stopped, to await orders where we should take our stand. We heard a confused firing, and caught the smell of wood smoke, and away beyond us we could discern a shuddering flare; where the fighting had raged, trees and underbrush had burst into flame. Near us were dense thickets and uncertain clearings, dim with moonlight, where the whippoorwills were crying.

Again our halt was short. We were soon making our way to the right along another forest road, and startling the hollow way with a great roar of "John Brown's Body." If we glanced behind us, we saw above the trees the night sky sparkling with the flight of burning fuses and the fiery pang of shells. It was about midnight when we came to a clearing and went into position along the road with our right refused. Pickets were sent out, and one regiment, the 104th New York, was posted as a guard in advance of our line. The pickets were soon engaged in a skirmish and sent in some prisoners, who said that our right would be attacked in the morning. The regiments in line were set to work throwing up breastworks, and our tired men did their task so well that by daybreak our defenses were respectably strong.

Early Sunday morning the battle was resumed beyond our left, near Chancellorsville, and all through the forenoon it raged furiously. We continued to strengthen our works, details of each regiment standing under arms while other details were busy with axes and shovels. All day we expected the promised attack, but there was only a skirmishing of pickets in our front. We could see nothing of what was happening anywhere; the forest shut us in. We could only conjecture how the battle was going.

III

HEADQUARTERS, 2D DIVISION, 1ST CORPS,
May 3d, 1863, 4½ o'clock P.M.

COLONEL—

You will please send an intelligent officer to the right of your line to ascertain and report upon the condition of affairs on the Rapidan. Observe particularly whether the enemy is making any movement in that direction. The information is wanted this evening.

JNO. C. ROBINSON,
Brig.-Gen., Com'dg.

To COL. A. R. ROOT,
Com'dg Brigade.

Respectfully referred to Adj't Small, 16th Me. Vols., who will execute the duty and report thereon.

A. R. ROOT,
Col., Com'dg Brigade.

In obedience to this order I mounted my horse and, with an orderly, jumped the breastworks and proceeded down the road towards Ely's Ford. Passing our picket line half a mile out, and the cavalry vedettes but a short distance beyond, I slackened pace and moved cautiously some three miles, and drew rein at the edge of the woods, where the road made a sharp bend to the left in the direction of the ford. The quiet hush of the forest and the stillness of the air betrayed no presence of a living creature. I at once left the road, and came upon a shabbily clad and villainous-looking tramp, possibly the owner of the shanty that was now in sight directly in my way. I bade him good evening and asked if he objected to my crossing his yard and field. A surly grunt was the only reply he made. I felt uneasy about leaving him at large, but time was precious, my orderly was unarmed, and I couldn't invest in a rebel and proceed; so, thanking him politely, I rode on past the shanty. A mile or more beyond, I came to the crest of an elevation some fifty or seventy-five feet above the Rapidan. There I stopped and made note of what I saw.

Directly across the river, and from one to three miles to the left, fires from deserted camps and several buildings were still burning. Two long columns of infantry with artillery were moving rapidly from our front in the direction of Fredericksburg. I saw no other signs of the enemy, and, believing that my information was valuable to an army waiting behind breastworks for an attack from a force which, unseen, was withdrawing, I started on my return, elated with success accomplished with so little danger.

Riding back towards the road, I passed through the farmer's yard, and as I reached the shanty I was startled to see, a hundred yards to the left, a rebel outpost, the men lying on the ground near their stack of arms, and, over by the road and following the woods both ways, a line of pickets. A rapid and cautious excursion showed me that the line extended out of sight to both right and left. I couldn't risk attempting to ride around it. There was nothing to try but a dash through.

Rebel prison or the Union lines? My orderly and I were as yet unobserved. I pointed past the enemy; he understood; we struck spurs into our horses and bolted across the yard. The first plunge of the animals aroused the outpost. We heard loud shouts of "Halt! Halt!" as we dashed past into the clearing. We were in for it. The pickets were alarmed; there was more shouting, and bullets came whistling past our heads as we made for their line and burst through it and galloped madly away. The outpost, crowding the road behind, sent after us a scattering fire, but luckily for us the rebels were armed with carbines, not rifles; we were soon out of range, unharmed.

Nearly a mile out from our lines was General Reynolds, our corps commander, with members of his staff, anxiously waiting for the intelligence requested through General Robinson. When I rode up, he said quickly, "Well?" I gave him my information. He thanked me cordially, turned, and hurried away; to carry the news to Hooker, I supposed. As for me, I rode inside our lines and gave my horse in charge to my orderly. Tired from two days of excitement without rest, I lay down on the ground behind the breastworks without removing any of my equipments, and in a moment I was fast asleep.

I had slept only a short time when I was waked up, and an aide with a verbal order from Colonel Root directed me to report at once at brigade headquarters. I hastened to obey, wondering what more would be required of me. Not more than half awake, I heard a staff officer tell me sharply that I was to go with him from the right of our line to the Rapidan, where I was to remain while he established a line of vedettes between our position and the river. Since he represented the brigade commander, I listened to him; but I didn't like his looks or his tone, I thought him a fool, and doubted his capacity to establish anything.

As we set out, he desired me to go first. I demurred. Why should I precede my superior?

"I'm ready to follow you; lead," I said.

He led; and we went out into a black tangle of forest, in search of a river that ran silently somewhere off to the right. We were soon where no remark of mine would be "prejudicial to good order and military discipline," and I didn't care a damn for my guide personally, so I thorned him about the lack of respect shown to his rank and station by the Wilderness. Vines tripped him, branches mashed his hat and whipped his face, and every now and then a hole would open under his feet and take him down sprawling.

We were hours in getting nowhere. We tore through briery thickets and stumbled into stony ravines, all for nothing. The silent river kept away. More than once as we stopped to listen we heard the gurgling rush of a brook, but there was no sound of widely flowing waters. All of a sudden my guide pitched headlong with a splash. I may have been unkind, but I had to laugh, and between spasms I asked him if he had found the Rapidan.

"Yes, damn you," he replied, "I have found the Rapidan."

I knew he couldn't have found it, and told him so, for at the rate of our slow groping we shouldn't have got to it before daylight; but no argument would disabuse him of the notion that he had fallen into the river. I think he was in Hunting Run. Whatever it was, he ordered me to stand facing it in the position of a soldier and to stay there while he went back and brought out his line of vedettes. He thrashed away into the blackness, bumping and cursing, and silence closed in behind him. I felt sure that he didn't mean to come back; revenge was what he wanted, at my expense.

It must have been near midnight, as dark and quiet as the grave. If Nature had a heart, it ceased to beat. My own beat the faster. My duty seemed plain; I had been ordered to stay; but common sense advised me to return, and I started back for my regiment. Every few moments I stopped, and kept still, and listened for some guiding sound. After a while I heard ahead to the left the whop of an axe, and presently, ahead to the left again, I heard another. I took a direction as nearly between the two sounds as I could, and at the end of half an hour I turned sharp to the left and came in over the works in front of my regiment. As the pickets had been told to fire, without challenging, upon anyone approaching, my escape was lucky.

In the morning I learned that by nothing short of a miracle my late guide had blundered back to safety. I half expected that he would raise hell about my part in the expedition; but the incident was closed. I heard nothing about his having established his line of vedettes. What he had reported to the brigade commander, I never knew.

All that day, Monday, May 4th, the brigade was under arms and strengthening its works. The 107th Pennsylvania was sent out on guard duty, relieving the 104th New York. Paul's brigade of Wadsworth's division moved up on our right, lengthening our line towards the Rapidan. There was comparative quiet, though now and then we heard cannonading away to our left.

The higher commanders were still curious about the situation on their extreme right. In the forenoon our skirmishers were active, and General Reynolds, with a few officers including Colonel Root, made a reconnaissance to the front of our position and found that rebel pickets were close beyond our own. In the afternoon General Robinson took the 12th and 13th Massachusetts and a section of Hall's battery and made a reconnaissance along the Ely's Ford road, where I had gone the evening before. He satisfied himself that the rebels were there in force to his left. His skirmishers were fired upon, and several were wounded.

After nightfall, when everything was still, there was a sudden outburst of firing close on our right that brought all the men of my regiment to their feet, muskets in hand, just in season to be targets for a wild broadside from the 22d and 29th New Jersey, posted in reserve in our rear. Fortunately for us, the Jerseymen were short in service and hadn't yet learned to aim low; their bullets whizzed over us into the treetops. The firing had started in one of the regiments extending our right towards the river; it was their first night in the Wilderness, and probably they were nervous. Triggers were pulled all along the line. Captain Waldron, commanding the pickets in front of us, collected some of his men and charged in over the works, roaring at the blunderheads to cease firing. The scare was soon over. No one was hurt.

Again the next day, Tuesday, we were under arms and ready to fight, but we only spent the day in discomfort; a heavy rain fell, flooding our trenches and drenching the men. Late in the afternoon the 22d New Jersey was moved from our rear to the right, and the line was extended all the way to the Rapidan. Relieved of the presence of Jersey lightning, we felt safer. Late at night the brigade was ordered to evacuate its position, but the movement was hardly begun when we were ordered to return; the river was rising, the pontoon bridges were in danger, and we couldn't withdraw until the crossing was made safe. The position at the front was again occupied, not agreeably; we knew that evacuation meant retreat, and we hadn't been given a fighting part in the battle. We felt that if our corps had been used—but speculation, we knew, must yield to fact.

Before daylight of Wednesday the pickets were drawn in and deployed to right and left as a rear guard; the works were evacuated; the brigade marched back to United States Ford, crossed the swaying, bumping pontoon bridge over the swollen river, and continued the march in the direction of Falmouth. It was still raining. We bivouacked in the mud of a bleak hillside, without wood for fires; our men chewed by turns their dry hardtack and the cud of discomfort, and saved their coffee for the morrow, when they might have a reasonable hope of acquiring a front-yard paling or the always popular farm fence.

Thursday we marched on, and bivouacked for the night in a patch of woods near the Fitzhugh house. We stayed there till Sunday, when we moved a few miles farther and went into camp near White Oak Church. The army was again occupying the country between the Rappahannock and Potomac rivers. The rebels returned to their old position below the Rappahannock, near Fredericksburg.

IV

THE campaign, hopefully begun, had ended in a bloody repulse for the Army of the Potomac. Our brigade, having done no fighting beyond a little skirmishing, had suffered few casualties. Our regiment went into camp with no losses to mourn. We made a model camp, a Virginia mansion supplying us with much handy material. Our tents were pitched in trim lines; the company streets were graded and policed; an evergreen arch was set up at the head of each street and decked with a wreath of boughs and flowers encircling the letter of the company; our garrison flag floated proudly above us; the band played, the men sang. It was a holiday scene that met the eye of visitors.

Our bitter chagrin at the outcome of the battle was soon abated. We were pleasantly sheltered, fully supplied, and well fed; our mail came almost regularly; our duties were performed with a reasonable regard for comfort. We drilled early in the morning or late in the afternoon, avoiding the heat; it was soon very hot at midday.

We stayed near White Oak Church a month. Towards the end of that time there was a change in the organization and command of the brigade. The strength of the army was reduced by the discharge of many regiments, as their terms of service expired, and many consolidations were made. The three brigades of our division were reduced to two. Paul's brigade was broken up, four of its regiments being assigned to Baxter's brigade, and one, the 13th Massachusetts, to Root's; and the same day that this latter regiment joined us, the 94th New York marched away for duty elsewhere, Colonel Root went with it, and Colonel Leonard, of the Massachusetts regiment, became our brigade commander. We rather liked the appearance of Leonard, shrewd and kindly; but we should have preferred to keep Root.

We expected another campaign; and soon we had it, after two false starts. June 4th, at two o'clock in the morning, we received orders to be in line at daylight, ready to march. Towards noon the order was countermanded. Again, June 6th, we were up early and in line; our guns were in stack nearly all day; at night-fall our tents were pitched again. Friday, June 12th, we went. At half-past five in the morning we struck tents, packed up, and bade a last good-bye to our camp, and a brief farewell, we hoped, to Lieutenant-Colonel Farnham, whom we left sick at the Fitz-hugh house.

We marched all day in dust and burning heat. Water was scarce; we drank from occasional muddy pools by the roadside. Fence rails had almost disappeared from this part of Virginia. When we bivouacked for the night, near Deep Run, our men could hardly collect enough wood to make fires for coffee. Our spell of light duty in camp had unfitted us for heavy going; we lost, as stragglers, in that march of twenty miles, four officers and eighty men. Saturday we got to the Orange & Alexandria Railroad, and bivouacked, in rain, between Bealeton and Rappa-hannock Station; we marched twelve miles. Sunday we tramped all day, and kept on going almost all night, arriving at Manassas Junction at half-past three Monday morning; twenty-five miles. At nine o'clock we pushed on, and arrived at Centreville at two in the afternoon; seven miles more. Tuesday we stayed at Centre-ville, and I refreshed my memory of going to the first Bull Run battle, almost two years before; it seemed two centuries past. Colonel Leonard was now superseded in the command of the brigade by General Paul. The general was an old regular, frosted with age and long service. He was a man of distinguished ap-pearance; he had a noticeably wide head and large eyes and a foreign look that was doubtless an inheritance from his French forebears.

Wednesday we marched twelve miles in blistering heat to Herndon. This took us through a farming country which didn't appear to have suffered much; fences were standing, fields were under cultivation, and houses were occupied. Thursday we stayed near Herndon. Wood and water were plentiful; and some of the fences vanished. In the afternoon a welcome rain fell, which continued all night. Friday we marched five miles to near Guilford Station, went into bivouac, and sent out a picket line towards Leesburg.

As we neared the end of our march to Guilford we passed an old plantation, shabby and serene, the house and grounds undisturbed except by time. A tottery board fence fronted the road, and perched on the fence were darkies of all shades and sizes. The crazy contortions of their bodies and the grimaces of astonishment that spread over their faces as they saw regiment after regiment massed in a field and batteries parked beyond, would have driven a circus crowd wild. I drew rein to watch them.

One old Sambo bared his woolly poll, stretched forth a long and bony hand as if to cover us with a blessing, and sang out in a cracked voice:

"Praise de Lawd fo' de glory ob dis yer 'casion! Heabenly Massa bress de Linkum sojers, an' show dese yer eyes de golden chariot b'fo' Ah die!"

Old hats, jackets, and shoes went high in air, and shouts of "Glory! Hallelujah!" burst from along the fence. An excited patriarch got down and hobbled to the roadside and right up to the marching men, exclaiming:

"Great King! How many mo' you'uns comin'? 'Spec's fo'ty milyuns toted by hyer since mo'nin.'"

"Well, uncle," said one of our boys, "you can stand here three weeks and see the Yanks go by."

"B'fo' God, Ah reckon so! Massa Linkum mighty sojer, Ah reckon. He gwine by hyer, too?"

"Oh yes, uncle, he's at the rear of our corps, miles back; he'll be along in his chariot tomorrow."

Limping back to the fence, now alive with squirming legs and shining faces, the patriarch yelled:

"Chilluns, cotch off yer hats an' jine in de chorus!"

And swaying from side to side in grotesque attitudes, the old man leading, they sang in their peculiar way:

> "Don' yer see 'em comin', comin', comin'—
>   Milyuns from de oder sho'?
> Glory! Glory! Hallelujah!
>   Bress de Lawd fo' ebermo'!
>
> "Don' yer see 'em goin', goin', goin'—
>   Pas' ol' massa's mansion do'?
> Glory! Glory! Hallelujah!
>   Bress de Lawd fo' ebermo'!
>
> "Jordan's stream is runnin', runnin', runnin'—
>   Milyuns sojers passin' o';
> Linkum comin' wid his chariot.
>   Bress de Lawd fo' ebermo'!
>
> "Don' yer hear him comin', comin'?
>   Yes, Ah do!
> Wid his robe an' mighty army?
>   Yes, Ah do!
> Want ter march wid him to glory?
>   Yes, Ah do!"

Long into the night I seemed to hear their chorus:

> "Glory! glory! Hallelujah!
>   Bress de Lawd fo' ebermo'!"

We were five days at Guilford. Stragglers caught up with us. It rained. Major Leavitt fell ill, and was sent to Washington. Thursday, June 25th, we tramped northwards over muddy roads to Edwards' Ferry, crossed the Potomac into Maryland, and marched to Barnesville; twenty-five miles. Friday we marched fourteen miles to Jefferson; Saturday, four or five miles farther to just above Middletown, in the Catoctin Valley. We didn't know where the rebels were; we only knew that they too had crossed the Potomac, and supposed that they might be not very far to the west of us. Our regiment went on picket duty. We saw no enemy. At half-past seven Sunday evening we were ordered to Frederick City, ten miles to the east. We got there at two o'clock Monday morning, rejoining the brigade, and found that our old comrades of the 94th New York were with us again. We left at five o'clock, and marched through Lewistown, Catoctin Furnace, and Mechanicstown to Emmitsburg, arriving at Emmitsburg at a quarter to six Monday evening; thirty-six miles in twenty-five hours, with a two-hour stop!

Hooker was now forced to give up the command of the army, and was superseded by Meade. The change was almost a surprise, and was not altogether to our liking. We should have chosen Reynolds. General orders from the old and new commanders were read, the one a farewell and the other a soldierly acceptance of duty. Among other things, the order from Meade said:

"The country looks to this army to relieve it from the devastation and disgrace of a hostile invasion."

Tuesday we marched northwards a few miles farther, into Pennsylvania. The "invaders" must be there, too, somewhere north of the Mason and Dixon line.

GETTYSBURG

When, sudden, over hill and dell
The gloom of coming battle fell ...
—ANON., "The Battle of Gettysburg"

AT NINE O'CLOCK in the morning of Wednesday, July
1st, we began to march towards Gettysburg, our division bringing up the rear of the corps. The road was hazy with the dust of
the marching column, and the farm lands, drifting by, were dry
and shimmering in the sultry heat. As we neared the town from
the southwest we heard away ahead to the left an unexpected
warning of battle. It was cannon. We quit the road and set off
through lanes and fields in the direction of the firing. Just as we
left the road we met a black servant with a horse, and the servant
said that the horse had belonged to General Reynolds; the general was killed.

We hurried on towards a low ridge a little west of the town.
Along the ridge was a scattering of trees and houses, and lording
it over them was a brick building, the Lutheran seminary, which
gave the ridge a name. Our brigade went around to the western
face of the building, and there we threw up a barricade of fence
rails and anything else that was handy. The barricade took the
shape of a crescent, bending to the west. Beyond it the ridge
sloped away through trees into fields, and beyond the fields was
another low rise of ground, topped with woods. There was fighting along that farther ridge, and the action appeared to be spreading beyond our right. I recall that as I looked up at the building
behind us and saw some officers in the cupola taking a view, I
noticed them pointing northerly. Baxter's brigade soon marched
off in that direction, and General Robinson went with it. Our
brigade was left in reserve.

As we waited by the seminary, Captain Whitehouse came to
talk with me.

"Adjutant," he said, "I wish I felt as brave and cool as the colonel appears."

"Why, Captain," I said, "he's as scared as any of us. Cheer up! 'Twill soon be over."

He tried to cheer up, and made sad work of it; his face wore a look of foreboding, and his smile was a stiff mockery. While we were talking we heard the command to fall in; and he looked me full in the face and said:

"Good-bye, Adjutant. This is my last fight."

We moved around the northern end of the seminary, and passed in rear of a battery there, and slanted northeast. We crossed the Cashtown pike, which led to our left across the ridge, and a little beyond the pike we crossed an unfinished line of railroad, which ran through the ridge in a sharp cut. Then we slanted northwest towards the ridge again and went across a field towards a grove. Along the edge of the grove were low heaps of stones. They had been hauled from the field and dumped there by some farmer, years back, and among them now were thick bushes. We clambered over the stone heaps and bushes, wheeled to the right, and went up through the trees to a rail fence. This brought us under fire, and some of our men were hit, and Captain Whitehouse was killed.

We went into line along the fence. Beyond it was another field, and from behind a fence at the farther side of the field a rebel line was firing. Corporal Yeaton of our color guard was shot dead. Captain Waldron, shouting to his men to keep cool and aim low, was struck; I saw him put up his hand as blood gushed from his neck. He clung to a tree, and stood there stubbornly, keeping his place and refusing to be taken to the surgeons. Colonel Tilden rode up to the line, his mount was shot, and horse and rider went down; but the colonel was on his feet in a moment, unshaken. Under his steady eye and voice our men poured a hot fire across the field. Other regiments were blazing away. The rebels took to the rear. Up went our colors and over the fence, and the regiment followed with a shout; but our line was recalled. As we came back over the field a rebel battery shelled us, and some of our men fell.

We returned to the grove, and presently we moved around to the right and took up a position by a stone wall near the crest of the ridge. We joined with Baxter's brigade there and beat off an attack. I remember the still trees in the heat, and the bullets whistling over us, and the stone wall bristling with muskets, and the line of our men, sweating and grimy, firing and loading and firing again, and here a man suddenly lying still, and there another rising all bloody and cursing and starting for the surgeon. Lieutenant Deering picked up a musket and fired without first removing the rammer, and the rammer went hurtling away with a crazy whizz that set the boys of his company to laughing. It was strange to hear laughter there, with dead men by.

After the attack was beaten off, Baxter's brigade, now wanting ammunition, was withdrawn, and our brigade took over that part of the ridge, the extreme right of the corps line. It was a hard place to hold, the rebels half surrounding it; but a skillful defense was made under the direction of General Robinson. I don't know who was in command of the brigade. General Paul had been disabled, shot through both eyes; and Colonel Leonard, succeeding him, and Colonel Root, succeeding Colonel Leonard, had both been wounded. Our regiment was under the direct orders of the division commander.

As the afternoon wore by, the rebel forces increased and ours didn't; their army was coming fast towards Gettysburg, crowding the roads from both west and north, and their lines formed and moved in with overpowering strength. All along the ridge behind our left the battle was still raging. The defense was stubborn against repeated attacks from the west. But east of the ridge in the fields beyond our right the fighting was soon over; Howard's troops there were driven back rapidly towards the town. Our right flank was exposed.

I should say it was after four o'clock when our regiment moved yet farther along the ridge. My recollection is that we crossed the Mummasburg road. We saw a brigade of rebels coming against us, and we looked around for support, and saw none, and were falling back for a more favorable position, when an aide came from General Robinson with an order for us to advance and hold the ridge as far north as possible. A few moments later the general himself rode up to Colonel Tilden and repeated the order. The colonel protested that our regiment without support couldn't hold the ridge; we numbered fewer than two hundred, all told; as well set a corporal's guard to stop the rebel army; but the general insisted:

"Hold it at any cost!"

"You know what that means," said Colonel Tilden, turning to us, and in the same breath he gave the commands that sent us hurrying back towards the Mummasburg road again. The stone wall came along on the left, and bent sharply ahead of us to face the road. (Or was it a fence by the road? It doesn't matter.) We made a dash for the corner, and planted our colors in the angle. We got there just as a flag and a line of battle showed up across the way; we heard distinctly the commands of a rebel officer directing his men to fire; and a volley crashed, and we saw some of our men fall. Our line blazed away in reply, and the rebel flag went down, and the officer pitched headlong in the stubble. In the field across the road were dead men and scattered equipments, wreckage of a rebel repulse earlier in the day; and now there were more. But the attacking line came on, and following behind it was another, and we knew that our little regiment could not withstand the onset. With anxious hope we looked again to the rear for support—and saw that the other regiments of our brigade, our division, were falling back rapidly towards the town. The rebels were sweeping in through the fields beyond our right. The ridge could be held no longer. We were sacrificed to steady the retreat.

How much time was then passing, I can't say; it was only a matter of minutes before the grey lines threatened to crush us. They came on, firing from behind the wall, from fences, from the road; they forced us, fighting, back along the ridge; and Captain Lowell fell, and some of our men. We got to the railroad cut, which offered a means of defense against the rebels following us, but just then we saw grey troops making in from the west, and they saw us. We were caught between two fires. It was the end. For a few last moments our little regiment defended angrily its hopeless challenge, but it was useless to fight longer. We looked at our colors, and our faces burned. We must not surrender those symbols of our pride and our faith. Our color bearers appealed to the colonel, and with his consent they tore the flags from the staves and ripped the silk into shreds; and our officers and men that were near took each a shred. I have one with a golden star.

Though the rebel lines were fast closing in, there was yet a chance for some of us to escape, and nothing now forbade our risking that desperate hazard. We that took the chance bolted across the Cashtown pike, and made our way, in a fever of anxiety, to a hill south of the town. There were batteries on the hill, in a cemetery; and Howard's reserve division, with some of his troops that had been driven through the town; and what remained of Reynolds' corps, under Doubleday. Directing the placing of troops where we turned up was Hancock, whose imperious and defiant bearing heartened us all. We found a remnant of our brigade, with what was left of the 11th Pennsylvania added to it, and Colonel Coulter of that regiment in command.

Once more we formed in line; more gap than line. The survivors of the 16th Maine then numbered only thirty men, four line officers, and myself. Captain Marston, our one captain present, assumed command of the regiment. The brigade was moved to the left, to Cemetery Ridge, and placed in position facing west and overlooking the Emmitsburg road, not far from where we had left that road in the morning. We threw up breastworks and stayed there in support of a battery until fresh troops relieved us, late in the forenoon of the next day. Hancock's corps, under Gibbon, had come up on our left.

July 2d our corps had a new commander, General Newton, whom we didn't know; an old regular, rather quiet in his bearing, and with a large, kindly face and level eyes. Doubleday had earned the command, but was returned to his division. Towards noon, we were moved to the right and placed in support of batteries on Cemetery Hill. All around our front and along the ridge beyond our left there was a continuous stir of preparation for more fighting. Colonel Coulter acquainted himself with the condition of the brigade, and made some staff appointments. I had a change of duty by the following order:

HDQ'RS, 1ST BRIG., 2D DIV., 1ST A.C.,
July 2d, 1863.

General Orders, No. 44.

.   .   .   .   .   .

Adjutant A. R. Small, 16th Reg't Me. Vols., is hereby detailed as Acting Assistant Adjutant-General of this brigade. He will be obeyed and respected accordingly.

.   .   .   .   .   .

By command of R. COULTER,
Col., Com'dg Brigade.

Until midafternoon the day was not noisy; only the movements of troops near by, the occasional bark of a gun on the hill, and farther away the scattered rattle of skirmish fire, disturbed the sultry quiet. Our men caught snatches of rest. About half-past three some rebel guns east of the town opened fire against batteries not far from us, which replied, and the quarrel was kept up through more than an hour. At the same time we began to hear other cannonading away to our left, and towards evening we heard from that direction the confused uproar of battle.

About sundown our brigade was hurried to the scene of action. Our way was swept by rebel artillery fire. As we passed the little house on the Taneytown road that was Meade's headquarters, a shell burst in our regiment and severely wounded Lieutenant Beecher and seven men. The brigade dashed on at the double quick. We heard the shouted command, "By the right flank—march!" In line of battle we hurried on through smoke, over rough ground, into the uproar, just as the rebels were driven back. The rush of grey had swept up through a battery. If I remember rightly, two of the guns were brought off by our men. The enemy did not renew the attack. We were marched back to our position on the right.

After dark, I should say about nine o'clock, we were moved down the front of the hill, under our batteries and near the town. Rebel sharpshooters were firing from the windows of houses near by. A stone wall offered some protection to our brigade, and the men lay on their arms until morning.

At daylight of July 3d, we were withdrawn and moved up to the left. As we came up the hill, we heard to the east the boom of cannon on the morning air; a little later we heard musketry; and by snatches we caught the noise of fighting until late in the forenoon. Near us, all was quiet. Colonel Coulter established brigade headquarters on the brow of the hill, at the left of the cemetery, pitching his tent in the edge of a small grove of trees and planting defiantly in full sight of the rebels the brigade flag.

From this point I could see almost all the Union position from Cemetery Hill to the Round Tops, two miles to the south, and the opposing curve of Seminary Ridge, now held by the rebels, and the valley between. The skirmish lines in the valley were clearly defined by streaks of curling smoke that faded upwards in the shimmering heat. A false calm possessed the field.

Noon came, and the sun blazed fiercely hot, and the silence fretted us. Time was counted through minutes that seemed hours and an hour that seemed an eternity. Then away down the Emmitsburg road a rebel cannon flashed, and a puff of smoke blew and hung on the still summer air; then another; and then from all the rebel line there was one vast roar, and a storm of screaming metal swept across the valley. Our guns blazed and thundered in reply. The earth groaned and trembled. The air, thick with smoke and sulphurous vapor, almost suffocated the troops in support of the batteries. Through the murk we heard hoarse commands, the bursting of shells, cries of agony. We saw caissons hit and blown up, splinters flying, men flung to the ground, horses torn and shrieking. Solid shot hit the hill in our front, sprayed battalions with fountains of dirt, and went plunging into the ranks, crushing flesh and bone. Under that awful fire, continuous, relentless, our brigade and all our line held tight and unfaltering.

About two o'clock our brigade was moved from the left to the right of the cemetery and placed in support of batteries there. How that short march was made, I don't know. The air was all murderous iron; it seemed as if there couldn't be room for any soldier upright and in motion. We stayed an hour in our new position, exposed not only to shelling from both east and west, but also to the galling fire of rebel skirmishers.

Colonel Coulter, tearing up and down the line to work off his impatience, all of a sudden drew rein and shouted:

"Where in hell is my flag? Where do you suppose that cowardly son of a bitch has skedaddled to? Adjutant, you hunt him up and bring him to the front!"

Away I went, hunting for the missing flag and man and finding them nowhere; and returned in time to see the colonel snake the offender out from behind a stone wall, where he had lain down with the flag folded up to avoid attracting attention. Colonel Coulter shook out the folds, put the staff in the hands of the trembling man, and double quicked him to the front. A shell exploded close by, killing a horse, and sending a blinding shower of gravel and dirt broadcast. The colonel, snatching up the flag again, planted the end of the staff where the shell had burst, and shouted:

"There, Orderly; hold it! If I can't get you killed in ten minutes, by God, I'll post you right up among the batteries!"

Turning to ride away, he grinned broadly and yelled to me:

"The poor devil couldn't be safer; two shells don't often hit the same place. If he obeys, he'll be all right and I'll know where my headquarters are."

Recklessly he dashed down the line. In a few minutes he returned, with one arm dangling. I recall the expression of his pain-distorted face when I, in my anxiety, asked him if he would not dismount; it was almost one of reproof.

"No, no," he said; "not now. Who in hell would suppose a sharpshooter would hit a crazy-bone at that distance?"

His pain drove him to have the wound dressed. The command of the brigade was transferred to Colonel Lyle of the 90th Pennsylvania, but for a short time only; Colonel Coulter remained with the brigade and resumed the command.

About three o'clock we were again moved to the left, from the hill to the ridge. Many of the Union guns were now ceasing their fire; damaged batteries were going to the rear, and others were hurrying up from the reserve. Shot and shell from the enemy still pounded the hill. The ground was strewn with dead horses. Here and there were dead men. We wondered, as we passed through the cemetery, that we weren't smashed into the earth to mingle with mouldering citizens of peace.

As we hastened toward the ridge we heard a thunder of artillery there, and musketry that wasn't the crash of volleys or the harsh rattle of scattered firing, but one continuous din. The long-awaited assault had come. As we topped the ridge we caught another tone of the uproar, strange and terrible; a sound that came from thousands of human throats, yet was not a commingling of shouts and yells, but rather like a vast mournful roar.

Down the slope in front of us the ground was strewn with soldiers in every conceivable vehemence of action, and agony, and
death. Men in grey, surrounded and overwhelmed, were throwing up their hands in surrender. Others were falling back into
the valley. Many were lying in the trampled fields, dying and
dead. The assault had failed. I felt pity for the victims of that
ruined hope. Looking down on the scene of their defeat and of
our victory, I could only see a square mile of Tophet.

Our brigade moved forward as the enemy fell back, and we
took part in a general skirmish fire that was kept up by both
sides until after dark. We threw up breastworks; and when it was
learned, about eleven o'clock, that the rebels in our front were
taking down fences, perhaps to clear the way for another attack,
we strengthened our works with rails from fences within our
reach. The brigade was busy with this labor almost all night.

July 4th the armies kept their opposing lines all day without
attacking or being attacked. Skirmishing continued. The morning was lowery, and some rain fell, and shortly after noon there
came a drenching downpour and a wild wind. The wounded
lying on the ground, and protected only by trees, were in a sorry
plight. All the wounded along our front had been brought in
by the morning of this day, and were being cared for by medical
officers with ordinary supplies; but the trains had not come up
yet, and the field hospital could provide little shelter.

My duties permitting, I went among the wounded in a grove
on the left of our position, where lay many hurt survivors of the
rebel attacking force; men of Pickett's division, and Heth's, and
Pender's. I proffered what assistance I could. I remember stopping beside one poor fellow who was shot through the body.
His wants were few. "Only a drink of water. I'm cold; so cold.
Won't you cover me up?" Then his mind wandered, and he mur-
mured something about his mother. Then he had a clear sense
of his condition. Would I write to his home, and say how he
loved them, and how he died? "Tell them all about it, won't you?

Father's name is Robert Jenkins. My name is Will." I thought I heard him say that he belonged to the 7th North Carolina and came from Chatham County. His words faltered into silence. I covered his face.

Near by I saw a handsome youngster; a Virginian, of Kemper's brigade, I think. I knelt beside him, and wondered if perhaps he were sleeping, he was so calm and still. He unclosed his eyes, and looked into mine with an intense questioning gaze, an appeal most beseeching, most eloquent; but I had no answer to the riddle. I asked him where he was wounded. He drew a hand slowly to his breast, and I knew there was little chance for him. I asked him if he was afraid to die. He whispered, "No; I'm glad I'm through." A spasm of pain closed his lids. I couldn't bear to leave him. I put my head down close to his; and suddenly he opened his eyes again; and I shall never forget their unearthly beauty, nor the sweet, trusting look that spread over all his face as he said to me, with a motion as if he would throw his arms around my neck, "I'm going home. Good-bye." I did weep; I couldn't help it. I don't remember his name; he may not have told it me. I only recall that boys of my regiment took him to a field hospital, though they saw that there was no hope for him.

Heavy though the rebel losses were, in their attack of the third day, ours in the fighting of the first day had been heavier. The survivors of my regiment grieved at thought of comrades dead, and of many, our loved colonel among them, now prisoners in the hands of the enemy. We hailed with joy a few that escaped from the rebels and returned to us. One, I recall, was Benny Worth. Captured on the first day of the battle, he had been set to work the second day at carrying muskets from the field. The third day, he had worked his way into a rebel field hospital, acquired some bloody bandages, and bound up an imaginary wound that supposedly disabled one of his legs; and when the prisoners that could walk were started for Richmond, he was left behind. He made his way back to us the next morning. In the evening of that day, July 4th, Major Leavitt arrived from Washington and took command of the regiment. He had been ill, but, hearing of the battle, he had at once applied for leave to rejoin us. What he found on arriving was not the regiment as he had known it. There were few voices to greet him. Yet these assured him that the regiment still lived, and wouldn't say die.

II

AFTER a night of blank and dreary vigilance, we saw, in the morning of Sunday, July 5th, that under cover of the storm and darkness the enemy had quit the field. Early in the afternoon our pickets were relieved and the brigade was moved a mile to the left and rear. We rested there, and bivouacked for the night. Colonel Coulter was obliged to leave us, by reason of his wound, and Colonel Lyle again assumed command of the brigade. Lieutenant Lord of our regiment, escaping from the rebels, rejoined us, and in the morning Lieutenant Plummer likewise returned. It cheered us to know that not all our losses were permanent.

The army was set in motion, in pursuit of the enemy. Three days of marching, and we had crossed the Catoctin range again, and the valley beyond it, and passed through Turner's Gap over South Mountain. On the western slope of the mountain we built breastworks. The enemy was somewhere below us; we heard firing; but we spent a day inactive on the height, grumbling, and staring into the western haze. We marched next day into the farther valley, and halted there a day, and then, on Sunday, July 12th, we crossed Antietam Creek and twice threw up breastworks facing intrenchments of the enemy. The rebels were cornered. The Potomac River was behind them and our army was closing in slowly against their front.

We expected a battle; our men were impatient to advance; but nothing happened. Monday there was some light skirmishing. Tuesday we were up early and ready to move, but we stayed behind our works until after noon, and then advanced leisurely and met no enemy. The rebels had abandoned their position. We learned, as we halted within a mile of Williamsport, that they had built bridges and crossed over the river and were safe.

Our army was drawn away to cross east of the Blue Ridge. Wednesday, July 15th, we began to tread familiar ground, marching in summer's heat where once we had marched and suffered in winter's cold. We crossed the Antietam battlefield and passed through Crampton's Gap in South Mountain, turned south, and crossed a pontoon bridge over the Potomac at Berlin. I seem to recall that there were two of those bridges, both crowded, long columns of blue-clad men going over on one and caravans of white-topped army wagons on the other. We marched once more down the Loudoun valley. The marches were rapid and the weather was hot and sultry. In Virginia the rebel bushwhackers, hanging about our rear, were a foul nuisance.

Our regiment was now so reduced in numbers that we mustered only forty-seven guns. One company mustered one gun. A report by Major Leavitt, dated July 19th, and forwarded by me, gave our total strength, present and absent, as four hundred and thirty-seven; number of recruits wanted, five hundred and forty-three. We all hailed with pleasure the following order:

HDQ'RS 1ST ARMY CORPS,
July 21st, 1863.

Special Orders, No. 167.

The following named officers and enlisted men will . . . proceed to rendezvous in their respective States, and nearest to where their regiments were enrolled, for the purpose of conducting to their commands the drafted men to fill them up.

.   .   16th Maine   .   .

Captain J. D. Conley	Sergeant Jones Whitman
Lieutenant A. R. Small	Private Joseph Dunnells
Sergeant W. H. Chapman	Private George Peabody

.   .   .   .   .   .

By command [etc.]

We were then in camp near Middleburg. I obtained a pass, and in company with Lieutenant Mathews of the brigade staff I rode into the village to make some necessary purchases. No luck. The town was completely secesh. There was scarcely a building that wasn't shuttered tight and barred, and no visible sign of life except on one street corner, where lounged a ragged contraband.

More marching in the dust and heat, and we saw that we were heading for the Rappahannock. Friday, July 25th, at Warrenton Junction, Lieutenant-Colonel Farnham rejoined the regiment from sick leave and took command. The day was infernally hot and sultry, threatening a storm, and that night a fury of lightning and thunder and rain broke over us as we marched to Bealeton, on our way to Rappahannock Station. Next day the detail named in special orders left camp for Maine. I was sorry to leave the regiment and glad of my opportunity to visit home.

SERVICE NORTH AND SOUTH

Hdq'rs, Volunteer Recruiting Service,
Augusta, Maine, August 19th, 1863.

Order, No. 203: Lieut. Abner R. Small, 16th Me. Vols., having reported at these headquarters by verbal order from Maj. Whiting, commanding the camp of drafted men at Portland, Maine, will immediately proceed to Camp Keyes, Augusta, Maine, and assume the charge of a detachment of drafted men who are to be forwarded to Portland.

In taking command, Lieut. Small will exercise great care to prevent desertion. After turning over the men and their descriptive rolls to the officer in command of the general rendezvous, at Portland, he will take a receipt for the same, and return to these headquarters without delay.

By order of Capt. T. C. J. Bailey, 17th U.S. Inf.,

Act. Sup't., Vol. Rec. Service.

T. C. Webber, Lieut. of Me. Vols.,

Post Adj't.

In accordance with the foregoing and similar orders, I took drafted men to Portland, and found the performance of that duty a diversion. Other duties of mine, apprehending deserters, and taking arrested deserters to the forts in Portland and Boston harbors, I found most disagreeable. I had to forget that I was a man like themselves and prone to military sin, though my sin and theirs might not be the same one, and to remember only that I was a soldier and must obey orders. I had to forget that they were sent to the front, perhaps to face a firing-squad. My sympathies, I admit, were often moved for deserters whose love of family was apparently stronger than their love of country. They weren't running away; they were merely going home.

Under orders, I once traveled down to Bath to find a homing deserter and arrest him. When I discovered where he lived, in a poor quarter of the city, I placed guards around the house and knocked for admittance. I'm afraid my knock was a feeble one, yet it brought to the door a woman, who turned pale as a corpse when she saw my uniform. She tried to shut the door. I prevented that, and asked for the man. She said he wasn't there, but I knew that the only truth in her words was that she loved him. She was his wife. It was a bitter task for me to go in and take him. My authority compelled him to show himself, and I marched him under guard to the city jail to await a train for Augusta. I never performed a more disagreeable duty. I shouldn't have cared to repeat it for a ninety days' leave or a brigadier-general's commission.

Quite different was another affair at Bath, that same day. I had eaten my dinner at the Sagadahoc House and afterwards wandered down to the busy wharves, to see the shipping and catch a breath of salt air from the tide. While I was idly watching the unloading of a large schooner, I saw pop out of her hold Henry Barney, one of my old comrades in Company G, 3d Maine. Before I made any sign of recognition, he sang out cheerily:

"Hullo, Small; excuse me, I meant to say 'Lieutenant'; just wait till we get this cargo ashore and I'll go right along with you."

He must have thought I was after him, for as he rattled on he admitted that he was "absent without leave," which meant, no doubt, that he had deserted. I had no specific authority for arresting him, and when he offered his promise to meet me at the Sagadahoc House as soon as he should have finished working off his passage in the schooner, I left him.

I was sure that he would turn up, for I knew him; knew that he was bound for home; knew that he hadn't a cent, and that he would rely upon me for transportation to Augusta, at least. His home was in Waterville. I knew also that this wasn't the first time he was "absent without leave." The term "deserter" was not in his vocabulary; it never applied to him, in his own view of his aberrations. To lay down his gun and start for home on the impulse of the moment seemed to him the most natural thing in the world. He would go about as boldly as if he had a pass, and when he got ready he would return to his duties—and his punishment.

He did turn up, and told me a sad tale; pictured to me the utter destitution of his family; shed tears over the pleadings of his wife that he should come home "to get some wood and water." Please would I furnish him transportation to Waterville? No; I told him that I should turn him over to the provost marshal at Augusta, first landing him in jail.

As we left Bath, Barney locked arms with my other prisoner and started a speech. I was astonished, amused, and disgusted to hear this deserter lecture his companion on the enormity of desertion. No one could have condemned the crime in more scathing terms. He would have kept it up all the way to Augusta if I hadn't stopped him.

Barney pleaded with me not to land him in jail; he couldn't bear the disgrace of it, he said. He wanted me to take him straight to Major Gardiner. He would "argue his case" to the major; and he hadn't any case. I don't know how I dared to do what he asked; however, I did, and stated the case just as it was, leaving the argument to Barney. The major, after listening for about five minutes, turned to me and asked, "Is this man crazy?" Then he ordered that Barney should be put to work as post cook; and Barney promised to serve faithfully and stay, pending final decision of his case.

While Barney was cook the kitchen department flourished, everything was cleanly, and the food was superb. Guards kept an eye on him; but there came a morning when Barney was missing. I didn't see him again until after the war was over, and then he didn't know me.

I am quite sure that I used handcuffs only once. My prisoner was George Hutchinson, of Gardiner. I think his offense was that he had retreated all the way home from Bull Run; at any rate, he had deserted from Company C, 3d Maine, and in course of time had been arrested and put in jail at Augusta. From there I was to take him to Fort Preble in Portland Harbor:

> Hɒq's, Volunteer Recruiting Service,
> Augusta, Maine, October 13th, 1863.
>
> Order, No. 48.
>
> Lieut. Abner R. Small, upon the receipt of this order, with a guard sufficient to prevent escape, will proceed to Fort Preble, Portland harbor, in charge of the deserter, George L. Hutchinson. Lieut. Small, after turning over said deserter to the commandant of the fort, and taking a receipt for the same, with his guard will return to these headquarters without delay.
>
> By order of Maj. J. W. T. Gardiner, U.S.A.,
> Supt. Vol. Rec. Service.

Everyone seemed to be down on Hutchinson. There was a general suspicion that he would take great risks to relieve me of his company. By advice of the jailer at Augusta I put the handcuffs on him. He caught his breath as the iron touched him, and hove a shuddering sigh; and he went with lowered head to the train. As we drew into the station at Gardiner I half made up my mind to take the handcuffs off. Possibly some member of his family, if he had a family, might come to the train, and I didn't wish to humiliate him or his visitor. The only person that did come to see him was Charles White, who was, as I knew, a copperhead. He stood outside the opened car window and said to George:

"So they've got you at last."

Then he lowered his tone, but I caught enough of his words to know that he was advising my prisoner to escape. I interrupted him.

"Such advice, Mr. White, could only come from a copperhead. Another word to the prisoner, and I'll take you along with him."

He shut up, then, and I was disappointed. I should have been delighted to take him.

The train started on again, and Hutchinson was quiet. At Brunswick I removed his irons and saw to it that he had a good dinner. He said nothing, but I thought he looked grateful when I put the handcuffs in my pocket to stay.

At Portland, as we went by boat to Fort Preble, I watched him closely. He was fidgety, and his face was pale, and I saw as we neared the fort that his eyes were measuring the distance to the water. I pointed to the weapons of the guard, and said, "I wouldn't try it." He didn't try it. I was glad to take a receipt for him, and sorry to see him led away downcast into the fort.

Orders relieving me from duty in Maine and directing me to report to my regiment in the field were received on October 23d. My leave was extended, however, and Captain Conley and I rejoined the regiment at Liberty, a few miles north of Bealeton, November 11th. We had missed no battles; only the rapid marches, executed by Meade in preventing Lee from outflanking him, which were known generally among our soldiers as the "Culpeper-Centreville Express."

II

WHEN I rejoined the regiment I found it in good spirits and visibly strong. More than five hundred recruits had been sent from Maine, convalescent sick had returned to duty, and a few of our captured comrades had been recovered from the enemy; our aggregate present was six hundred and fifty men. The day before my return, the enlisted men of the recruiting detachment had reported, and had brought from Maine new colors to replace those which we had torn up at Gettysburg. We were ready for a winter campaign, if there was to be one.

Sunday, November 15th, we received orders to pack up and wait. We packed up and waited nearly a week before anything happened. Saturday, about noon, a cavalryman, bareheaded and pistol in hand, dashed into camp, shouting:

"The guerrillas are coming! Mosby!"

Then there was action, fast enough; for we ached to lay hands on Mosby and all his men.

"Turn out! Turn out the regiment!"

We turned out, and set off at the double quick. Around a bend of the road, about half a mile from camp, we found three loaded supply wagons and two ambulances, which a party of Mosby's guerrillas had swooped down upon. They had routed the escort, but not before the drivers had cut loose the mules; the marauders had not been able to carry off the supplies, and lacked time to destroy them; they rode away with wild yells as we came on the ground. We thought the excitement was all over, but just as we were starting back to camp a squadron of cavalry dashed up, mistook us for the raiders, and charged, and two of our men were wounded.

Monday, November 23d, the regiment broke camp at daylight and marched to Bealeton, where the division was massed, and then to Rappahannock Station, and went into camp near the river. Tuesday and Wednesday we stayed in camp, in a drizzling rain. Thursday we crossed a pontoon bridge over the river and marched to Richardsville; then southwards to the Rapidan, crossed a pontoon bridge at Culpeper Mine Ford, and bivouacked for the night. Friday, guarding a wagon train, we made a slow march into the bleak forest of the Wilderness, turned westwards on the Orange Court House plank road, and halted at Parker's Store; then pushed ahead to Robertson's Tavern, turned off to the left, and bivouacked.

Early in the morning of Saturday, November 27th, we moved about a mile to the right and formed in line of battle. A rain was falling, and the roads and paths, already soaked by other rains, were turning into ditches and bogs. Artillery floundered forward, and some batteries opened fire, developing the position of the enemy; and the infantry, moving up, formed a new line, overlooking the valley of Mine Run. We could see all too plainly the strength of the rebel position across the shallow valley. The Johnnies had thrown up breastworks, felled a slashing of timber in front, and dammed the run; or if they hadn't dammed it we thought they had, for between them and us the stream was now a widish pond. We didn't like that for a battlefield; it had too much the appearance of a Red Sea. We rested in line till sundown, then moved to the woods in our rear and bivouacked.

Sunday we rested in the woods all day. Rations were issued, and we were cautioned to husband our supplies, as the army was far from its base and living on its trains. Reconnaissances were carried out, and orders were given for a general attack to be made at nine o'clock Monday morning, the cannonading to begin at eight.

Monday morning came, and we moved out for the attack; knapsacks were unslung, bayonets fixed; we nerved ourselves for a mad and bloody assault that would probably fail. The guns were banging away, and shells went shrieking over, bursting on the farther hillside. Nine o'clock neared, and an officer came riding hell-for-leather up the line. As he passed in rear of our regiment his horse failed to clear a slough, and plunged in shoulder deep, tumbling the rider under and crushing him in the cold mud. Some of our men got him out. He gasped a few words:

"I'm General Meade's son. Send to the right and say the order to attack is countermanded. Quick! Quick!"

Lieutenant Davies, I think it was, mounted at once and dashed off with the message. Young Meade was plucky; as soon as he got his breath he insisted upon finishing his errand. He was helped to mount, and reeling in the saddle he galloped on up the line. The awaited hour came, and passed, and the attack was not made.

We could study more calmly the prospect in our front. It was noisy, but no longer fatal. The opposing lines of skirmishers were firing, wasting ammunition trying to shoot each other across the run. A flock of sheep, let out of a barn near by, were scurrying up and down on our side of the water. The Johnnies couldn't reach them and wouldn't let us have them. Our boys were madly hungry for mutton. They determined to make a raid and damn the risk. About two o'clock, a party from the 16th and the 20th Maine made a gallant effort to drive the sheep into our fold; but the rebel fire became so hot that the enterprising shepherds had to retreat, amid wild yells from the Johnnies and laughter from the Yanks. Then a man of the 20th rose up in his place on the skirmish line, took deliberate aim, and shot a fine lamb, and laid down his gun and went out and brought in the carcass. Under the protection of his shelter he took off the pelt, and hung it on a fence rail and stuck it up, inviting the Johnnies to fire at a fixed target. His brigade cheered.

We stayed in line all day, shivering with cold. About sunset a happy grin settled on the faces of the regiment. I inquired of Major Leavitt the cause of this.

"What pleases the men, Major?"

"Why, they saw an aide give a billet to Colonel Farnham."

"What of that? They don't know what it says."

"Oh, they caught the word 'picket,' and they know that when he's in charge of the picket line at night we're bound to move in the morning."

Move we did, early the next day, back towards Robertson's Tavern; and then, as all the army fell back, we marched again through the Wilderness, over one of its worst roads. We reached the Rapidan at Germanna Ford at eleven o'clock that night, and bivouacked.

Two more days of marching, and we went into camp just below the Rappahannock, near Kelly's Ford. Lacking orders to go farther, and seeing that the place was good, we decided at once to build winter quarters. Wood was plentiful, springs of excellent water were near at hand, and rebel barracks of good lumber were still standing a short distance away. The men raced for those huts and marked their claims, the first man to strike one with his hand establishing his title, which no one disputed. The slow men cursed their luck; but there was always a happy generosity among our soldiers; the winners each gave up a share of the spoils, and all was distributed even-handedly, as if by a quartermaster.

Our second day in camp was a day of annoyance, owing to the vacillation of someone in command above us. There came an orderly with a message saying, "Colonel, you will have your regiment in readiness to move at a moment's notice." Then came an orderly with the welcome intelligence that we were not to move. Hardly had this messenger gone when out from the woods, like a jack-in-the-box, popped a third orderly, who handed to Colonel Farnham an order to hold the regiment in readiness to move. Good God! Had there been a time since we joined the army when we hadn't been in readiness to move? The three orders were duly entered, quietly folded up, and, with a piece of red tape tied around each end, laid gently away; and our men continued to put the camp in shape.

We were soon comfortably housed in an evergreen village, attractive and well ordered. A look of contentment spread over the collective face of the regiment, and peace reigned. At this time, as I recall, Colonel Lyle left us, and the command of the brigade was taken over by Colonel McCoy of the 107th Pennsylvania. Christmas approaching, applications for leaves and furloughs were numerous, but few were approved. One of our men, who was handy with Bible texts, composed an application based on Deuteronomy, twentieth chapter, seventh verse:

"And what man is there that hath betrothed a wife, and hath not taken her? Let him go and return unto his house, lest he die in battle, and another man take her."

A FIELD HOSPITAL

This quotation won him his furlough, while the formally worded petitions of two officers for leaves were disapproved. He consulted his oracle again, and said, with what result I don't know, that he would ask for an extension, referring to Deuteronomy, twenty-fourth chapter, fifth verse:

"When a man hath taken a new wife, he shall not go out to war, neither shall he be charged with any business; but he shall be free at home one year, and shall cheer up his wife which he hath taken."

Three days before Christmas, Colonel Farnham went home on leave and Major Leavitt took command of the regiment. The next day we were ordered to be in readiness to move, and the next we went. In the frost of early morning the brigade bugler sounded a blast long and loud enough to wake the dead; we broke camp, and soon were marching away reluctantly from a comfortable home. The cold was so sharp that in less than five minutes the band froze up, and the tune of "The Girl I Left Behind Me" shrilled into silence. We marched all day westwards, past Brandy Station, to Culpeper Court House, and turned south towards the Rapidan. Christmas Day we spent in a marshy forest, bleak and dismal; nothing merry about it. The next day we marched two miles farther and bivouacked in the mud near Mitchell's Station, awaited orders, and kept in readiness to move.

When we turned up on our calendar the last day of the year, we were still stuck in the mud, in a cheerless and exposed position on the extreme front of the army. It was a stated day for our being mustered for pay. Major Leavitt was assigned to muster the 39th Massachusetts, and Lieutenant-Colonel Peirson of that regiment was to muster the 16th Maine. Our men, frozen and muddy, were not in temper for ceremony, but regulations required an inspection before the muster and a review before the inspection.

I had the bugler sound the call; our companies turned out under arms; but the band, which should have assembled, was

nowhere to be seen. I had the call repeated; still no band. Then I
went up to the right, found the trouble, and fell into temptation.

"Mr. Shea, did you hear the call?"

John Shea was always a gentleman. He doffed his hat and
managed to say slowly and politely:

"A'jutant, I hope you'll 'xcuse me; I'm drunk."

"How's the B flat, Mr. Shea?"

"He's bad off 's I am."

"And how's the bass?"

"Dre'ful tired; 's lain down."

"Are any of you sober?"

"Well, I'd say, A'jutant, we simply shouldn' play."

"Oh, nonsense! There's a cold spring of water down there.
Send for a pailful or two, bathe your heads, and drink a quart
of it, every one of you, and you'll be all right. Hurry up!"

I returned to my quarters, thinking of what would happen
when the water should get warm. A few minutes later I heard
the notes of "Adjutant's Call," clear and correct. The band, all
present, played the companies into line. On notice from me, the
captain of the first company stepped a pace to the front and
gave the command:

"Order—arms! Parade—rest!"

From captain to captain down the line the order was repeated,
and smartly obeyed by the men. All right so far. But now the
band was to march, playing, down the front of the line and back
again. With some misgiving, I ordered:

"Troop—beat off!"

Away went the band, and the ground seemed very uneven
under its feet; and now and then the leader would lose a note
and, trying to catch it, would clash into the B flat; and the bass
drum persisted in coming down heavy on the up beat; and the
cymbals forgot to clang when they should, and closed with a
crash when they should have been still. The musicians, counter-
marching, started in quick time together; but now the water

was warm, and somehow the orders of Mr. Shea were not understood, and half the band struck up one tune, the other half another. This was too much. I heard above the discord a loud and angry voice:

"Parade is dismissed!"

I received a reprimand, but the show was worth it. The band had enjoyed the performance, and I think everyone else had, too, from the smile that went down the line. The men of my regiment soon burst out laughing, and laughed so loud and so long that the other regiments took it up; and so the good nature spread; and I was forgiven.

III

AFTER a week of cold storms, the sun rose bright on New Year's morn and shed its warm rays on as dirty, despondent, and disgusted a brigade as could be found on duty; and after roll-call, when the men had drunk their hot coffee and thawed out, something like good nature began to prevail. Our soldiers entertained once more a notion that the regiment was to settle for the winter. Some had already made collections of fence rails, though none had dared to start building huts. At nine o'clock there was a visible stir at brigade headquarters. At ten our regiment was ordered to change direction to the left, in line parallel with the railroad, and go into camp. Tents went up, streets were policed, a parade ground was cleared; by nightfall we were again at home. Log huts were to be erected as soon as possible. Regrets for our lost houses at Kelly's Ford were banished.

At this time Frank Richardson came to us from Maine to reorganize and drill the band. The officers had engaged him for this service, and paid him out of their personal funds. Instruments of the best quality were provided, the men sharing with the officers in meeting the expense. The band became the best in the division, an honor to us, and a pleasure, and a good influence upon us all. We were better men, and our sleep was sweeter, for its playing.

Through late January and early February I was at home on leave. When I returned, Colonel Leonard commanded the brigade. Colonel Farnham was again in command of the regiment, and we had a new chaplain, the Reverend Uriah Balkam of Lewiston. Farnham and the chaplain and I rode out to the home of a Mrs. Fessenden to see the renowned Mose and Robert, who were reputed to have been servants of George Washington. Robert was "a hundred and six years old," he said, "but not so old as to forget Massa George." His appearance would have warranted a belief that he was five hundred. Blind, bald, and toothless, and shriveled as a mummy, he sat facing the winter sun like one outstaring time.

"Robert, can you sing?" asked the chaplain.

"Oh yes, Massa!"

"Perhaps you would sing us a hymn."

Sing! There wasn't the most distant approach to anything like tune, time, or harmony in the noises that Robert made. We rode away, and left him solemnly croaking the tenth verse of some darky song.

Sunday, February 21st, Chaplain Balkam spoke in memory of Captain Lowell, killed at Gettysburg. Where the body of the captain lay, we didn't know; I'm not sure that anyone knows now. What I take to have been the last news of him, as I here set down, I have had from Luther Bradford, who was then a corporal in Company E. Corporal Bradford, taken prisoner on the first day of the battle, and being allowed on the second day to search for wounded of ours within the rebel lines, found Captain Lowell a short distance from the Mummasburg road and near the stone wall. The captain was yet conscious, but not able to speak. Corporal Bradford and other prisoners carried him to the seminary, which was then in use as a hospital, but before they could find a surgeon to look after him they were marched off to the rear. The captain had been robbed of his valuables and all papers on his person; his pocket diary had been torn up and the pieces scattered, perhaps by his own hands; there was nothing left on him to say who he was, and he could hardly have recovered speech to make himself known. He must soon have died, and his body have been buried among the unidentified dead.

Before the next Sunday came, our chapel was completed; a large hut built of hewn logs and roofed with canvas. The interior was decorated with evergreens, which were hung in festoons and fashioned into crosses, anchors, and circles upon the walls. Familiar Bible texts met the eye from over the pulpit. The chaplains were happy. All the shepherds of the brigade took part in the formal dedication. Propriety was gained for them and comfort for us, when we went to church.

Early March brought us talk of General Grant, though not the man himself. March 10th he visited Meade at Brandy Station; but that was some miles up the line from where we were. March 12th orders were published announcing that Grant was in command of all the Union armies. We thought he would do; yet we were inclined to wait and see. Meade was continued in command of the Army of the Potomac, and orders were issued in his name.

Meanwhile there were alarums without excursions. The winter camp of the enemy was just across the Rapidan, only three or four miles from our position, and there was always the chance that the rebels might move first. March 10th, before daylight, something excited our picket line, and our regiment was turned out; but nothing happened. A rainstorm began, which lasted nine days. March 18th the enemy was reported to have crossed the Rapidan at Raccoon Ford; the regiment was ordered under arms, in readiness to move; but we didn't move. The next day it snowed, and two days later it snowed again, and a violent storm made the night howl.

Before the end of March the five corps of the Army of the Potomac were reduced to three, and ours, the 1st Corps, was consolidated with the 5th, and thereafter was to share the name of the latter corps. The change was not relished by any that had helped to win glory for the 1st Corps at Gettysburg. We appreciated and applauded what General Newton, retiring from the command, said in his farewell order of March 24th:

"The 1st Corps gave at Gettysburg a crowning proof of valor and endurance in saving from the grasp of the enemy the strong position upon which the battle was fought. The terrible losses suffered by the corps in that conflict attest its supreme devotion to the country. Though the corps has lost its distinctive name by the present changes, history will not be silent upon the magnitude of its services."

Commanding the 5th Corps was General Warren, who had brought himself rapidly to notice and preferment, chiefly by securing the defense of Little Round Top in the Gettysburg battle. He was younger than the other corps commanders, Hancock and Sedgwick. His hair was jet black; and so were his sharp eyes, which put life into his darkly sallow face. He was a thinnish man with a liking for big horses, and he wore full uniform, sash and all, when he rode into action; a rather odd figure. Our division was commanded for a short time by General Baxter, but General Robinson presently returned to us. Colonel Leonard continued in the command of our brigade.

March 28th our regiment was made happy by the return of Colonel Tilden. After seven months in the hands of the enemy, he had escaped from Libby Prison and made his way across heartbreaking miles of hostile country to safety; and now, being strong again, he came back to his command. Our veterans were wild to hail his return; our new men were excited to welcome the colonel they had never seen; every soldier was trim and shining, and our camp was swept and garnished. As the hour neared for the train to arrive from Culpeper, the band, its brass gleaming, assembled on the parade ground, the companies were played into line, and Lieutenant-Colonel Farnham prepared them for ceremony. Major Leavitt and I went to the station, with a superb black horse for Colonel Tilden to ride; and when the train had come, and the colonel appeared, we escorted our commander formally to camp. The regiment presented arms; he acknowledged the salute by raising his cap; and we knew not which to admire the more, his soldierly bearing and splendid horsemanship, or the perfect discipline of the ranks. After the salute, cheers; the band played; parade was dismissed, arms were stacked, and the men, all smiles, pressed around their loved commander until he happily waved them away.

That evening, the colonel was the guest of honor at a reception in the chapel, attended by the officers of the regiment and the field officers of the brigade. Colonel Farnham presided. I was the toastmaster. Major Leavitt had somehow conjured up a Washington banquet; and with good food and drink and speeches we made merry until late, while the wind raged outside and rain beat furiously on the canvas overhead.

Next day, some four or five hundred men of the brigade assembled, and this battalion, under the command of Sergeant-Major Stevens, formed in front of regimental headquarters, the band playing; and when Colonel Tilden appeared, there was presented to him as a gift from the enlisted men the black horse ridden by him the day before, and with it a complete set of equipments. The presentation was made by the sergeant-major, in a speech that taxed his powers of oratory and emotion. The colonel replied, and then shook hands with men that had been captured with him at Gettysburg. The day was declared a holiday. In the afternoon there were field sports. In the evening the officers entertained the brigade commander, his staff, and officers from other regiments, at a merry dinner in the chapel; and again it stormed.

March went out like a drowned lamb, and April floated in like another; yet between rains there were lovely spring days, and Chaplain Balkam and I took frequent rides. Once, I recall, he suggested that we should pay our respects to a Mrs. Major, who lived near Cedar Mountain. I was not pleasantly impressed with our reception; our proffers of sugar and coffee were gracefully declined. We knew that nothing could have been more welcome in that house than coffee; but Yankees bearing gifts were not welcome, and we were turned away. Soon after we left, we saw a young woman of the family fighting a fire, which was running rapidly over a dry field and threatening the fences and buildings. We dismounted and offered to assist, but were told with the utmost scorn that our help would not be acceptable. She said we had better ride on. She made a handsome figure in her shortened skirts, her head bare, cheeks red, and eyes flashing. We rode on with a sigh.

We visited the next house, and went in; the chaplain appeared determined to make a round of calls. He introduced himself, and after some attempts at general conversation, which was all uphill work for him, he asked if he should offer prayer. There was no answer that I heard; but he knelt down, cleared his throat, and opened up to the Lord the necessity of helping the Union cause, and then besought Him to grant unto the family, there present, patience and reconciliation to the hardships of war. I wished to show respect to the occasion; yet I couldn't help watching, through half-closed eyes, that family group. It was made up, I guessed, of a married woman, her aged father, and her children; her husband, no doubt, was in the rebel army. The faces of the old man and the woman were sad and fearful, and sharp with hope long deferred. The children showed a half-frightened curiosity. It was a stiff reception they gave us, and we had no right to expect anything different. I felt that our intrusion was unwelcome, almost an insult. It was plain that the family was in urgent need, yet I couldn't make to these proud poor the usual presents of coffee and sugar; their eyes forbade me. As the chaplain and I rode back to camp, I was downcast, while he wore a happy expression of having done his duty with faith that the Lord would do the rest.

LEAVING WINTER QUARTERS

Another day, the chaplain, Captain Conley, and I rode to the signal station on Cedar Mountain. I felt a sudden lightening of the heart as we went up. For a moment I was happy in the foolish and wonderful certainty that where we were going there would be no war nor memory of war, no troubling dreams, no dread of returning to the land of agony. A little higher, and we should be rising lightly into a region that we had never quite ceased to hope might be above us. I almost saw the glow of it brightening. Perhaps it was only sunlight among the trees. When we got to the top of the hill there was nothing but the signal station and the view.

Away on every side spread a broken country, shaggy with forest and thicket, creased with many watercourses, and dotted sparsely with hamlets and the clearings of lonely farms. I saw it green and smiling with spring; and I looked away, because it was grinning with dreadful ghosts. The chaplain didn't see any ghosts. He was pointing out the beauties of nature and the tented field. Far along the northwestern horizon rose the hazy splendor of the Blue Ridge. Nearer, to the northeast, perhaps we could discern where the Rappahannock wandered. Miles away to the east, we knew, it was joined by the swifter waters of the Rapidan, tumbling up from the south. Beyond the Rapidan and below the Rappahannock was the vast green covert of the Wilderness. It was lovely with the careless innocence of nature; yet I remembered that in lonely hollows under those trees lay horrors of charred bones and rotting flesh. Only last spring we were at Chancellorsville. I was there again; it was dreadfully quiet; from under a haggard pine a grey and sunken face was staring at me emptily. I started, and heard the chaplain rattling on. Where he was pointing now, to the north, were the Union camps; but every detail of them I could see with my eyes shut. We turned to the southeast and looked at the camps of the enemy, just across the Rapidan. We gazed through powerful glasses mounted on a frame, and the rows of rebel tents and huts and the soldiers on guard duty were brought so near that it seemed we might touch them. We saw men lounging in their shirt sleeves and smoking their pipes, and talking, very likely, of home; and others playing ball. Captain Conley, after watching the ball game a while, turned to me and said solemnly:

"My God, Adjutant, they're human beings just like us!"

IV

GENERAL GRANT had set up his headquarters at Culpeper Court House, March 26th. When it came our turn to be reviewed, April 8th, we strained our eyes to see what the man was like; but he rode past our regiment so rapidly that we hardly saw him at all. My clearest recollection of his appearance must be from a later occasion. After the debonair McClellan, the cocky Burnside, rosy Joe Hooker, and the dyspeptic Meade, the calm and unpretentious Grant was not exciting, anyway. In my mind's eye I see a plainly uniformed general of common size and build, wearing his campaign hat squarely on his head, and sitting his horse squarely and without distinction. The figure was not impressive, nor the face under the hat inspiring. It would be easy now to say that we all perceived in the square and bluntly bearded jaw the force of relentless persistence; but I doubt we more than glimpsed a quiet solidity.

After a month of final preparation, the army was ready for a new campaign. April 26th our regiment broke camp and moved across Cedar Run, half a mile up the railroad, where we got rid of all surplus baggage and accustomed ourselves to sleeping on the ground, preparatory to field duty. May 3d the expected order to march was received; and at two o'clock in the morning of Wednesday, May 4th, we started. Our division brought up the rear of Warren's corps.

Under the bright stars our long column went north towards Culpeper Court House, then turned to the east and marched into a glorious spring day. Wild flowers were up; I remember them nodding by the roadside. Everything was bright and blowing. A little way beyond the clump of houses that was Stevensburg we topped a ridge commanding a wide view, and saw a splendid sight; all the roads were filled with marching men, the sunlight glinting on their muskets, and here and there on burnished cannon. We followed a narrow road that turned south into somber woods, and after a while we came to the Rapidan, crossed a pontoon bridge at Germanna Ford, and marched away from the swift stream into the green quiet of the Wilderness. The day had not been oppressively warm, but in the narrow defile among the trees no air was stirring, and the heat of long marching under a heavy load provoked some of our men to throw away overcoats and blankets. We lost a few stragglers. When orders came down the line for us to halt and bivouack for the night, we were nearing Wilderness Tavern.

Early Thursday morning we were up and ready to resume the march. By five o'clock there was a stir of troops ahead of us. We followed them a little way and came to a large irregular clearing of rough ground, broken by the ravines of Wilderness Run. In the clearing, the plank road that we had followed from the ford led on southeastwards and crossed, near the tavern, the Orange Court House turnpike. A rougher dirt track led southwestwards to the Orange Court House plank road. We turned down the dirt track and halted, beyond the pike, near the Lacy farm, where General Warren set up his headquarters. Our division was held there in reserve, while Crawford's and Wadsworth's divisions, moving on towards Parker's Store, and Griffin's division, heading westwards on the turnpike, disappeared in the forest. Soon, mounted orderlies came dashing out of the woods, hastening towards the crossroads near the tavern, to the headquarters of Grant and Meade, and then dashed back into the woods again; and more than once General Warren went hurrying off; and after a while the Maryland brigade shouldered arms and disappeared in the green thickets. Now and then we heard a muffled sound of firing, and saw smoke rise from the farther reaches of the forest and vanish in the still air; so we knew there was fighting; but how the fight was going, we could only guess.

About noon, orders came for our brigade to move. We hurried across bushy fields into the forest and out along the turnpike a mile. A scattering of men was running in, some of them crying disaster, and ahead of us there was an uproar of yelling and firing. We came to a clearing and filed off to the right of the turnpike and went into line along the edge of an old field. The field, ragged with bushes, sloped down to a hollow and then up to the forest beyond. The fight had swept across it and back again, and now the hollow was filled with wounded, and out where the pike went over it were two fieldpieces, abandoned, the dead horses lying near by. The rebels wanted those guns and tried to get them, but our brigade, and the reserve of the troops that were in action before we came up, were now in line, and sent so hot a fire from our side of the field that the rebels drew back to their side and stayed there. The wounded in the hollow called vainly for water. The guns on the pike stood lonely in the sun.

Later in the afternoon, when batteries were firing across the field both ways, we were ordered to the left across the pike. Our men lined up close to the roadway. A shell would burst with a roar in the green defile, and over would rush a battalion with a defiant answering yell; or a dozen men would cross to draw the fire of the enemy, and then over would go a hundred in about three leaps. Few were wounded, and none, I think, was killed. We formed again, under the pines, and moved out to the edge of the clearing; and there we stayed, while our skirmishers blazed away in front.

About sunset, a charge was ordered; someone must have decided that the lost guns ought to be recovered. Out into the open went the brigade, and the enemy let fly with everything he had. The noise was terrific; the forest walls around the field echoed and magnified every sound. Under that crashing din we groped for our foes; but the charge failed. We were ordered to retire, and fell back to our line in the swiftly gathering dusk. The lost guns were still on the pike, with no takers, and the dead and wounded lay more thickly on the field.

Night was falling when I was ordered to beat the woods behind our line for stragglers. I found a few. They were badly frightened men, going they didn't know where, but anywhere away from that howling acre. I urged them to go back to their companies; told them that they would be safest with their comrades and sure to be more than thankful, later, that they had followed my suggestion. I feel sure that they all went back, as they told me they would, though more than one of them started with shaky knees. I didn't blame them for dreading the return.

Shells were still coming over, and here and there one that burst as it hit the ground would start a blaze in dry leaves. A crash and a flare, a scurry of great leaping shadows, and then the fire would die out and the night would be blacker than before. Once, when the darkness was torn suddenly away, I saw a dogwood all in flower, standing asleep and still. I groped on, stumbled, fell, and my outflung hands pushed up a smoulder of leaves. The fire sprang into flame, caught in the hair and beard of a dead sergeant, and lighted a ghastly face and wide-open eyes. I rushed away in horror, and felt a great relief when I found our line again and heard the sound of human voices.

We manned our works all night in the edge of the woods. There was no moon to light the clearing, only dim stars, and the air was hazy and pungent with the smoke and smell of fires yet smouldering. We couldn't see the wounded and dying, whose cries we heard all too clearly; nor could our stretcher bearers go out to find them and bring them in; the opposing lines were near, and the rebels were fidgety and quick to shoot.

At daybreak we were relieved and sent to the rear to make coffee and breakfast. Colonel Leonard then being absent, sick, Colonel Lyle was assigned to the command of the brigade. We were moved back nearly to our old position. Ahead of us throughout the morning there was fighting, but we were not engaged. Early in the afternoon the brigade was withdrawn, moved to the left, and placed in reserve with some heavy artillery troops near the Orange Court House plank road. Later there was fierce fighting near by, but again we were not engaged. We threw up breastworks under skirmish fire, and stayed behind them that night.

Saturday, May 7th, we stood in expectation of more fighting, and strengthened our works; but the battle was over. Neither side had driven the other. Rumors came that Lee was retreating. We doubted that. What would Grant do? By evening we had our answer; the right of the Union line moved in rear of the left. We heard on the still evening air a sound of distant cheering from the rebels. Had they seen the move? Did they suppose that Grant was falling back? Our division was massed not far from Wilderness Church, and from there, we knew, the turnpike led to Chancellorsville. Would Grant, like Hooker, draw back, and then retreat to the north side of the Rappahannock? No. When we started, at eight o'clock that night, we headed south. Our men knew what that meant. Somewhere, Grant was seen, and a great burst of cheering greeted him as he rode swiftly and silently by.

SHOOT, SHOVEL, AND MARCH

Come, Freemen of the land,
Come meet the last demand!
—ANON., "Put It Through"

W E WERE BOUND for Spotsylvania Court House; and so were the rebels, though we didn't know it then. We were delayed in starting, mounted troops of the provost guard blocking our way; it was eleven o'clock before they moved out the Brock road and we followed them. We marched, that night, through a forest of black pines; the road was narrow, and the trees made it very dark; it was a desolate and dismal track. Before daylight we passed Todd's Tavern, where the road turned to the southeast, and about a mile beyond the tavern we halted while the division closed up, and our men caught a snatch of rest. By dawn we were marching again, and presently we overtook the advance guard of cavalry. They had met the enemy in the dark and failed to make headway, though they must have tried; some of them were lying dead by the roadside.

Our division pressed ahead and deployed, our brigade in the lead. We soon found rebel skirmishers in our front, and drove them back through a mile of woods. Hard going, that was; the rebels had felled trees across the roads and paths. It was broad day and scorching hot when we reached the cleared lands of the Alsop farm. We pushed on beyond the farm and came to a rise of ground and a wooded knoll, and halted to gather our scattered ranks. We were fully two miles from where we had first deployed; our men had run a part of the way, and many had dropped out, overcome by heat and weariness. My regiment at that moment numbered fewer than two hundred.

Beyond a clearing ahead of us there was a forested ridge, and we could see where the rebels had felled a slashing of trees and thrown up breastworks. We were ordered to charge them. Out into the open we went, over rough ground, under fire. We crossed the clearing, and smashed a rail fence at the farther side, and rushed up among the felled trees. We could go no farther. Our men took to cover and fired at any heads that appeared over the works. The rebels were there in force, too strong for us; and they had come to stay.

We heard a great uproar as the fighting spread; and then we were ordered to retire. The brigades coming up on our right and left had each been taken in flank by a savage outburst of musketry and artillery, and General Robinson, leading the charge, had been hit and disabled. We all fell back in some confusion; but the men steadied when clear of the flanking fire, and beat off an attempt of the enemy to take advantage of our repulse and our loss of a commander. Not far from the Alsop house we threw up a barricade of earth and fence rails. General Robinson was carried to the rear, and Colonel Coulter assumed command of the division.

My regiment took count of its losses. Two of our line officers, Captain Belcher and Lieutenant Fowler, were wounded severely. Lieutenants Wiggin and Richards were missing; they, and some of our men, were taken prisoners in the running fight when the brigade fell back. Three of our men certainly, and perhaps more, were killed, and more than fifty were wounded. One of the first men hit was Corporal Palmer, carrying our national color. While we had been in the woods, the color had been carried in the case to protect it from being torn; but when the charge was ordered, Palmer stripped off the case and flung the ensign to the air. A bullet struck him in the arm and side, yet he held up the flag until it was taken from his grasp by our other color-bearer, Corporal Manchester, who gave the state flag into the hands of Corporal Fairbanks. The banners went forward together in the charge. Palmer crawled painfully to the rear until exhaustion overtook him. We found him when we fell back to the farm, and sent him, without hope, to the surgeons.

About eight o'clock in the evening we advanced again, to the right of the place where we had halted before charging, and threw up breastworks. Our men were digging all that night and Monday forenoon. Troops of Sedgwick's corps were busy on our left. Early in the morning I caught sight of General Sedgwick, standing with an officer of his staff near a battery in the corner of a field. A moment later he slumped against his companion, and they both fell to the ground. The officer got up, but the corps commander lay still. A rebel sharpshooter had killed him.

Monday afternoon and evening, as Hancock's corps came up on the right of Warren's, our regiment several times changed position to the right and each time threw up breastworks. By nine o'clock that night we were at right angles with our line of the morning, and facing south, and our weary men were still digging. When at last the work was done we got some rest, but the dawn of another day was near; we slept only two hours.

About eleven o'clock Tuesday forenoon we were moved from the right to near the center of the corps front. We were on a low ridge, in woods, facing the enemy across a narrow ravine. The slopes of the ravine were grown up with trees and underbrush, and the bottom was choked with a dense thicket of tangled cedars. We were engaged there, skirmishing, more than four hours continuously; and all that time we were under a sharp fire, not only from the rebel works in our front, but also from a battery of theirs that raked our line from beyond our left.

About four o'clock in the afternoon there was a general attack. I don't recall that our regiment took part in it except to give dubious support to troops that went in ahead of us. We could see hardly anything of what was happening. We learned later that where the ground was more open some men and colors got over the rebel works, and the fighting was stubborn; but the attack failed.

Then we heard that another attack was to be made at sunset, and that when we should hear the troops on our right going forward, we should join the advance. A little after sunset we caught the noise that we had been listening for and praying that we shouldn't hear. We moved down the slope of the ravine and thrashed into the tangle. As we came out on the other side, we saw, up the farther slope, a slashing and a tier of breastworks among the darkening trees. The works flamed and roared with a sudden outburst of fire. The bullets of that first volley went over our heads, but a regiment behind us blazed away in reply, and we were threatened from both front and rear. Our men were ordered to lie down, and they did, until the fire from the rear was stopped. Then they, and all the brigade, rushed yelling up among the trees and tore madly at the abattis, in a wild effort to get over the works. No use; we were beaten off, and then ordered to retire. Cursing and stumbling, and helping away our wounded as best we could, we made our way back to our starting place. At nine o'clock that night our brigade was relieved, supplied with ammunition and rations, and moved to a position on the right.

My regiment, reckoning its losses, counted seven or more men dead and four line officers and more than forty men wounded. Again a color bearer was one of the first men hit. Corporal Fairbanks, carrying the state flag, was struck and severely hurt by a splinter from a shattered tree. He gave the flag to Corporal Bradford, who bore it forward in the attack. Then Corporal Manchester, carrying the national color, was hit, the same shot breaking the color staff. Bradford then carried both flags, and found it hard work when he had to take them back through the tangle; but with the help of Private Barney Boyle, who swore by all the saints that he would "stick by the ould flag as long as there was a grey divil in front," the colors were got through.

All day Wednesday the weather was wet and stormy. There was no fighting, only a scattering of skirmish fire. Our division was broken up, presumably because it had "behaved badly" in that unsuccessful attempt to break the rebel line on the road to

Spotsylvania, two days before—an attempt made bravely enough, but by exhausted men. Colonel Coulter was returned to the command of his brigade, and that brigade was assigned to Crawford's division; our brigade, Lyle's, was assigned to Cutler's division; and the Maryland brigade was retained by the corps commander under his personal direction.

Before daylight, Thursday morning, we were ordered to move, and by seven o'clock we were again near the center of the corps front. This was the morning of the assault on the "Bloody Angle." I am quite sure that we heard no sound of it. The fight was begun about a mile beyond our left, and a stretch of woods intervened; perhaps the conditions were right for one of those local silences occasionally remarked in the vicinity of a battle. As I remember it, the quiet was almost unbearable. Our men, yet weary from continuous marching and fighting and digging, lay at full length on the cool, fresh earth; silent, too tired even to grumble. The air was foggy and sultry. About eight o'clock a heavy rain began falling and was most welcome.

Time dragged. We had no hint of what was developing elsewhere. Nine o'clock came, and passed. Then out of the watery haze on our right came an aide, who made his way quietly along the line, dropping a word to this and that commander; only a ripple, and all was still again.

"What was it, Colonel?" I asked.

No answer from Colonel Tilden; he merely pointed towards the rebel works. Then he took out his watch and looked anxiously to the right. Then suddenly a commotion ran down the line; there was a great stir of troops; and we heard the command to go forward. We passed through the works, and were formed in rear of two lines of assault, which pressed ahead, forcing their way through the tangled brush; and we followed them to act as their support. Shells were soon bursting all around us; our position was uncomfortably hot, but we stayed there, and were ourselves engaged, until noon. Colonel Lyle then sent me to General

Cutler to ask for ammunition or release. Hurrying to the rear, I found the general nervously watching the effect of shells that went crashing into the trees above his head. He caught sight of me and came forward to meet me.

"What is it, Lieutenant?"

I repeated the verbal dispatch.

"Don't know that I can get a round of ammunition to your brigade," he said. "Tell Colonel Lyle to hold his position. I'll relieve him when I can."

I hurried back with the reply. It was not ten minutes that I was away, yet death had been furiously busy in that little time. "Look here!" said Colonel Farnham; and where he pointed I saw, partly buried in leaves and dirt, the headless body of an officer of the 90th Pennsylvania, and heaped around and upon the body six dead and dying men, all silenced by one shell. While we were looking at this sight, another shell came over and exploded so near that Colonels Prey and Farnham were knocked down and I was whirled round like a top. None of us was hurt.

Relief came just as the last bullets were rammed home in the muskets of our men, and our brigade was moved to the left and rear. It was then a little after noon. About two o'clock we were again moved to the front, in rear of an active skirmish-line, and prepared for another assault; but the assault was not made. Beyond our left a savage fight raged, and kept up all the afternoon and late into the night.

This was the bloodiest day of all the Spotsylvania fighting. Our regiment was not in the worst of it, yet we suffered a great loss; Major Leavitt was severely wounded by a musket ball, which ripped through his chest. Our loss in wounded men was slight; only two had more than minor hurts. Acting Corporal Foss of the color guard was killed without being hit directly. He had stumbled over the root of a tree and fallen headlong, and as he lay sprawling a solid shot struck into the earth beside him and passed under him, tossing him slightly from the ground.

A moment later a comrade spoke to him and, receiving no reply, touched him and found that his unbruised body was lifeless.

II

FRIDAY, May 13th, after nine days and nights of almost continuous activity, I had my first real rest. At eight o'clock in the morning the brigade was moved to the right into a position of comparative quiet. I went to the rear and slept, with the sound of cannon for my lullaby. There was no call to action all day. At ten o'clock that night our corps began a march around the northern end of the rebel position. It was rainy and foggy and black dark, and the roads were beaten into sloughs. Here and there to mark the way were log fires, flaring and hissing in the rain, and lonely and miserable guides huddling up to the smoky blaze. The going was slow. There was much straggling. After a while the groping columns left the beaten roads and went by a farm track to a ford of the Ny, crossed the stream, and made their way across fields to the main road leading down from Fredericksburg to Spotsylvania Court House, and followed that road southwesterly across the Ny again. It was then after six o'clock in the morning. Warren was supposed to have made an attack at four. It was late for that, and the troops, wearied and scattered by their night march, were in no condition to do anything beyond establishing a line.

Did I make that march? I don't know. Surviving pages of my diary indicate that I slept, and rode with a train next day almost to Fredericksburg, and returned to my regiment Saturday evening. I have no recollection of making either journey. I may have had proper business with the train; but if I had, I must have been more asleep than awake.

Our corps having rounded the "Bloody Angle," we were facing west, not two miles from where we had last been fighting, facing east. There was no apparent advantage in the move; the rebel works were just as strong on this side as on the other, and the defenders were as stubborn. The weather was interrupting the battle. Through Sunday and Monday, in the rain, we pushed our intrenchments forward and called them "water works." Tuesday the weather cleared; our batteries were better established; we joined our trenches with those of Burnside's corps, which had come up on our right. Wednesday at daylight our corps artillery opened fire, and the troops beyond our right attacked. Our brigade was moved to the left, below the Fredericksburg turnpike and in rear of corps headquarters, in support of the batteries. When the guns ceased firing, soon after ten o'clock, we knew that the attack had failed. By noon all was quiet again. We were moved back to the right. After nightfall, Burnside's corps was withdrawn.

Once again, our corps formed the right of the army. All Thursday forenoon our regiment strengthened its works. Then there was a lull. Awaiting orders, Colonel Tilden and members of his staff, including myself, were seated on the ground and filling pipes to quiet the calls of empty stomachs when Chaplain Balkam rode up. He greeted us cordially and began to unstrap a healthy-looking package from his saddle. At that moment the enemy opened fire on us with artillery, but the warm smile of the chaplain only broadened as he unloaded his saddlebags. The good things revealed made our hearts glad, and when our godly friend produced a corkscrew and opened a bottle we blessed the rule that required us to have a chaplain and exempted him from active combatant service.

Just as we finished our unexpected luncheon, the cannonading ceased and a double line of rebels emerged from the woods and came on at the double quick, yelling like demons. Word was passed for our men to hold their fire and keep down out of sight. At the left of our position the line of works turned a corner, and in the corner was a brass battery. As soon as the Johnnies came within range of the battery, it opened on them with grape and canister. They couldn't stomach that. Their yelling stopped, and they headed back for the woods. It was fun to see them turn and run, and our men jumped up on the breastworks and swung their caps and hurrahed and called to the Johnnies to come on; but the Johnnies didn't come on any more, that time. Probably they had only been feeling our new line.

Towards evening they attacked in earnest, beyond our right, threatening to seize the road which was then our main line of supply; but it chanced that some raw troops under General Tyler had come down from Fredericksburg and were halted on that road, not far from us, and these troops held their ground until they were reënforced, when the rebels were driven off. We heard with regret that the 1st Maine Heavy Artillery, here acquitting itself heroically as infantry, sustained a record loss (eighty-two killed, three hundred and ninety-four wounded).

Saturday, May 21st, we packed up, and at half-past nine in the forenoon we started away. The enemy tossed over a shell or two. Was he going to come out of his works and attack us retiring? Our brigade hurried back, but nothing happened; we regained the breastworks without firing a gun; casualties, one chair stolen. Early in the afternoon we moved to the left of our corps line, and at half-past two we started away again, and this time we kept going. Our general direction was east. We noticed a change in the character of the scene. There came over us the happy realization that we were leaving the Wilderness behind us. There were woods aplenty, but the countryside in general was more open, and farms and dwellings were not so sparse. By six o'clock we were at Guiney's Station on the Richmond & Potomac Railroad. From there we took a road to the southwest, marched about two miles from the station, and bivouacked for the night.

Sunday afternoon we resumed the march, crossing Guiney's Bridge over the main branch of the Mattapony and pushing west towards the telegraph road, along which the telegraph line had run between Fredericksburg and Richmond. The rebels had been going down the telegraph road in the night. We saw some stragglers of theirs, but didn't bother about them; they would be gathered in by our provost guard at the rear. Once, when we halted, I saw a little boy in grey sitting on a log and embracing a small drum. He was watching our troops as if in a dream, unaware that he was now with the Army of the Potomac. I felt drawn to him because he was so young and lonely. I dismounted and sat down beside him and looked my questions. Without any show of fear or hesitation, he said:

"I'm a drummer boy. Couldn't keep up. I'm hungry."

Of course I shared with him what food I had. He took it without a word and began to eat. Then, looking me over from cap to boots, he caught sight of a gold Masonic shield attached to my coat, and reached out a hand and touched it, and asked:

"Is it gold? Real gold? May I hold it?"

"Certainly, my boy."

I took it off and put it in his hands.

Again he asked: "Is it gold? Real gold?"

He caressed it fondly, as if it were something inexpressibly dear, and rubbed it on his cheek. He passed it back reluctantly.

"I reckon I must go, now," he said.

He got up, but where he was to go he couldn't have had any valid idea. A bugle sounded. Our troops were starting on, and I rose to go, too. I left the boy; but he stayed vividly in my mind, and when we bivouacked and built our fires near Bull's Church, that night, I wondered what had become of him. I never knew.

Monday we marched down the telegraph road, went beyond Mount Carmel Church, then back to the church again, and took a winding way that led us to the North Anna at Jericho Mill. It was late in the afternoon when we went down the steep bank and crossed a pontoon bridge over the shallow stream. As we moved up and forward on the farther side we saw woods ahead and troops going into them, but we were directed towards open ground on the right. Just then, the rebels opened fire against our

PONTOON BRIDGE, JERICHO MILL

corps front with shot and shell. Union batteries replied. One that was on a knoll in the open had a duel at close range with a rebel battery just across a ravine, and as we moved ahead we could see them pounding each other as hard as they could, so near together that the smoke from their guns would meet when they fired at the same moment. We were out in the open without breastworks or any natural protection. Our brigade was in the second line. The position soon got uncomfortably warm; the enemy attacked; and we saw the troops ahead of us give way. The rebels came on, yelling, with a rush, intending to drive us into the river; but our batteries broke the attack, and the Johnnies were driven off. The fight was brief. My regiment suffered a few casualties; four of our men were hit when shells from the depressed guns of our supporting batteries burst near us.

We went ahead to the western edge of the woods and threw up breastworks, and loafed. Our soldiers were singularly peaceful after the fighting. In the cool hush of the trees they sprawled comfortably on the ground, some munching hardtack, others whittling, a few peering into the sky through the branches overhead as if to force the secrets of the morrow. Darkness fell; and out of the silence came a wavering moan, strangely continuing. Men looked around in wonder and silently grasped their weapons. The waver steadied into a cadence, the moan swelled into a song, and from all our front there rose in mighty voice the music of "Old Hundredth." That hymn tune was popular among all the Union soldiers. They would take it up, as now, without any apparent occasion for it and without the least suspicion of irony. They didn't bother to think how many voices the war had stopped from praising God. They sang merely because they liked it; the tone was pleasing and the volume of sound was grand.

Tuesday morning we pushed ahead and threw up breastworks near Noel's Station on the Virginia Central Railroad, which here ran parallel with the river and about a mile south of it. Early

Wednesday morning we advanced again, moving to the left, and threw up a line of works about a thousand yards south of the railroad in a farm field. Our division formed the first line of battle; but no battle developed, only skirmishing. The day was showery.

Thursday morning the rain fell in torrents. We welcomed "out of the wet," as our humorists were quick to say, Lieutenant Wiggin and eleven men recaptured from the enemy. After the battle of the Wilderness, and while we had been fighting near Spotsylvania, the cavalry under Sheridan had gone south on a raid. May 9th, Custer's brigade had swept into Beaver Dam Station, about ten miles up the Virginia Central from where we were now, and had captured there some trains of cars carrying wounded men and a great store of supplies, and several hundred Union prisoners. Among the surprised and happy captives thus recovered was Lieutenant Wiggin, who had been taken prisoner May 8th in the fighting near the Alsop farm. Instead of undergoing, as he had expected, heartbreaking months of horror in Libby Prison, he had been in rebel hands only one day, and his soldier captors, he told me, had treated him well.

Thursday afternoon we learned that our corps was to recross the North Anna that night. We withdrew unmolested; before midnight, we were over the water and marching away. Friday morning we were at Chesterfield Station on the Richmond & Potomac Railroad, a little way north of the stream. Leaving there towards noon, we marched to the southeast until evening. Somewhere off to our right the North Anna flowed in the same general direction, the South Anna joined it, and the two streams became the Pamunkey. Saturday, marching on, we crossed the Pamunkey near Hanover Town and threw up a line of works along the low heights rising beyond the river.

We were now on the far landward end of the Yorktown peninsula, the scene of McClellan's campaign of two years before. We couldn't help thinking how McClellan had got the army almost to Richmond with hardly the loss of a man, while Grant had lost already more thousands than we cared to guess; yet we felt that this time there would be no turning back.

III

SUNDAY, May 29th, we pushed ahead. The ground of our advance was flattish, wooded, and sparsely inhabited except by rebel skirmishers. The weather was sultry. All afternoon we skirmished and sweltered. At evening the brigade moved to the left, crossed the swampy Totopotomoy Creek, and threw up a line of breastworks at a crossroads near Old Church.

Monday forenoon we moved over to the right and rejoined the corps; and the 94th New York rejoined the brigade. We found that our old division was brought together again and placed under the command of a Brigadier-General Lockwood, whom we didn't know and didn't care for; he looked like a crabbed schoolmaster. This general, with a batch of green aides, was running things in a feeble way.

Monday afternoon we advanced again, following an active skirmish line. We encountered the rebels near Bethesda Church and drove them back and threw up a line of works. Our regiment twice changed position, throwing up breastworks each time, and our men were digging all night.

Tuesday some raw recruits came up, and just as they arrived a huge shell exploded over their heads with a shattering crash and a spatter of iron. It was like the splash of a great stone in a frog pond. The startled recruits jumped and dove in all directions. One man went head first, like a solid shot, into the midriff of Colonel Farnham, who fell in a heap, convulsed with laughter. Some went shooting among the old settees in the churchyard, where General Warren and his staff were sitting. One man was hit; a fragment of iron took his right thumb off. He started running aimlessly around, holding up the bleeding stump and howling; but a veteran corporal stopped him with a scolding.

"What ye makin' such a hell of a fuss about a thumb fer?" he asked. "There's a man over there with his head shot off, and he don't say a damn word. I'm ashamed of ye."

Skirmishing was active all that day and the following night. Our lines were pressed nearer to the rebel works. Wednesday our division was pushed ahead and deployed, but we got more or less bogged in a swamp and arrived at no place in particular. Towards evening our regiment moved to the left into an open field, and after nightfall we moved up a slight ridge and built, very quietly, a line of breastworks. When the rebel skirmishers found us there at daylight, they fired a few startled shots and fell back. Our skirmish line followed them into a strip of woods and came suddenly upon some large tents, with horses hitched close by; perhaps it was a brigade or division headquarters of the enemy. A few shots into those tents brought out some officers, active as hornets. They rallied their men and drove our skirmishers back to the edge of the woods, where we settled the controversy and established our picket line.

Thursday we did more shooting and sweltering. Early in the afternoon, when heavy firing was heard beyond our right, we were marched to the rear and towards the right of the swamp, and then marched back again; and General Lockwood was relieved from the command of the division. We supposed that the intention had been to put us into the fighting, but somehow we had been led away from the action while apparently going towards it; a fatal error for any general to make. Late in the afternoon it began to rain, cooling us off, and the rain continued in showers all night.

Early Friday morning we heard a great thunder of artillery away beyond our left, near Cold Harbor. The Union troops there, as we learned later, advanced to the assault and suffered a more costly repulse than any other sustained in the entire campaign. Our corps did some fighting, but not much, as our corps front was very thin, stretched out to a length of perhaps three miles. The pickets of our division covered more than a mile of this front, but were too near our works to protect our men from the almost incessant skirmish fire of the enemy. Colonel Tilden, as division officer of the picket, was directed to advance the entire picket line. We held our breath as he sprang over the works and alone advanced to the front and down the line, rapidly issuing his orders under fire. He escaped unscathed, but Captain Washburn of the 13th Massachusetts, who joined him in a reconnaissance to the left, was severely wounded. The pickets pushed forward, driving back the rebel skirmishers; and Colonel Tilden brought in the wounded captain.

Towards noon we moved to the right—across the swamp, this time; not around it—and went into a line of works near the church. Saturday we moved to the left near the works that we had thrown up beyond the field. Sunday, at nightfall, we left our intrenchments under a heavy skirmish fire and moved southerly to a position near Cold Harbor. We learned, to our sorrow, that Major Leavitt, wounded in the fighting near Spotsylvania Court House, had died in a hospital at Washington.

Our corps was now in reserve. Monday our baggage train came up, clothing and shoes were issued, and we went into camp. We stayed in camp three days. General Crawford, who had been directing the movements of the division since the Lockwood affair, was now formally assigned to the command, and Lieutenant-Colonel Farnham was detached from our regiment to be Crawford's chief of staff and division inspector-general. We didn't think too much of Crawford. He was a tall, chesty, glowering man, with heavy eyes, a big nose, and bushy whiskers; and he wore habitually a turn-out-the-guard expression, which was, as we knew, fairly indicative of his military character.

Saturday, June 11th, we broke camp at four o'clock in the morning, marched at five, and headed southeast, crossed the Richmond & York River Railroad at Dispatch Station, and went into camp not far from the Chickahominy River. By the map we were near Bottom's Bridge, but all the bridges were down, destroyed by the rebels. Saturday night and Sunday we rested. Early Sunday evening we broke camp, at midnight we crossed a pontoon bridge over the Chickahominy at Long Bridge, and through the small hours we pushed cautiously westward on the Long Bridge road.

After a halt at daylight, Monday morning, we moved up the main road leading north across White Oak Branch towards Richmond, and formed in line of battle facing the swampy stream near White Oak Bridge. Troops of our corps were covering the passage of the Chickahominy by all the army in our rear. From our position on the brow of a rise we could see a force of rebels going into line less than a thousand yards away on the farther side of the stream. An officer on a white horse was a conspicuous mark for our sharpshooters, but apparently he bore a charmed life; he rode up and down his line unharmed. Our batteries, though occupying commanding positions, were unaccountably silent after one discharge. Not so, the fieldpieces of the enemy. Two men of my regiment were severely wounded by bursting shells. Our skirmishers were deployed and a smart peppering was kept up till late afternoon.

Towards evening our division was withdrawn, and at nine o'clock that night my regiment, after acting as a rear guard, was ordered away. We marched south to St. Mary's Church, arriving there at three o'clock Tuesday morning, and starting again at six we plodded over dusty roads in broiling heat until we went into camp near Charles City Court House. Ammunition and rations were issued. We rested all day Wednesday.

Thursday our division broke camp at dawn and marched to the James River at Wilcox's Landing, and our brigade crossed in the steamers *Joseph Powell* and *James Brooks*. We rested until afternoon, and then marched rapidly out the Prince George Court House road, halting at half-past three Friday morning. We pressed on at daylight, and later left the road and made our way over swampy ground and through tangled brush in the direction of Petersburg. Towards nightfall we came up on the left of troops attacking; for some time my regiment lay waiting under the steep and bushy bank of a ravine, and we heard fierce sounds of struggle in the darkness above us. Colonel Carle's brigade moved forward to the assault, carried the works in its front, and sent back prisoners and colors; but the troops on our right gave way, the rebels opened fire from a battery to our left, and Colonel Carle was ordered to withdraw. Our brigade moved up to relieve his, a strong skirmish line was pushed ahead, and we threw up breastworks.

Early Saturday morning there was a general advance; but instead of moving into a storm of fire, as we had expected, we went up and over abandoned works manned only by the dead of the night before. The rebels had drawn back nearer to the town. We pushed ahead nearly a mile, driving their skirmishers out of sudden and deep ravines, and finally clearing them out of the narrow and steeply sided cut of the Petersburg & Norfolk Railroad. Beyond the cut the ground rose away in a swelling slope, and along the crest of the slope the rebels were strongly intrenched in their new line. We withdrew from the cut and fixed our line about halfway up a hill overlooking and near the railroad. Our men worked all night at building intrenchments.

We took cover through five days following. Our men lay close to the ground all day, and at night deepened the trenches and dug approaches to the wells and other works in the rear. The rebel sharpshooters had a clear range of our entire front, and were quick on the trigger; my regiment suffered a daily loss. Captain Stevens, while sitting behind a tree and reading a newspaper, inadvertently exposed his head and was shot through the neck. He bled to death in the arms of Sergeant-Major Stevens, his brother.

Regimental headquarters had the protection of a large oak tree and a small redoubt. The oak was about six feet in diameter and the wings of the redoubt extended a like distance to right and left of the tree. Here reports were made and callers received. In the daytime, military courtesies were generally ignored; aides and orderlies came in with a jump and landed on all fours. One orderly, rocketing over, struck the top of the earthwork and fell sprawling in a shower of dirt and official papers. He had a circular for Colonel Tilden to sign. The colonel signed in ink, and I handed out a blotter, and just at that moment, incredibly in the outworn tradition, a bullet hit the edge of the redoubt and scattered sand all over the paper, and the colonel said not to mind the blotter. He shook off the dirt and handed the circular back to the orderly, who took it, gave a quick glance over the redoubt, and jumped for the ditch. Sergeant Mower, then appearing, was indiscreetly formal; he stopped to salute. The command of "Down, Sergeant!" was not quick enough; a bullet struck him in the shoulder. He went to the surgeon; but the shoulder was never much good after that.

Somewhere up the slope behind us there was an apple orchard. In spite of orders and friendly counsel, men of my regiment persisted in risking life for the possession of a green apple, which, if they got it, would only give them a bellyache. Some of the survivors told me that from the orchard they could see the spires of Petersburg thrusting up beyond the slope in our front. I don't recall that I viewed the town, myself; I wasn't so anxious to risk seeing another world at the same time. Our regimental loss while we occupied this position was one officer and six men killed, and twelve men wounded, by sharpshooters.

Friday, June 24th, our brigade moved to the left, under a furious fire from the rebel batteries in our front. We took up a position just west of the Jerusalem plank road and about a thousand yards from the rebel line of defense. A large redoubt, later called Fort Davis in honor of Colonel Davis of the 39th Massachusetts, who was mortally wounded there, was built by the brigade and occupied by several regiments. My regiment had the honor of

IN THE TRENCHES AT PETERSBURG

holding a line of works several hundred yards in front of the redoubt and within speaking distance of the rebel pickets, who were sometimes more inclined to talk than shoot.

We spent seven weeks in our trenches, living in the ground and bearing the risk of dying there. Not far beyond our right, on the Jerusalem plank road, there was built a large redoubt, Fort Sedgwick, soon familiarly known as "Fort Hell"; and opposing this, in our front, was the rebel Fort Mahone, which we called "Fort Damnation." The cannon in these works often exchanged compliments, making a great racket, disturbing our rest, and sometimes annoying us more seriously. The skirmish lines between the intrenched armies were consistently busy. Yet, though we dwelt always in the land of Memento Mori, we enjoyed some extraordinary lapses into life.

As if by common consent, our troops and the rebels in our front would suspend hostilities. Men would lie lounging on the works and talking with their enemies across the way. Occasionally a Yank and a Johnnie would meet between the lines and exchange coffee for tobacco, or a New York *Herald* for a Richmond *Enquirer*. The Johnnies were careful to cut out some of their news, and the Yanks, equally cautious, clipped the papers which they gave into Southern hands. When a battery was about to open fire, some friendly skirmisher would shout "Down, Yank!" or "Down, Reb!" as the case might be, and down out of sight would go every man.

Our band was with the regiment, and for an hour in the morning, and just before sundown, it would play some of its best selections, generally closing the program with a national air. Often we saw the rebels crowding up to their works and listening to "The Battle Hymn of the Republic" or "America." None of the rebel bands had been heard since we had left the North Anna. Sunday evenings, "Old Hundredth" and "Pleyel's Hymn" would come rolling in over the works, from a thousand throats, to mingle harmoniously with thoughts of peace.

Towards the end of July we all talked about the mine that was to be exploded under the rebel works. At last the day came; it was July 30th. As early as three o'clock in the morning we were under arms and waiting nervously for the explosion. Shortly after four the powder was touched off, and we hardly knew it; there was a vague sound, heavy and muffled, which few of us heard, and from our brigade position we could see little of what was happening more than a mile to our right. The assault following the explosion was by all accounts a dismal failure.

IV

ALL through July and halfway through August the chief occupation of our corps was the strengthening of its works in front of Petersburg. We almost came to suspect that the war was degenerating into a digging match. We were pleased when early in the morning of Monday, August 15th, the corps was relieved and moved quietly to the rear. After two days of rest and a day of rain, we were put in motion early Thursday morning and marched, out of sight of the enemy, towards the left. The heat was terrific. Our progress was pardonably slow. It was about noon when our brigade was halted near the Yellow House, on the Weldon Railroad, about four miles south of Petersburg.

We were sent there to seize and hold the railroad; the rebels used it to get supplies to their army. We proceeded to take possession. Ayres's division was started up the west side of the track and Crawford's division up the east side, our brigade forming Crawford's left and my regiment forming the left of the brigade and moving nearest to the railroad. We were supposed to connect with the right of Ayres's division; but we didn't, whatever the official records may say to the contrary. A most unaccountable posting of our brigade, by a bewildered commander who moved it in all directions but the right one, left us pulling away at a slant, more than a hundred yards from the track and over ground thickly covered with trees and underbrush.

We were slowed up and somewhat disordered by the tangle of bushes, and proceeded cautiously. Regimental commanders were informed that a strong line of skirmishers was posted close in front, awaiting orders to advance; meanwhile, there must be no firing of muskets. Then suddenly we heard the rebel yell and the crash of a volley; and the skirmishers came running in, apparently without having fired a shot. Some officer ordered our men to lie down and blaze away, and we opened fire to our front; but the rebels, taking advantage of the gap between the divisions, filed through on our left and closed in upon us from both front and rear, and many of us were captured. I found myself looking into the muzzle of a gun with a determined face behind it.

Cursing the blundering stupidity of whoever had let us into that fix, we were started with a most willing escort towards the rebel rear. As we climbed the fence of a cornfield beyond the woods, we heard our batteries begin to fire. I was both angry and mortified at being a prisoner, and when a shell burst near me and drove a rebel through the fence into Kingdom Come, I was more than glad. I was double quicked out of range into open ground, and there I was astonished to see that the enemy had no infantry support whatever. For obvious reasons I used all my persuasive powers on my captor to allow me to escape. I sincerely believe that he thought twice about it, for he halted and looked me full in the face and said:

"Yank, I'm damned sorry you didn't capture me."

Naturally, I was in full accord with that sentiment and argued to effect the exchange; but the Johnnie didn't quite feel that he could swap places with me. My acute disappointment was tempered with admiration for his loyalty to honor; he was too conscientious to gain release from his starving service at such a price. He didn't scruple, however, to relieve me of my new hat and rubber coat. He offered me a grey cap to wear until we should reach the rebel quartermaster, when I would have to give it up. I didn't wish to wear any part of a rebel uniform, but just then it came on to rain, and the drenching downpour drove me to cover my head.

I was led like a lamb to an officer mounted on a sorrel horse and wearing stars on the collar of his badly fitting coat. He was a cadaverous, dyspeptic-looking man, with nerves all over him and an eye as cold as a glacier. This, I was told, was "Billy" Mahone. General Mahone was possibly in command, as he was exceedingly anxious to know what he was facing.

"What corps do you belong to? What batteries have you got? Any cavalry? Is Grant there? Who commands?"

He fired his questions at me in a breath. My only reply was:

"General, you are too good an officer to expect me to give you correct answers."

Smiling with the lower muscles of his face, he motioned me to the rear. Under the guidance of my captor, who clung to me like a brother, I started away. We were hardly out of earshot of General Mahone when an incident occurred that suggested a relapse of discipline in the rebel army. An officer spoke sharply to my guide.

"Go back to the front," said the officer.

"Go to hell," said the private.

"Keep nearer to the front," I felt like saying, "and you'uns will all go to hell soon."

We went towards Petersburg, all of us that were prisoners now being herded together. Remembering what my captor had said about a visit to the quartermaster, I dropped my watch through the armscye of my vest. As it left my hand and made its way down, with a short prayer from me at every stop, I had troubled thoughts of the suffering in store for me if I should land in prison penniless. Near the town, sure enough, we were halted and stripped of our outward valuables. I had the dubious satisfaction of seeing my captor despoiled of his plunder; the quartermaster was enriched by my hat, rubber coat, and an elegant silver corps badge presented to me a few days before by Colonel Farnham. I gave up the grey cap to its proper owner, with thanks which he didn't seem to appreciate.

Under a strong guard with loaded muskets and bayonets fixed, we were marched through the principal streets of Petersburg. The sidewalks were lined with old men, boys, and decrepit women, who vied with one another in flinging insults and venom. The women were the worst of the lot; they spat upon us, laughed at us, and called us vile and filthy names.

Our first night in rebeldom was passed in an old outbuilding, a sort of shed, strongly flavored with Africa. In the black darkness of the night I felt a hand light on my shoulder and glide towards my watch pocket. Thoroughly awakened, I grabbed something tangible and held on. I heard a whispered warning:

"Keep quiet! There are friends around."

This particular friend seemed anxious to supply me with greenbacks and directions how to escape. He said that he was a Northern man there to aid us. When next he asked me if I had a gold watch, negotiations were suspended, I requested him to move on, and he was kept moving until the hole called a door allowed him to crawl out with a kick in the rear. I later sold my watch to a more reputable tradesman, and put the money where I thought it would be safest hid, in odd corners of my clothes.

Towards noon of the next day we were moved to an island in the Appomattox River; and from there, the day following, we were sent to Manchester, and across the James into Richmond. Arriving in the rebel capital, Saturday evening, we were received at Libby Prison as if at a palatial hotel. Most courteously we were requested to announce our names for register. The commandant, Major Turner, asked us sweetly if we desired to deposit in the office safe our watches, jewels, or other valuables, and assured us that he would give us receipts which would redeem our property on our release. He was not at all anxious to receive our treasures. We soon learned why.

Ordered into line in a room adjoining the reception room, we were called by name, one by one, to the rear of the prison; and there, out of sight, a little puppy named Ross went through the clothes of every prisoner who denied the possession of money or valuables. Not a garment escaped inspection; yet the money that I had hidden stayed hidden for my use. One by one we went to that room, and none went back. We were shown up the stairs to the second floor of the prison. Only after the last of us had come up, and seen the stairs pulled up after him, did we know of the indignity inflicted upon our comrades. We cursed our keepers from that hour.

LIBBY, SALISBURY, DANVILLE

I see the gorgèd prison-den,
The dead-line and the pent-up pen ...
—FORCEYTHE WILLSON, "In State"

LIBBY PRISON was a large brick building, formerly the
warehouse of Libby & Son, ship-chandlers and grocers. It fronted
on Cary Street at Twentieth, and was three stories high where it
faced Cary Street and four stories high at the rear above a wharf.
Twentieth Street sloped past our end of the prison. An empty
lot sloped past the other; it was from that end that Colonel
Tilden had escaped, through the tunnel planned by Colonel
Rose. On the Cary Street level at our end were the prison offices.
Our room, next above, was a bare low loft, with barred windows
at front and rear and others on the long side overlooking Twentieth Street. I suppose there had once been glass in the windows,
but there was none then. No air seemed to come in, and the
room was smelly and hot and stifling. I took the place assigned
to me on the floor and tried to sleep, but sleep I could not.

My first day there, I seized what chances offered to look out
of the windows. The view across Cary Street was not inviting;
on the other side of the street was a row of empty lots and dingy
buildings, and behind them was a confusion of roofs and chimneys. Across the intersection of Cary and Twentieth streets were
the tents of the guard, and beyond were more roofs and chimneys.
A dozen blocks away in that direction was the rebel Capitol; I
couldn't see it, nor cared to behold the cause of my misfortune.
I went to the windows overlooking Twentieth Street; nothing
there but an empty lot, and then a large brick warehouse like
our prison. I went to the rear. The view there was better; close
below by the wharf was the quiet water of a dock, and beyond
an embankment at the farther side of the dock was the rippling
James. I looked across and saw open fields, and away downstream

I could discern rolling hills by a distant reach of the river. Across from the prison were some factories, and upstream beyond them was the village of Manchester. Between the village and the city were long, white bridges, the nearest half-hidden by green trees on a little island midway of the stream. A mile farther up was Belle Isle, a bigger island, where many Union soldiers, enlisted men, were held prisoners and died. I think there were only officers at Libby.

Major Turner, the commandant, might possibly have been a gentleman under favorable circumstances. It would be treason to common sense to suggest that Dick Turner, the turnkey, was anything but a scoundrel. I heard, and was willing to believe it, that his proper station in life, which he had ambitiously forsaken, was that of a bootblack. His heart was blacker than any brogans that he may ever have shined with a brush. He took pleasure in tormenting us, in subjecting us to little, stinging annoyances. He lied to us for sheer love of that fascinating vice. His vanity was often wounded, and then he was like a hornet let loose in a camp meeting. We ignored him as much as possible when he showed his ugly face in our room.

Our quarters were kept indifferently clean by negroes, who swept the floors every morning and sloshed them twice a week. James River water was used for washing, drinking, cooking, and bathing. We drew it from a single tap in our kitchen, or let it fill a trough there when we could get a chance. The kitchen was furnished with three old cook-stoves and a limited supply of utensils, for the use of those prisoners who preferred to cook their own food. I was at first surprised at this, but soon I was only too glad to take my turn as kitchen scullion, for human nature rebelled at scant rations of corn-and-cob bread, tough beef boiled dry, and bean soup flavored with rancid bacon and garnished with white worms.

We that had money fared well as long as it lasted. Greenbacks were exchanged for rebel currency, one dollar of ours for five of theirs, and food was bought at high prices from outside sources. We organized a commissary department, with Colonel Hooper of the 24th Massachusetts as chief. He divided us into messes, and each mess chose its own commissary, secretary, and treasurer. The members of Mess No. 6 were Captains Kinsley and Hutchins and Lieutenants Hanson, Tidd, Barker, and Chapman, all of the 39th Massachusetts, and Captains Conley and Lord and Lieutenants Broughton, Chapman, Fitch, and myself, all of the 16th Maine. To this original membership there was added Lieutenant Sage of the 144th Ohio and, later, Captain Goler of the 6th New York Cavalry. Captain Cook of the 9th Colored Troops was also a member of our mess for a short time, until he was transferred to Mess No. 7. Our first commissary was Lieutenant Chapman, of my regiment; our first treasurer was Lieutenant Hanson, and I was the secretary. I kept in my diary a record of our expenditures.

We were so anxious to get war news, even of the rebel variety, that we subscribed for Richmond newspapers. We got little comfort, however, from the columns of the *Enquirer* and the *Dispatch*. Our armies were always defeated there, the rebels always victorious. We discounted that, and looked for the announcement of a general exchange of prisoners; but we never found good news.

On September 29th, troops of Butler's army attacked Fort Harrison, a part of the defenses of Richmond, and carried it by assault. The heavy cannonading and bursting of shells only six miles down the river set us wild with hope, and the stay-at-homes of Richmond wild with terror. From the windows of our prison we saw housetops crowded with men and women looking anxiously in the direction of the firing. Bells rang, the "Long Roll" sounded; there was a general turn-out. We knew that down the streets of Richmond were straggling the last reserves of the capital city, to stop the breach; and we hoped they couldn't stop it. Next day there was more cannonading, which kept us in a fever of excitement. The rebels attempted, as we learned later, to recapture the lost fort, and failed; but they held their line of defense. They decided to send us to a safer place.

At three o'clock in the morning of Sunday, October 2d, in a drizzling rain, we were hustled out of the prison under a strong guard, marched across the James, and herded into cars at Manchester. Army haversacks were issued to us, with rations for three days; three hunks of corn-bread and three smaller ones of meat, hardly sufficient for a lunch. We were not permitted to take our blankets. None of us had more than ordinary clothing, and few had hats. The train started, and the miserable collection of crowded cars went rattling towards the farther South. We stopped for the night at Clover Station.

At every stop of the train, hucksters, both black and white, would crowd around to dicker. One old darkey had four sweet-potato pies in one hand and a peck basket in the other. "What do you want for the basket?" inquired Captain Conley. "Golly, Colonel," answered the black, "reckon couldn't 'spose of dat 'ere; brung dat to put de blue greenbacks in." Officers in the car with me sold personal property at fabulous prices in rebel currency. Captain Kinsley sold his meerschaum pipe to the engineer of an up train, crossed at Clover Station. He got two hundred dollars for it, and gave me fifty dollars for our mess if we should be separated.

We rattled on, and at half-past three Tuesday afternoon we reached Greensboro, North Carolina. Our cars were sidetracked to await an up train, which soon rounded a curve and came to a stop close beside us. In a worn passenger car, which was neither better nor worse than the one other car in the train, sat Jefferson Davis, and with him a woman, whom we took to be Mrs. Davis, and an officer who looked like General Beauregard.

No man could have sat for a photograph with a sadder face than that worn by Davis. Apparently oblivious of his surroundings, he was possibly seeking a solution of his difficulties. I wondered if he was moved by any feeling of remorse or regret for his suicidal folly. Whatever he may have felt, it was obvious that he imparted none of his feelings to the woman with him. Placid, comely, and well dressed, she got up and swished out to the platform of the car. Looking us over, she said, "Gentlemen, I am exceedingly glad to see you; I hope to see more of you." Was this sarcasm? Those of us that wore hats raised them without a word. The rebel officer stood near the woman, and fidgeted; his manner was nervous and disagreeable. When she went back into the car again, he followed, turned back a seat, and sat facing her. Their conversation may or may not have been interesting. To me, that car and its occupants appeared like a coach of mourners on the way to a funeral.

After Davis' train departed, we were turned out of ours and ordered to bivouac in a pine grove near the station. I saw few civilians. The town was as quiet as a graveyard. Surrounded by a guard, we chewed the cuds of discomfort and bitter reflection. Desperately hungry, we rejoiced when from a storehouse near by there came a detail of soldiers bringing boxes, which they left in our midst. The contents was quickly distributed, and as quickly defined with scientific profanity. No human being could penetrate with ordinary teeth that rice-bread, baked to a hardness equaled only by petrified wood. The cakes, about the size of government hardtack, were of no use as food. Indignant prisoners sent them skimming through the air in all directions.

Rebel soldiers came from a camp near by and looked us over, but with kindly eyes. One of them, noticing a peculiar badge I wore, spoke to the guard and started on the run back to camp. Returning, he placed in my hands a package, and stood near while I opened it. That package contained hot bacon, corn dodgers, and biscuits spread with butter. The smiling Johnnie that brought it won my heart; I have loved him in memory ever since. I gave him a note addressed to Colonel Tilden, "To succor J. B. Hobson, 1st North Carolina Sharpshooters, if captured."

Captain Conley had not got over his hankering for rum, and when a greyback winked several drinks at him, he passed over a five-dollar scrip to be invested in applejack. The Southerner looked honest; but the captain awaited his return in vain.

Wednesday morning, by kindness of my unexpected friend, I had a breakfast of broiled steak and hot biscuits. I began to think that if we could stay at Greensboro, I might at least be well fed; but we were herded into our cars again and started away. Our progress was slow. The road was sadly out of repair, the rolling stock was worn out, and fuel was scarce. Often on an ascending grade the train would stop, and sometimes would run back in spite of brakes. The trainmen replenished the tender with fence rails, and themselves with corn whiskey. The firebox was crammed with pitch knots, the heat became fervent, the steam hissed; the engine would creak and groan in every joint when the throttle was pulled wide open at the head of a long, steep grade, and the cars with their living freight would gather speed and plunge madly down the uneven track. We were slatted from side to side, thrown down, and piled in heaps, groaning and cursing. Several of our number saw their opportunity and leaped from the rushing train, preferring the risk to an indefinite stay in a stockade. The guard fired at them dutifully, but the shots must have gone wide. At nightfall we reached Salisbury.

II

THE stockade at Salisbury enclosed a piece of ground perhaps a dozen acres in extent, surrounding an old cotton factory and several smaller buildings which had served, I suppose, as quarters for negroes. Armed sentries paced a raised walk on the outer side of the stockade, and cannon commanded the main gate and pointed inwards from the corners of the yard. The factory was a brick building of three stories with a narrower fourth story; a dingy, shabby, stinking place. From the beginning of the war it had been used as a sort of slop jar, into which the Confederacy had dumped odd lots of political and military prisoners. When we arrived, perhaps eight hundred of these rogues and victims were confined here, and among them were desperadoes called "Muggers," who seemed to have the white card to beat, rob, and kill the weaker of their fellow prisoners.

How can I describe the horrors of our first night at Salisbury? We were forced up the factory stairway, step by step over nameless filth, to the monitor room under the roof. The fiendish "Muggers" crept in and robbed several of our number before an alarm was given. Two officers, then stationed at the door with billets of wood, will never be held accountable for the skull-crushing blows that beat back a "Mugger" as he attempted to force his way in. He fell backwards with a wild scream, and I heard him bound from stair to stair down, down, into what I hoped was the Bottomless Pit.

Early in the morning, the officer of the day was called and complaints were made to him. He denied responsibility and called the commandant, Major Gee, who came and asked who complained and why. Our ranking officer, General Hayes, ignoring Major Gee's extended hand, pointed in silence to the filth-drenched hall and staircase, and then, with a look that brought the color of shame to the commandant's face, demanded larger and better quarters for officers of the United States Army. The general's courageous words, that "ten thousand fresh prisoners would not bear for another hour such indignities," must have had some effect; for we were transferred to the small outbuildings and were permitted the use of open ground within the stockade. The huts were close quarters for us, and were filled with vermin; yet they were preferable to the factory.

My mess and three others occupied one hut, two messes upstairs and two down. Captain Conley and I bunked together, sleeping under the same dirty quilt and ragged blanket. Someone supplied me with a dipper, fork, and spoon; and I ate as decently as I might what food I could get, though my stomach would not always retain what little I swallowed. The prison rations were insufficient. Once or twice they increased, raising our hopes, but then they dwindled again, and we despaired of keeping our strength. We were often thirsty; there were crowded into the stockade seven thousand prisoners, and all the water available came from two or three ordinary wells. Our suffering became so apparent that two worn shovels were thrown to us and we were told to dig. We dug, and about fifteen feet down we came to water. An old bucket resembling a nail cask, and a rope, were then supplied, and a windlass was quickly made from green firewood. Mud and water were scooped up together. The water was held in dippers till the mud had partly settled, and then was drunk. But this was not enough. More than once I was so thirsty that my ears rang and my tongue swelled in my mouth. We would have dug another well, but an official came with a guard and took away the shovels. The prison authorities were always in a fever of suspicion that we were tunneling our way out; it was perhaps a compliment to us that a well was not excepted from the possibilities of escape.

Miserable as our condition was, that of the enlisted men was far worse. We were separated from them by a dead-line guarded by sentries, but we could see them and their sufferings all too plainly. There was no shelter for them. There was not enough food. They were thinly clad; many had no shoes, few had overcoats, and hundreds had only ragged trousers and shirt to cover their nakedness. There was no stream running through the enclosure to carry away filth. The ground was soon reeking, and the air was sour and heavy with the stench of offal. In that filth-glutted soil men lived, slept, and died. Some burrowed holes to lie in, and some lay on little clay-heaps in the open. When rain fell, the burrowers were flooded out, and the heapers were marooned on mudbanks only a few inches above the water, which floated offal full of maggots and vermin. When the sun shone, it could not lighten the misery of these wretched captives.

I saw men wander back and forth, their heads bowed, their eyes searching the ground for a stray bone or morsel of food dropped from some weaker hand. I saw men with clasped fingers and streaming eyes, praying for their dear ones at home, into whose loving eyes they would never look again. I saw men in delirium beat themselves and curse God. And I saw, shuddering as I looked, the dead-cart on its morning rounds, and in it God's images tiered up like sticks of wood.

Death or desertion were the only sure chances of release for our men. I will not censure those who went over to the rebels at Salisbury, as a life-preserving act. Escape seemed impossible. Bordering the yard, near the stockade, was an imaginary line which the men were forbidden to cross, and between their part of the yard and ours was another. These lines were significant, and all prisoners kept away from them, for the sentries would fire at anyone approaching within ten feet of their beats. On October 16th I saw Lieutenant Davis of the 155th New York shot dead as he stood near the line in the yard.

We planned to deliver all the Northern prisoners. Soon after arriving at Salisbury, we began secretly to organize a corps of two divisions, with a capable officer in command of each division and General Hayes directing the whole. So perfectly was this organization effected that every enlisted man over the line knew who his immediate commander was. Codes of signals were adopted and quickly learned. Orders were written, wrapped around stones, and after dark were tossed high over the heads of the sentries pacing the dead-line in the yard.

An attack on the guard, the gate, the batteries outside, the commissary, the railroad station, and the town, was planned for October 18th. We felt reasonably sure of success; but the afternoon before the attack was to be made, Lieutenant Gardner of the 13th Connecticut, in sending a last message of command, threw his carrier-stone too swiftly, and his message, which was not in code, became detached and fell fluttering at the feet of a sentry. The sentry at once called the corporal of the guard, and he the sergeant, and so on, until the officer of the day came, who, it was said, was the only one of the number who could read.

The officers on one side of the line and the men on the other stood as if paralyzed. Every eye was fastened on that little armed group in the center. Like a flash there came to the minds of hundreds the thought of seizing the rebels, holding them as hostages, taking their guns, and breaking out of the stockade; but the rebel officer shouted: "Turn out the guard! Turn out the camp! Man the guns!" Our moment for action was lost. The parapet bristled with muskets, and the black mouths of cannon grinned at us from the corners of the yard.

Then began a search for Lieutenant Gardner. No one knew him. He didn't even know himself when addressed. The rebels spent all the next day and the next in trying to spot him, without success. Finally, we were formed in one rank, and roll was called. Each officer, on answering to his name, was passed out through a gate in the stockade. Lieutenant Gardner, having disguised himself by dirtying his face and changing from his neat uniform into some ragged cast-offs, answered to the name of an officer who had jumped from the train on our way south. We all went out, taking with us Hugh Conway, a private in my regiment, who had been permitted to act as a mess servant on our side of the line. I forget what name he answered to.

We were marched to the station and herded into a train, and at five o'clock in the afternoon of Wednesday, October 19th, we were started back to Virginia. By ten o'clock the following night we were at Danville, a few miles over the state line, and there we were marched into another prison.

III

OUR prison at Danville, for officers only, was an old tobacco warehouse, known as Prison No. 3 in order to distinguish it from the prisons for enlisted men. It was a brick building of three stories, with a small yard at the rear. We were quartered on the upper two floors, and Mess No. 6 was glad to be on the top floor, since it was warmer there under the roof than on the floor below. The ground floor was used as a promenade, where limited numbers of prisoners were permitted to exercise in daylight hours. We had the use of the back yard for cooking; and there, too, were our sanitary conveniences, which were limited to a wooden trough for washing and one other institution more deplorable than any army sink. Sentries guarded the prison on all sides, and the ground-floor promenade, and the yard.

Lieutenant-Colonel Smith, the commandant, was almost an improvement over our former keepers. The Libby jailers had been bad, and the Salisbury jailers worse; at Salisbury I had even regretted the Turners, and would have taken any amount of Turner in exchange for Gee. It was difficult to believe that either Major Turner or Major Gee had ever been a soldier. It was our general experience that Southern fighting men were human beings like us, but that Southern prison keepers were mean-spirited brutes. Colonel Smith, though by no means inclined to pamper us, did occasionally show that he possessed soldierly qualities and a comprehension that we were prisoners of war. I doubt that he enjoyed keeping us.

We were thankful that water was plentiful. The prison was near the Dan River, and details of prisoners under guard brought water in buckets from the stream. It was possible to have a sponge bath, without the sponge, and on rare occasions a few of us could go under guard to the river and get into water all over. After Salisbury, we certainly needed a cleaning; but it was soon too cold for men in our weakened condition to risk a chill for the sake of satisfactory cleanliness. We couldn't, by any mere washing, have rid ourselves of vermin. This prison, like the others, crawled with them.

Our prison rations were hardly sufficient to sustain life. Corn-and-cob bread was the chief item supplied, to which were added at odd times uncertain portions of salt cod or boiled beef. When we could raise money, we bought flour and rice and helped out our diet with sorghum, a few vegetables or apples, and salt. We had utensils for cooking and eating, but no table or kitchen; Mess No. 6 inventoried six tin plates, ten pewter spoons, two tin dippers, seven case-knives, one fork, three jack-knives, and an old stove-hearth on which we fried our delicious flapjacks. These fritters were made of corn-and-cob bread and river water, and sometimes were flavored with dried-apple juice and pepper. We took turns at cooking. Captain Lord became an expert. It was humiliating to see an officer of the United States Army, with an old stove-hearth under one arm, a handful of splinters under the other, and a rusty can full of corn mush, starting for the back yard to prepare his dinner. I felt honored, but cried with shame, when an enterprising colonel sent his compliments and requested the loan of our stove-hearth.

Our mess underwent some changes in membership. Before we had left Libby, Lieutenants Fitch, Broughton, and Sage had gone to the hospital in that prison, and my recollection is that they did not return to us. I am not sure that Captain Goler stayed with us, either; he may have done so. Early in November there came to us Captain T. C. J. Bailey, of the 17th Infantry, the same Captain Bailey under whom I had served when on recruiting duty in Maine. A little later we also received as a member of our mess Captain Boice, of the 3d New Jersey Cavalry. The latter was not with us long, however, for early in December he was sent to Richmond as a hostage, to be confined in a Libby cell. Captain Conley and I were still bunking together, though now we had no bunk, only a place on the floor and a piece of quilt to cover us. We shared our quilt and our few other possessions with Captain Bailey, and he shared what he had with us.

Several of the messes on our floor clubbed together and bought an old cook-stove with two legs and some funnel of different sizes. The stove was set up and the funnel run through a broken window. When the wind was right we were happy, but as that particular window was in keeping with our other misfortunes, we were soon most beautifully bronzed. The smoke poured in as often as out. The fuel was coal, of poor quality, and the stove had to be cleaned out frequently, and with every cleaning there was a belch of gassy fumes that set us to coughing. Every hour, day and night, that superannuated relic of a stove did service. It was covered with dilapidated kettles, tin pails, cans, and old tin coffee pots without handles or noses. A dish once on, the owner must watch it with untiring vigilance until his food was cooked, or he lost his turn, which came only as often as he could steal a chance. If his back was turned for an instant, off went his pot and on went another. Since a hundred and fifty or more officers practiced cooking on that apology for a range, it required a miraculous ingenuity to have meals at regular hours. There were some hangers-on by the stove who did no cooking. They were trying to keep warm; but there was hardly room for such luxury.

Our quarters were so crowded that none of us had more space to himself than he actually occupied, usually a strip of the bare, hard floor, about six feet by two. We lay in long rows, two rows of men with their heads to the side walls and two with their heads together along the center of the room, leaving narrow aisles between the rows of feet. The wall spaces were preferred, because a man could brace his back there and sit out the long day or the longer night. There was a row of posts down the center of the room, but these were too few and too narrow to give much help; I know, because I had a place by one of them.

I remember three officers, one a Yankee from Vermont, one an Irishman from New York, and one a Dutchman from Ohio, who messed together by the wall opposite me. When they came to Danville they were distinct in feature and personality. They became homesick and disheartened. They lost all interest in everything, and would sit in the same attitude hour after hour and day after day, with their backs against the wall and their gaze fixed on the floor at my feet. It grew upon me that they were gradually being merged into one man with three bodies. They looked just alike; truly, I couldn't tell them apart. And they were dying of nostalgia.

It gave me the nightmare to lie down in front of those men, so I resolved to break the spell which held them over the grave. I fortified myself, one morning, with corn-and-cob bread and crust coffee, and took up a position directly facing the trio, and looked from one to another repeatedly. After a while the Dutchman raised his eyes and muttered: "Gott in Himmel! Vot for you shoost look on me?" Paying no attention to that, I concentrated my gaze yet more strongly on the others, until the Vermonter asked what the hell I wanted. This aroused the Irishman, who yelled an interrogation point at me. My medicine was working well. I only feared that my strength would fail before I could effect a cure. I stared and stared, and forced the Vermonter and the Irishman to their feet. The Dutchman was fast sinking back into apathy when I spat full in his face. The insult stung him to action, and I ran for my life around the room with Dutchy after me. He soon gave up the chase, but the warm current of blood which I had started did not stagnate. When the three had cooled off, I made them a morning call and explained matters. Perhaps they didn't believe all I said, but they forgave me, and lived. I don't remember what they did to occupy their minds after that; I only know they quit staring at the floor.

Some of the prisoners played chess, checkers, and backgammon. Captain Conley and I had made a set of checkers in Libby, and we still had them, but the game palled on us. Like the ungodly majority, we killed time and escaped insanity with cards. A few of our associates, pursuing the consolations of religion, found none too much time to study the Scriptures; games had no fascinating power over them. A few others, remembering what they had learned at college, engaged in the study of classical or modern languages. Many tried to read, but reading somehow ceased to be a comfort in prison; at least, that was my experience. Our library, moreover, was a small one; it consisted of a few books and some back numbers of monthlies brought to us by the Reverend Charles K. Hall, a Methodist minister of Danville, who occasionally preached to us.

Many of our comrades developed a wonderful talent at handicraft and made hundreds of ornaments from bone and wood. Crosses, rings, and pins were artistically fashioned and most beautifully chased. Busts were carved from bricks taken from the walls. Checkers with monograms and raised figures were cut from bone and bits of wood. Altogether, there was output enough to stock a respectable museum. These objects were not made wholly in the cause of art, nor to while away the time; they were valuable for barter and exchange.

As our money gave out, we sold things to get more, or swapped articles of value or works of art for necessities. Boots, spurs, watches, rings, jack-knives, buttons, even toothpicks, were commodities of traffic. Boots were a quick commodity and brought high prices in debased rebel currency; but we hated to part with them. Captain Conley's pride in a pair of nice boots lasted until his luxurious habit of smoking demanded a sacrifice. The officer of the guard, an inveterate haggler with the general manner and appearance of a Malay pirate, offered one hundred Confederate dollars and finally a pair of shoes also, for the boots, and the offer was accepted. The cash was paid, and the captain, almost in tears, gave up his fine footwear. After a wait of two weeks there was passed into the prison a package addressed to Captain Conley. "My shoes!" he cried. He tore off the wrapper, and for an hour sat and swore at two old army brogans, of different sizes and both for the same foot. My own boots went for cash the day after Christmas. I fared better than Conley; I got a hundred dollars and a pair of shoes that I could wear.

All sorts of makeshifts were adopted to cover our persons as decency demanded. When I was captured, I was the proud possessor of a new staff uniform ornamented with gold lace. Five months later, my most intimate friends would have failed to recognize me in the ragged tramp who sat naked on the floor at Danville and robbed the ends of his trousers in order to reseat them. It was not till after I was paroled that I took those trousers off; I couldn't have done so before, because, after sewing up the legs while I had them on, I couldn't get my feet through.

Although we all became disreputable in appearance, some of us kept up as best we could our proper relations of mutual respect. I am sorry to say that military rank was soon ignored by the majority of officers in Prison No. 3, and that selfishness and dishonesty added to our cup of humiliation and suffering; yet I know that much should be forgiven in men who had almost lost their natural humanity. Our nerves were worn ragged. The slightest of provocations would cause a quarrel. Two cavalry officers, Captain Harris and Lieutenant McGraw, fought over the possession of a few rusty cans. The captain's shirt was torn to shreds, and since it was the only shirt he had, and the remainder of his wardrobe consisted of a well-ventilated pair of trousers, he was to be pitied.

Happily, I remember some manly acts, and examples of Christian character maintained under the most adverse and depressing influences. General Hayes more than once rebuked severely those who indulged in profane and obscene language. Chaplains Fowler and Emerson, Captain Stewart of the 146th Pennsylvania, and Captain Burrage of the 36th Massachusetts seemed never to forget their Christian and moral obligations. I was not closely acquainted with any of these gentlemen, and was influenced by them only in a general way, but influenced I certainly was, and I have never ceased to feel grateful for their good examples. I believe they saved many from moral collapse; not by preaching, but just by being the men they were.

Freedom was more desired than salvation, more sought after than righteousness. We were no sooner in Danville than a start was made at digging a way out. From our windows overlooking open country, away from the town, we could see near the prison a deep ditch; and the plan was to dig a tunnel from the prison cellar to the ditch, and to escape by it at night. A way was found to enter the cellar, and the digging was carried on every night for two weeks; but the attempt came to nothing. The tunnel approached the surface of the ground too closely, and early one morning a sentry stepped on the undermined spot and fell through. The tunnel was traced, and access to the cellar was thereafter shut off. Some prisoners later escaped while returning under guard from the river, where they had gone for water; but these daring ones were few, and their chances were slim.

Tuesday, November 8th, which was election day in the North, we held an election of our own and cast our otherwise uncounted votes for President and Vice-President. The result was: for Lincoln and Johnson, two hundred and sixty-seven votes; for McClellan and Pendleton, ninety-one. I voted for Lincoln. Four days later we heard that Lincoln had been reëlected, and two days after that we saw the news in papers from Richmond. We knew that the war would be fought out and the Union restored, and we hoped that we should not be overlooked.

Thanksgiving Day came, and we had little to be thankful for, personally. We were alive, but that was about all. The prison authorities issued meat, such as it was, for our dinner, and a vile sort of bean soup for our supper. The Massachusetts members of Mess No. 6, having raised money by disposing of rings and other articles, astonished their stomachs with a real vegetable soup. The Maine members looked on with envy and unsatisfied appetite until they could stand it no longer. Then Captain Bailey raised thirty-five dollars by the sale of a ring, and on the strength of that I borrowed a pint of rice and bought a pint of molasses, and we made a "pudding" to celebrate with, and went to bed uncomfortable. Our only Thanksgiving happiness was in the good fortune of Chaplain Emerson, who left the prison that day for Richmond, to be exchanged.

Life became so unbearable, and the prospects of a general exchange so delusive, that on December 10th about a hundred of the prisoners, the most courageous, or the most wanting in judgment, made an attempt to break prison and escape, and failed miserably. Unaware of the attempt to be made, I, with five others, was walking the ground floor for exercise when I saw two officers close in on the sentry by the door that opened into the yard, one seizing his gun and the other taking him by the throat to prevent him from giving an alarm. At the same moment another officer tried to choke into silence the sentry by the stairs, but his grip was too weak, and the brave rebel, in spite of threats, shouted, "Turn out the guard!" The cry was at once repeated outside, and muskets were thrust in through the sashless windows. I have outlived the sensation of that moment, but I know that I was never more conscious of being in the presence of death than when I caught a glimpse of eternity in the black muzzle of a gun held within six feet of my breast. The other promenaders were as helplessly exposed, and we all might have been the victims of nervous and frightened sentries, but Colonel Smith came running and shouted, "Cease firing!" He was not quick enough, however, to save the officer who had grappled with the sentry by the stairs. That unfortunate prisoner was shot through the bowels, and his wound was cruelly aggravated as he made his way up the two flights to the top floor, hurriedly helped along by some of his associates. Colonel Smith came inside, ordered a number of prisoners into close confinement, and told us that a keg of powder was buried under the prison, and that if another attempt to escape should be made, he would blow us all to hell.

The prisoner that was shot was Colonel Raulston of the 24th New York Cavalry. He took upon himself the blame for the attempted break and the failure, and died without naming to the prison authorities the actual instigators of the uprising. I learned that the officer chiefly responsible was General Duffié, a swaggering and flashy fellow, who happened to be the ranking officer among the prisoners at that time. General Hayes was ill, and had been removed to the hospital on the other side of the town. If he had been present, I doubt the attempt would have been made.

Christmas came and went with little hope for us this side of the grave. I fell ill, and dragged through another month uncertainly, living in the flickering hope of an exchange. We heard many rumors of negotiations, but nothing seemed to come of them. With February came letters telling us that we should certainly be exchanged soon; and our hopes revived. On Sunday, February 12th, Dr. Hall preached to us from a text in 2 Timothy, which included the exhortation, "Thou therefore endure hardness, as a good soldier of Jesus Christ." Our endurance was nearly at an end.

Then suddenly the welcome intelligence at last arrived. At dusk of Wednesday, February 15th, Colonel Smith came hurrying in and announced that we were to leave for Richmond on the Friday or Saturday following. We cheered and laughed and wept, and sang "Hard Times Come Again No More" and "Home, Sweet Home." Few of us slept, that night, or the next night, either. Orders were read, and changes of orders, and the plans for our departure were uncertain up to the very moment of our going; but finally, at ten o'clock Friday night, we stumbled out of the prison into a darkness that was glorious with the light of promised freedom. We groped our way to the railroad station, where box-cars awaited us, and at midnight the train started for Richmond.

We arrived in the rebel capital at two o'clock Saturday afternoon, and were quartered once more in Libby Prison. Captain Conley and I had the pleasure of sharing our old space on the second floor near a post. We slept soundly, overcome by excitement and exhaustion. In the morning we enjoyed the luxury of hot coffee with milk and sugar, the first we had drunk in six months. At nine o'clock, corn-bread and corned beef were issued; and we noticed that the ration was smaller than ever. We signed the parole, that day. I believe I would have signed any promise without the least intention of keeping it. Monday, we rested on the raw edges of our nerves. Tuesday, we were told that we were to leave the next day.

At eight o'clock in the morning of Wednesday, February 22d, the door of Libby Prison opened to us for the last time, and we went forth free men. Slowly and painfully we made our way to the steamer awaiting us in the James. I fell to the ground repeatedly, but somehow I got there. The steamer was, I think, the *William Allison*. I found a place by the smokestack, and backed up to the stack for warmth, and fell asleep. When I opened my eyes again, the steamer was heading back to Richmond. I might have jumped overboard, but Captain Lord's happy face changed my thought, and I remembered how crooked the James was.

At ten o'clock we were put ashore on the north bank at Cox's Landing, and headed for Aiken's. Between the two landings we crossed the dividing line between South and North; to us, the border between hell and paradise. At half-past eleven we caught sight of the Stars and Stripes at Aiken's Landing, and soon we boarded the steamer *George Leary* for Annapolis. On the steamer we had a light lunch of ham, white bread, and coffee; also a half-ration of whiskey. I think the whiskey came first, and those who drank the portions refused by others, in addition to their own, had no need of the lunch.

The warm welcome for us at Annapolis, the earnest ministrations for our comfort, and the sweet words of sympathy, filled our eyes with tears. That long, linen-draped, well filled table; shall I ever forget it? We were cautioned to control our appetites, and warned of the fatal consequences of too free indulgence;

yet, alas for self-confidence and nonresistance, several of our number were soon dead and buried under the Annapolis sod.

We that survived were quartered and fed properly at Camp Parole, and nursed back to health and strength. When I arrived, I weighed ninety pounds. When I left, I was still thin, but gaining steadily. I had leave to go home; and then, being formally exchanged, I reported again for duty with my regiment. While I had been in prison I had received a signal promotion. From first lieutenant and adjutant I was advanced over all the captains and made major. How I had crept up!

CONCLUSIONS

Melt, melt away ye armies—disperse ye blue-clad soldiers,
Resolve ye back again, give up for good your deadly arms ...
— WALT WHITMAN, *Leaves of Grass*
Autumn Rivulets, "The Return of the Heroes"

I DID NOT BEHOLD the scenes attending the surrender of Lee to Grant at Appomattox Court House, April 9th. I wish I had. My regiment was at Appomattox until April 15th, when it was started on a leisurely march eastwards to Black's and White's Station on the South Side Railroad, where the brigade, commanded by General Baxter, went into camp. I rejoined it there April 24th, and was mustered in my new rank April 29th. Colonel Tilden went home on leave, drawn thither by the alarming illness of his wife, and, Lieutenant-Colonel Farnham being absent recovering from wounds suffered in the battle of Five Forks, the command of the regiment was turned over to me. I regretted having the honor at the expense of pain to my friends; yet, having it, I was beyond words happy and proud.

Our work was done. Monday, May 1st, the bugles sounded the order to pack up and march, and without regret we saw the sacred soil pass under our feet. Thursday we were at Manchester, across the James River from Richmond, and went into camp within sight of Libby Prison. How often, through those grated windows, I had cast longing eyes upon the field now occupied by our tents! The next day, many of the command went to look at the prison and other and less painful sights of the city. Saturday, May 6th, we crossed the James and marched through the principal streets of Richmond, our band crashing gayly among the ruins.

Northwards from the fallen rebel capital we marched to Hanover Court House, and northwards again to Fredericksburg. We crossed the old battlefield where the regiment had received its baptism of blood, and many now passed over that field in silence with uncovered heads. Northwards again to Fairfax Court House, then eastwards to Arlington Heights we continued the march, and went into camp near the river from which the Army of the Potomac had taken its departure and its name.

Once more the heights opposite Washington became a great armed camp. All our corps, the 5th, was there, now under Griffin, and the 2d Corps, once Hancock's, now under Humphreys. Later the 9th Corps came up, with a division of the 19th, and the Cavalry Corps. Drills were held daily, and camp duties were performed, to keep the men in hand, for all were impatient at the delay that postponed the supreme moment when we should end with being soldiers and become peaceful citizens of the restored Republic.

I don't remember that our men were happy at the reading of general orders announcing, for May 23d, a grand review in the streets of the national capital. To the soldier it meant the making of the best toilet his means would permit, at an ungodly hour in the morning; a long day of continuous movement without food, not even the solace of a pipe; a return to camp late at night. Of all the marches made by the regiment, for rapidity and length, without rest, none would compare with that inhuman tramp for display.

Our parade day began at four o'clock in the morning, when the 5th Corps started its march across the Long Bridge into crowded Washington. The parade movement was to be up Pennsylvania Avenue and past a reviewing stand by the White House where President Johnson would receive our salutes. For hours my regiment lounged in a street at right angles to the broad avenue. When at last I saw the extreme right of our division form at the head of the street, I heard at the same moment the sharp voice of an officer saying, "Get your men into line at once, sir!" It seemed to me that I should receive the order from my brigade commander, so I remained passive. The little peacock of an aide to somebody then repeated the order, and added as he looked condescendingly at my worn and faded uniform, "I mean you, sir!" I could only suppose that he was a recent graduate of the Military Academy, as no volunteer officer that had seen service would have exhibited so conspicuously the signs of vain officiousness. It was yet an hour before we moved.

The line of march was bordered by a vast throng of spectators, and happy faces and gay colors contrasted strangely with the black draperies which everywhere proclaimed grief for the martyred President Lincoln. The gloom of the capital city could not modify the heartfelt joy of everyone that our days of fighting were done.

The review was indeed a magnificent spectacle. The vanity of Halleck, that prince of military humbugs, and of President Johnson, must have been fully gratified. I can't say one good word for it, in principle; yet I must admit that I enjoyed my part in the show. I was conscious of great honor and good fortune in riding at the head of my regiment; and because I was riding there, I was showered with flowers and bouquets. My colored servant, George, walked all the way beside my horse, and I handed the flowers down to him, when I had kissed them to acknowledge the kindness of the givers. He was fairly smothered in the fragrant blossoms. From their midst rose his contented and continual gurgling laugh; they made him forget his hunger.

Monday, June 5th, we were mustered out of service. Colonel Tilden returned to us and resumed the command. Our journey home to Maine was uneventful. Saturday, June 10th, we reached Augusta fairly early in the morning. We had been expected in the afternoon of the day before, and a large crowd had gathered and waited until late in the evening; but we hadn't come, and the disappointed throng had dispersed. When we did arrive, there were few to greet us. There had been few to see us go. I remembered that when the regiment had left for the front, there had stood by the track a big fellow with a chest like a bellows, pumping a whistle to the tune of "The Girl I Left Behind Me."

That was the most voluminous whistle I had ever heard; equal to a steam band, for it had filled the air, voicing a sentiment over and above all other sounds, and following us until our train had rounded the southward curve. Did I hear it again? Yes, upon my soul, there was the whistler! He pulled out all his stops and poured upon us his loud welcome in a whistle that drowned our clatter as we tumbled out of the cars.

The news that we had come, or the proclamation of that whistle, was carried fast through the city, and by the time we started our march for the old rendezvous near the State House the streets along our way were astir with hurrying welcomers. Windows were filled with joyous faces and waving handkerchiefs and little flags. The governor and some other state officials reviewed us from a balcony. Our drums ruffled, our colors dipped, the swords of officers flashed in salute for the last time.

At our rendezvous we formed in line, but only to break ranks and say good-bye. That was hard; I prefer not to speak of it; I cannot. Neither can I find words for what I saw in other faces; in the happy rush of our home folk there were troubled fathers and mothers whose sons had gone with us and had not returned, and these unhappy ones had been drawn to us as if somehow we must have brought their dead boys back with us, alive.

By invitation of Governor Cony, the officers of the regiment gathered in his room in the State House; and there we gave into his keeping the colors of the regiment, the symbols of all that we had dared and suffered and done. I suppose he made a speech, said the expected things; I don't remember. Somehow, everything was suddenly commonplace. Without my knowing when it had happened, I had already taken my leave of war.

II

IT IS perhaps needless for me to say that I have neither attempted nor intended to tell the story of the war. It has been told officially; it has been critically discussed from all points of view by historians, participants, and lookers-on, who majestically tell us what should have been, what was, and what might have been. My simple purpose has been to mingle facts of history with a personal experience.

Any member of a regiment, officer or private, can have but little knowledge of movements outside of his immediate command. In all engagements with the enemy he has his special duty to perform, and no time to look with a critical eye upon his comrade's conduct; he has all he can do to obey orders and keep from running—many failed even in this. Almost the first thought that comes home to a brave man is one of self-preservation, and the second, the safety of his honor, when pride comes in as a powerful auxiliary and, oftener than courage, keeps him to the front.

The idea that a soldier, whose duty it is to remain in the ranks and move in geometrical lines, has an opportunity to view a Gettysburg as he would a panorama, is absurd. After the first volley of musketry, he is a rare man who theorizes, or speculates on the action of his comrade, or of his regiment, much more on that of the commanding general, three miles distant. The inequalities of the ground, the wooded slopes and deep ravines, the fog, the dense smoke, and the apparent and often real confusion of troops moving in different directions under different orders, utterly preclude the possibility of a correct detailed observation of a battle of any magnitude. Hence, I have drawn material from all sources considered reliable, and have refreshed my memory as justly as I could.

Naked history is pitiless; its searchlight is too powerful and leaves no background for the relief of simple objects, which give life and coloring. War without the fascination of music, of flying standards, brilliant uniforms, and galloping generals, wouldn't be war as we had it from '61 to '65. I am not ignoring that, with all these and many more pleasing adjuncts, "war is hell." The privations and sufferings have become history indeed.

Bravery and courage.—These remain deep mysteries. In the heat and turmoil of a fight, the word "bravery" has no significance to the combatants; men are heroes or cowards in spite of themselves. All the demands of active service call for courage; but the real test comes before the battle—in the rear line, under fire, waiting. The true perspective of danger is observed and comprehended by the man attached to the edge of a battle—not in it, but near enough to feel its fierce pulsations and get an occasional shock of its power.

A young author, his boyish fancy stimulated by books, has written a story in which he takes a raw recruit into, through, and out of a battle and represents him with a brain fully alive to reason and revealing a cunning course of deception, all in a way apparently realistic, and intensely interesting, but only possible in an imaginative mind before a parlor grate.

That any man in my regiment, or in the army, analyzed his feelings and marked out any specific line of conduct while under fire, or even thought for five consecutive minutes of the past, present, or future, or measured out or acted upon any theoretical course of conduct irrespective of the arbitrary military law which held him in obedience, is absurd. Afterthoughts are in a sense real, and give a correct résumé of what might have been; but to put an endless and connected train of thought in the brain of a green soldier, so thoroughly scared—by his own admission—that he is not accountable, and set it in systematic motion which shall develop the "Red Badge of Courage," is sheer rot.

The bravest front, bolstered by pride and heroic resolution, will crumble in the presence of the agony of wounds. Wading through bloody fields and among the distorted dead bodies of comrades, dodging shells, and posing as a target to hissing bullets that whisper of eternity, is not conducive to continuity of action, much less of thought. The shock from a bursting shell will scatter a man's thoughts as the iron fragments will scatter the leaves overhead.

Danger and death.—Buncombe, too, is talk often made from the speaker's platform, of "eyes glazing with rapturous delight" as they rest on the Old Flag, that "'tis dying in an ecstasy of sacrifice that makes the glory of the world." To die, under any circumstances, is not an act that brings thrills of "voluptuous sweetness" to anyone, unless it may be to a lunatic. It can safely be asserted that a very large number of men volunteered to "go for a soldier" from motives of patriotism; but ambition, love of adventure, personal courage, and lack of other employment gave the largest numbers to our army, and, I doubt not, to the rebel army, too. There ever was, there ever will be, a fascination in danger that appeals to youth, that calls men to arms at the beat of a drum. Yet no soldier desires—not even to save his country—to be torn in pieces by a shell, made a disfigured and hopeless cripple. A man of sense is not built that way. He simply takes his chances, always believing that as an individual he is immune. It is the buoyancy of youth, the hopefulness of his nature, that makes the man with a gun cheery and light-hearted as he locks step with fate, with death. It is a part of his temperament, his philosophy, to be a humorous optimist, to laugh in the face of peril. To him, it is always the man in the next rank who is to be the victim.

Defeat and loyalty.—The defeats sustained, the terrible lists of casualties, and the hardships endured could not dishearten or sour the loyal men of our army. Roseate bulletins describing victories when we knew we were whipped, and general orders of congratulation for successful movements which covered up marches made in the dark, and inglorious retreats, did not deceive the rank and file. Men knew it all; knew that they stood with one foot in the grave all the while; and for this were better men and better soldiers.

Sickness and other adversities.—Disease took more victims in our war than the bullet did. The pathetic pleading of the sick, the half-sick, and the homesick to go home to wife and family, or to a sweetheart, was a daily occurrence. The army hospital was an institution never to be forgotten by a patient. At first, the "Surgeon's Call" suggested care for the sick, and certain remedies for nostalgia; but our soldiers became disinclined to heed the call, and shrank from the mysteries of that long, white tent, with its rows of cots so close together that a patient could reach over and clasp the feverish hand of his neighbor. The interior arrangements were horrible in suggesting illness, suffering, and death away from home, and between the sick man and eternity there was only a thin canvas which flapped restlessly in the wind as if impatient to open its loose seams and let some tired spirit through.

If one visited the sick, one's impressions would be lasting. The row of fair, boyish faces drawn with suffering—how eagerly they scanned each new face as it entered under the raised flap, as if, by some possibility, friends from distant home had come to them! Here and there would be seen the wrinkled face of an old man more patriotic than wise, the seams and lines of age made more conspicuous by the fading of hair- and whisker-dye. If he lived through his first hospital experience, in a few months he was home again with a satisfied consciousness of having done what he could; and later in life he enjoyed a comfortable pension from a grateful government. It did seem strange that some men grew old so rapidly. A few months since, they swore they were only forty-five, and now they were just as ready to swear they were seventy-five.

Early in the war, "hospital bummers" were unknown. Only after one or two skirmishes did they develop a wonderful capacity for bellyaches. The favorite disease was "diarrhoea," which became chronic in a week. The general order for "three days' rations and forty rounds of ammunition" was equal to croton oil in its effects; "winter quarters" was the only antidote, although "numbers six, nine, and eleven" were prescribed as a remedy.

Mingled with pity was a feeling of indignation at seeing so many able-bodied men fall into line at the head of each company street every morning, at "Surgeon's Call," and march to the hospital tent, and swallow with evident relish a blue pill, bitter morphine or quinine, and brandy. Boys of seventeen would watch this funeral procession, so filled with disgust and anger that no discipline could prevent the most extreme profanity.

The regular prescriptions were numbered six, nine, and eleven, which were blue pill, quinine, and vinum. We soon learned that "vinum" meant either wine or brandy. I have seen men count from right to left, "six, nine, eleven—six, nine, eleven—six, nine, eleven," and step into the line just where "eleven" would strike. It was a sure thing, since the surgeon gave in regular order, as the men filed past him, something as follows:

"Well, what's the matter with you?"

"I don't know, Doctor, I've got an awful pain in my bowels; guess I've got the chronic diarrhoea."

"Let's see your tongue! Give him number six! Next, what's the matter with you?"

"I was took with an awful griping pain in my bowels—guess I've got the chronic diarrhoea."

"Give him number nine! Next, what ails you?"

"I've g-g-got an almighty b-b-bellyache, g-g-guess I've got the chronic d-d-diarrhoea."

"Run out your tongue! Give him number eleven!"

Growlers.—We had a few—very few—pessimists among us, constitutional growlers, who on the opening of every campaign were attacked with a dyspeptic foreboding that defeat and disaster would follow us. While they were under the influence of this malady, which happily was not contagious, the ruin revealed to them as being stored for our brigade was enough to unbalance a healthy mind. We always marched faster than they cared to go, but never fast enough to get ahead of their dismal prophecies. They had an ingrained hatred of discipline, cursed red tape by the great gross, and itched with a desire to "see a live Johnnie and draw a bead on him." Their desire was never gratified, for the Johnnies seemed to have an intuitive perception of these ferocious fighters' intentions and kept out of their sight; hence the few casualties in the immediate front of these rascally "bummers."

Grumblers.—Plain grumbling, of course, was one of the concomitants of the service; everybody grumbled, from the general down, and it was often mixed with profanity of the strong quality that convinces. No one was as positively wicked as the expletives would indicate; we swore, as one of the boys said, "prayerfully." The chaplains—some chaplains—endeavored to raise the moral tone of their charges, and labored earnestly, at times, for the adoption of more reverent expressions. One private, as I recall, was taken to task for cursing the lively condition of his underwear, while, stripped to the skin, he hunted vermin. He looked up smilingly at the chaplain and said, "See here, Chap, don't you worry; you pray a little and I swear a little, but neither of us means anything."

Chaplains.—As members of the military family of commanders, chaplains were not a necessity, but they helped to swell the "pomp and glorious circumstance of war," and filled a place that no other commissioned officer could. While amenable to army rules, as noncombatants they were enabled to do many things for the comfort of others (aside from giving spiritual advice), especially during and after a battle. Of course, courageous qualities varied in chaplains as in others. Chaplain Balkam, of the 16th Maine, while looking after the physical needs of his flock, incurred every danger incident to a soldier's life, and bore himself like a brave man. Chaplain Cook, of the 94th New York, would gather the surplus savings of the men of the 1st Brigade [2d Division, 1st Corps], go to Washington, and express the different sums to their destinations. He carried thousands, and I doubt a single dollar was ever lost. When I consider the responsi-

bility he voluntarily assumed, and the great personal risk he ran
when on his way to Washington through the woods and, worse,
through the frauds and scoundrels who always flocked like vul-
tures in the rear of our army, I place this chaplain among the
bravest officers of his regiment.

War correspondents.—Many chaplains and Christian Commission men were useless, I fear; and many war correspondents
were worse. At times, "war news" was manufactured in a slip-
shod manner from raw material raised in the brain of a penny-a-
liner for the special occasion, and wickedly sent North to elate
or depress the overanxious millions. Sometimes a Northern paper would reach us with its startling headlines of news from the
front, relating in thrilling and picturesque style the particulars
of a great battle that was being fought, the unparalleled deeds
of daring, what Grant said, what Meade did, what Warren was
going to do. We, resting in camp (and we were part of the troops
said to be engaged), would read it all with amazement—as an
interesting piece of romance, for it was mighty interesting; but
it snarled us all up as we tried to learn where we were—if we
were really anywhere. The fact was that a battle had been reasonably expected, and the correspondents had it all written up in
advance, like the obituaries of great men who are expected to
die soon. Meade had changed camp, Warren was not going to
do anything, and Grant never confided in correspondents. It all
might have been, and then some paper would have won out
in an early edition of important news, and the correspondent's
name would have been hoisted alongside of Grant's—perhaps.
Some history now in print was created at so much a line in the
brain of an ambitious and imaginative scribbler.

That old Springfield musket.—Of course, we laughed at the
romance and grumbled at the reality. Our days were always full
of duty, of study, drill, and evolutions, of marches, inspections,
and practice in musketry. The musket we first carried, the old
Springfield, was perhaps good enough when pitted against its

fellow, but in action against an improved weapon it was worthless; and prejudice and profit deprived the army of a more efficient and desirable arm for more than two years. It was certainly discouraging to the soldier who bit his cartridge with his teeth and rammed it home with a rod.

Drill.—First to last, drill was a necessity. The first drillmaster I remember was then a marvel to me. I sometimes wondered if he had ever smelt gunpowder, or wore scars, and whether he would have any new ones when he got to be a general. He, and all others, had their work cut out for them. Some men could never even learn to keep step. The explosive "Hep! Hep!" of the officer would cause a racking gait which would break the step of the whole company. I remember Dyer, of Company H, 16th, who would invariably perform all movements by inversion, always halting with his right foot and faced to the rear. Hours in the guard tent and nights tied to a wheel failed to bring him to time. No argument, coercion, or gentle persuasion could convince him that his left foot was the right one. There was no time in him but mealtime and time to halt.

Dust.—The infantry were often—too often—a footsore and weary multitude, sometimes from a long and exhausting tramp through mud ankle-deep, and again through blinding clouds of dust, hot and choky, that filled our noses and mouths, sifted down our necks, up our trouser legs, filled our shoes, and with sweat made a cement that fastened shoes, socks, and feet together. It painted us with an ochre tint that would delight an artist. We were a mud-spattered blue at Fredericksburg; at Gettysburg, pale yellow.

The dust of Pennsylvania, or Maryland, or Virginia, would close us in between walls and fences that were an indistinct whole showing scarcely an outline. An impenetrable veil hid from view everything beyond a distance of a few feet. Troops would lie down wherever they halted for rest, without disturbing the monotony of the landscape in the least.

Portrait of a private.—The ideal picture of a soldier makes a veteran smile. Be a man never so much a man, his importance and conceit dwindle when he crawls into an unteaseled shirt, trousers too short and very baggy behind, coat too long at both ends, shoes with soles like firkin covers, and a cap as shapeless as a feed bag. Let me recall how our private looked to me in the army, in the ranks, a position he chose from pure patriotism. I can see him exactly as I saw him then. He is just in front of me trying to keep his balance and his temper, as he spews from a dry mouth the infernally fine soil of Virginia, and with his hands— he hasn't a handkerchief—wipes the streaks of dirty sweat that make furrows down his unshaven face. No friend of civilian days would recognize him in this most unattractive and disreputable- looking fellow, bowed under fifty-eight pounds of army essen- tials, and trying to suck a T.D.

His suit is a model one, cut after the regulation pattern, fifty thousand at a time, and of just two sizes. If he is a small man, God pity him; and if he is a big man, God pity him still more; for he is an object of ridicule. His forage cap, with its leather visor, when dry curls up, when wet hangs down, and usually covers one or both ears. His army brogans, nothing can ever make shine, or even black. Perhaps the coat of muddy blue can be buttoned in front, and it might be lapped and buttoned be- hind. The tailor never bushels army suits, and he doesn't crease trousers, although he is always generous in reënforcing them with the regulation patch.

The knapsack (which is cut to fit, in the engraving) is an unwieldy burden with its rough, coarse contents of flannel and sole leather and sometimes twenty rounds of ammunition extra. Mixed in with these regulation essentials, like beatitudes, are photographs, cards, huswife, Testament, pens, ink, paper, and oftentimes stolen truck enough to load a mule. All this is crowned with a double wool blanket and half a shelter tent rolled in a rubber blanket. One shoulder and the hips support the "commissary department"—an odorous haversack, which often stinks with its mixture of bacon, pork, salt junk, sugar, coffee, tea, desiccated vegetables, rice, bits of yesterday's dinner, and old scraps husbanded with miserly care against a day of want sure to come.

Loaded down, in addition, with a canteen, full cartridge-box, belt, cross belt, and musket, and tramping twenty miles in a hurry on a hot day, our private was a soldier, but not just then a praiser of the soldier's life. I saw him multiplied by thousands. A photograph of any one of them, covered with yellow dust or mosaics of mud, would have served any relation, North or South, and ornamented a mantel, as a true picture of "Our Boy."

The soldier a composite.—Merge men together for a time in the army, and the individual begins to lose, in some degree, his individuality. When there is nothing that is even seemingly familiar in his surroundings, the loss of identity is the more apparent; he no longer claims his enrolled name; he becomes simply an indistinguishable unit. In the first year of the war, the distinctive marks of environment were observed at a glance. The Wolverine, the Hoosier, and the Down-East Yankee were clearly defined. But long association and a oneness of purpose gradually merged individual characteristics, and men became composite—almost developed a new type. Marks of birth were always apparent, but there was no aristocracy among the privates; they were thoroughly democratic. A graduate of Harvard and an illiterate from the wilds of Maine were often seen affectionately picking lice together. Rich men and poor, Christians from pious back-country homes and heathen bounty-jumpers from the slums of New York, would cheat one another at seven-up. All would bathe in and drink from the same stream, whether prior or subsequent to the watering of the brigade mules.

His education.—It was wonderful how quickly our soldier fitted himself to the new conditions that now shaped his life, and accepted all the good and bad surroundings that to him had become living facts. At first it shocked him immeasurably that his old life should have become a far-away, indistinct thing of memory. The explosion of shells, the continuous rattle of musketry, the waste and ravage, the sight of gutted and half-ruined houses, distorted carcasses of horses and mules, and shattered caissons, and scattered arms and accouterments and knapsacks and canteens, and dead men and men in the agony of wounds, and every variety of wreck and horror that go to make up a battle, very soon taught him that war was a profession with passion behind it.

There was something singularly shocking to him in the stiff disorder of the dead lying where they fell; in torn clothing; in the waxy arm yet hugging a gun. Some men lay as if asleep, with a smile of peace and contentment on their faces. Others showed the lingering agony of their death, their very attitude one of protest and unreconciliation. Never before had our soldier been brought so near to the unseen, the unknown, and now it was always surrounding him, and possibly for months and years to come there would be endless repetitions of these horrors which stirred him to the depths. Yet the time came, and soon, when he was indifferent to the sight of thousands dead.

He resented it all, and at times his resentment grew into a hatred for those who forced the whirlpool of war—a whirlpool that had so soon engulfed him. He hated his surroundings and all that war implied; it was drudgery, it was cruelty; yet he forced himself to resist whatever was inimical to the interests of a hated service. If he had at times any longing to lay down his arms, he carefully concealed it.

Always in front of him was the enemy, a something which, the more he thought of it, the more he hated; and as likely as not he never quite knew why. He might try to determine the sense of his antagonism that arrayed him in opposition to men like himself. His restlessness would occasionally develop. Then his face would grow into a smile as though carved, as he refilled his cartridge box and his pipe, and reburnished his gun. He might have the courage of his convictions, yet behind his bravery there lay something that mystified and repelled him. He didn't know what it was, so inevitably he went to find out. I don't know that he ever got an answer. I didn't.

His heroes.—Our soldier had great and unbounded admiration for the pomp of war—as exemplified in a richly dressed general with his nobby staff at a review, or when dashing by as if the devil were close behind. To him they were a distinct species, developed from molecules of an advanced state, and the more conscious of this they appeared to be, the greater the attraction to him. Our private had no desire to tear down the barbed-wire fence of discipline that necessarily separated officers from men, but he would have liked to crawl through and see where the difference lay, what made up the quality of distinction. Sometimes he wondered if "tearing the watch to pieces would show where the tick came from." He would stand at dignified attention when Sedgwick rode by, throw up his cap and yell with delight at sight of Chamberlain, and look with awe at Grant's silent figure. He cried at the loved Warren's unmerited disgrace, and hissed Sheridan as the cause. He felt a personal loss when Sedgwick died. He never tired of telling about his favorite officers, and would fight a comrade in defense of the good opinion. Some officers well deserved this. Howard, cold, selfish, and inordinately vain, would go to a soldier's tent and pray with him, and perhaps write a letter home for him; but Coulter would swear at a man, send him something to eat, and permit him, when exhausted, to ride Coulter's own horse.

Inferior superiority.—On the march it was seldom that men were permitted to file into the woods, or even to rest in the shade, however hot might be the day. Once I ran the risk of a court-martial in calling to account Captain Atwood of my regiment for striking one of his men with a sword. The march had been a long and weary one in the scorching rays of a summer sun, when men, exhausted, fell out by the wayside. It was evident that one man in particular could no longer keep in the ranks. He looked like a corpse, with eyes rolled up as he dropped, yet Atwood abused and struck him. He might as well have struck the dead limb of a tree. I told that captain what I thought of him, and his threats to have me court-martialed for disrespect to a superior officer only increased my vocabulary. With all the contempt possible to convey in words, I said, " 'Superior officer' be damned!" I assisted the fallen man onto my horse, and he came into bivouac with a smile that made me happy. This little act of mine that counted for so much to the private was not wholly unselfish, for I had been in the saddle all day. And I must add that the field and staff times without number helped many a poor fellow over the rough way.

Marching on.—Occasionally an independent command would leave the dry, dusty road and file into the woods, when the men would drop dog-like at length on the cool, mossy ground. A few minutes' rest, and they would come up as fresh as flowers after a shower, and, singing "John Brown's Body," would go marching on, oblivious of the dust and heat; over hills and through ravines, slipping and falling, bruising bodies on stones and stumps. Somewhere in front of them was the enemy, they neither knew nor cared where, and behind them the supply train.

Beans.—Long, weary marches were patiently endured if in the distant perspective could be seen the company bean-hole, and no well-disciplined New England regiment would be in camp thirty minutes without the requisite number. When we went into bivouac, every cook would have one dug and a fire over it before the companies broke to the rear and stacked arms. In the early morning I would hang around a particular hole, and ask Ben to just h'ist the cover and let me get a sniff for an appetizer; and how Ben would roll his orbs, till only the whites were visible, and say, "Golly, Adjutant, dem yalla-eyes don' got dere kivers off yet; you'll just natchely have to wait a while!"

But many's the time we would have to "git up and git," eating our beans half-cooked, and then would come an internal disturbance—not that infernal demon, dyspepsia, of civil life, but an almighty bellyache that would double a man up and send him into line at "Surgeon's Call."

Desiccated vegetables.—Too many beans with salt junk demanded an antiscorbutic, so the government advertised proposals for some kind of vegetable compound in portable form, and it came—tons of it—in sheets like pressed hops. I suppose it was healthful, for there was variety enough in its composition to satisfy any condition of stomach and bowels. What in Heaven's name it was composed of, none of us ever discovered. It was called simply "desiccated vegetables." Ben once brought in just before dinner a piece with a big horn button on it, and wanted to know "if dat 'ere was celery or cabbage?" I doubt our men have ever forgotten how a cook would break off a piece as large as a boot top, put it in a kettle of water, and stir it with the handle of a hospital broom. When the stuff was fully dissolved, the water would remind one of a dirty brook with all the dead leaves floating around promiscuously. Still, it was a substitute for food. We ate it, and we liked it, too.

Food "off the country."—Headquarters of my regiment occasionally embodied its kitchen and parlor departments in the person of one Tibbetts. He was the boss forager, the king of cooks, and the chiefest of liars where the rations of headquarters were concerned. He was like an *ignis fatuus* when the patrol went for him, but as come-at-able and innocent as an infant after he had unloaded, which he often did at unheard-of hours and places. Two o'clock in the morning would see him near the picket line, and, meekness personified, he would creep into camp, and crawl under his old army blanket. If he snored in the course of twenty minutes, we knew that his conscience was clear, and that somebody's "critter" was born into another life. Breakfast would prove the correctness of our conclusions.

Honey, with bees.—When we were lying in camp and enjoying misery, the trials were sometimes accompanied by grotesque incidents. Chenery, armed with a pass, went out about seven o'clock one evening, to "make a call." Returning after "Taps" with a hive of honey, and finding me asleep, he aroused the sergeant-major, who got a tub and received for headquarters a liberal donation of the delicious luxury.

"George, are there any bees in this?" asked Max.

"Oh, only a few," replied Chenery, "and they are too cold to sting."

With a peculiar chuckle, Max quietly deposited the tub close up to and partly under a corner of my blanket, and waited. The heat warmed up the bees, and they crawled over me; the uncomfortable sensation made me thrash around, and this stirred up the insects, and they just wreaked vengeance for the theft. I thought of enormous lice, of bedbugs, of fire, and danced around the tent like a lunatic. Honey always makes me sick.

Sinks.—Camp life was ordinarily a tedious monotony, relieved only by unwelcome tasks. Our private was not at first impressed by the fact that army sinks were a governmental institution, duly recognized in the regulations, and as necessary as they were objectionable. He questioned how digging a hole in Virginia would redound to his credit and add anything to the laurels of a soldier. General orders wouldn't say anything about them, unless demanding five to a regiment. Army correspondents, safely seated behind a redoubt, with a pipe and some rum, would write all about the forts, the long lines of breastworks, how strong they were, how many bastions and angles, how much repelling power, and charmingly congratulate some pioneer corps on the splendid engineering qualities of—its general. But they never dilated upon a line of army sinks, or complimented a regiment for the masterly, ingenious manner in which it covered up its unfaithfulness in the discharge of an irksome duty.

Regimental character.—Time brought experience, and experience stimulated a desire to please the colonel and establish a reputation for the regiment. Men and officers soon performed all disagreeable camp duties. Orders which at first were called hard knots in a long string of red tape, and were denounced as arbitrary, were cheerfully complied with as for the best interests of the regiment. I myself used to call it part of a "damned military despotism," and was about as unreconciled to orders and restraint as any other member of the command, until a shadow of insubordination brought in Colonel Tilden's authority.

Regimental character will always be determined by the character of the officers. Lack of confidence in officers brings disaster. Men are not overburdened with regard for rank as rank; they measure the individual, not the grade of his commission, and lucky is the officer seeking honor and promotion if he meets the specifications and fulfills the demands made upon his courage and ability.

The line officers of the 16th Maine were fair samples of the life from which they came, and were as good, I suppose, as any in the volunteer service. Of course they varied in ability, and in appreciation of the position they held, but working in harmony with their commander they helped to make one of the most effective and reliable bodies of fighters in the army. It won an enviable reputation for willing and prompt obedience. The rank and file were self-respecting; they looked for promotion, and gave what they expected to receive. Men promoted from the ranks proved among the best of our officers. I have heard the same of other regiments, too.

Patriotism and practicality.—Lieutenant Chapman has happily preserved the reply of Sergeant Dunbar to General Robinson, when the general expressed the opinion that "it must be very hard to march without shoes or stockings."

"I do it," said the sergeant, with a grim smile, "for my country, for sixteen dollars a month, and *clothes*."

The practical necessities of any situation were important to our soldier, and usually he met them; one of the advantages of being a volunteer was independence in thought and speculation, in prognosticating an important movement and preparing for it by the "drawing" of an extra blanket and the laying in of an increased supply of pork and coffee.

My regiment had a weakness for fence rails, and notwithstanding the ground had been prospected, occasionally struck a bonanza. As the day's march drew to a close, every Sixteener had an eye on either flank, and held himself ready for a dash at the word "Halt." Knapsacks, canteens, and everything that would impede his progress was loosened ready to drop, and, with one eye on the colonel and the other on a particular rail, he waited for the order. Sometimes an aide would come dashing down the column with orders "holding the colonel strictly responsible" for all property, including fence rails, on his flanks. A peculiar expression would mingle with the color in the colonel's face, as he loudly repeated the orders and added, "Now, boys, I don't want to see one of you touch a rail!" He would give his entire attention to a study of the landscape to the rear, there would be the hurried sound of many feet, and he would be quickly relieved of the responsibility that was supposed to cluster around forty rods of split cedar. Whether or not this was "prejudicial to good order and military discipline," it certainly improved the landscape, and enriched the slave-worn soil.

Fortunes of war.—The colonel would wink at a reasonable amount of vandalism, when the health and comfort of his men were concerned, but there was a limit. There was the poor woman who lost her all: her rails were burned, her outbuildings stripped of boards, and her home intruded upon. When she came to Colonel Tilden, and, with a face full of suffering, told him that someone had taken the only kettle she owned, which was a tea kettle, and killed the last poor calf left by those who had preceded us, his anger was just. He at once called the officers around him, and put the case before them in language that mantled every face with shame. From his own wallet he paid for the calf; he ordered the kettle restored; and he forbade anyone's approaching the house. The officers pooled their ready cash, and I think left the old woman in better circumstances than she had been in for a year. (As for us, we felt for a long time the cords of discipline drawn closely about us; the advantage taken of the colonel's good nature could not be easily forgiven.) I have often thought of that poor old woman, grey, wrinkled, and worn, bent with the cares of many years, alone on the edge of a clearing hardly large enough, if cultivated all over, to bear food for three months, perhaps awaiting the return of a husband or son, and daily hoping against hope for the presence of either to shield her from insult and keep her from starvation. Visited first by one army and then by the other, both trampling into earth her scanty crops, what a life she must have led! Who wonders that it takes time to heal the wounds and quiet the spirit of that man, be he never so much a rebel, who, if spared, found his mother's heart broken, or in vain hunted for her grave in a place changed beyond recognition?

Tribute and condemnation.—When I remember what I saw when Chaplain Balkam, Captain Conley, and I visited the signal station on Cedar Mountain and looked into the rebel camps, I can't help wondering how many of the apparently happy fellows over the Rapidan would have favored and approved the barbarous treatment of Northern captives, which (we are compelled to believe from published reports) was permitted if not authorized by their government. If General Gordon's statements in his *Reminiscences* are true—and I believe them—there was not one man in a division of the rebel army who would not condemn the administration of Southern military prisons. I judge fairly, from the treatment I myself received from my captors until they gave me up to the brutes in charge of prison-pens and stockades.

That the enlisted men of the rebel army were humane, and at times more than kind, goes without saying from me. It is conclusively shown in deeds of mercy, like risking life under fire to give a drink of water to an enemy who within the hour had tried to shoot the "good Samaritan"—the frequent warnings, at Petersburg, of "Lie down, Yank, we're going to shoot!"—the frequent exchange of tobacco for sugar and coffee, all hostilities suspended until both parties had left the "clearing-house."

Only a love of humanity could have prompted a private of the 1st Battalion, North Carolina Sharpshooters, to give me half if not more of his limited rations, when I was *en route* to Salisbury Stockade. In all my life I was never more deeply touched, never more conscious of the brotherhood of man, and from that moment war was hateful to me. This generous-hearted fellow gave me his name and address, at my earnest request. Immediately after my exchange, I wrote to him, not once but several times. Receiving no reply, I concluded that the poor fellow must have been killed. Had he been captured, my note to Colonel Tilden, which I left with him as the only earnest of my gratitude that I could show, would have proved my sincerity. I can only imagine the blessings my good colonel would have showered upon him.

Our other enemies, the war correspondents, likewise showed themselves to me in a glowing light when I was a prisoner. At Salisbury, Albert D. Richardson, of the New York *Tribune*, shared our quarters for a while. I shall always see his pallid face, greasy coat, and threadbare trousers. Junius Henri Browne, another correspondent of the same paper, also partook of our misery. His cheerful heart and bright smile were better than sunshine, and warmed into new life the fading hopes of many a poor devil. Richardson and Browne bluffed their way to freedom some time after we were transferred from Salisbury to Danville.

After so many years, it may be that I should erase the more or less bitter criticisms recorded in my captivity. But no! In prison I saw my fellow man, both friend and enemy, at his worst; selfishness and savagery; and I understand how Swift could call men "the most pernicious race of little odious vermin that nature ever suffered to crawl upon the surface of the earth."

Yet I remember, too, that I saw my friends heroic, and our enemies meriting our sincere tribute to their fighting qualities. I only wish that a war so hard fought could have been succeeded by an honest peace. The soldiers of both sides would, I think, have had it so. But the politicians would not. There were those among the victors who would prey upon an honorably beaten and defenseless foe, and there were those among the vanquished who proved unwilling to abide by the arbitrament of arms, which they themselves had invoked.

Sometimes I wish I could forget it all, and again I rejoice that it is indelibly stamped into my being, that my sons cannot but inherit, along with their father's loyalty, some of the conclusions of a life offered in the cause of making secure, lasting, and forever free, the government under which they are living.

CALENDAR FOR 1861

JANUARY

SU	MO	TU	WE	TH	FR	SA
		1	2	3	4	5
6	7	8	9	10	11	12
13	14	15	16	17	18	19
20	21	22	23	24	25	26
27	28	29	30	31		

FEBRUARY

SU	MO	TU	WE	TH	FR	SA
					1	2
3	4	5	6	7	8	9
10	11	12	13	14	15	16
17	18	19	20	21	22	23
24	25	26	27	28		

MARCH

SU	MO	TU	WE	TH	FR	SA
					1	2
3	4	5	6	7	8	9
10	11	12	13	14	15	16
17	18	19	20	21	22	23
24	25	26	27	28	29	30
31						

APRIL

SU	MO	TU	WE	TH	FR	SA
	1	2	3	4	5	6
7	8	9	10	11	12	13
14	15	16	17	18	19	20
21	22	23	24	25	26	27
28	29	30				

MAY

SU	MO	TU	WE	TH	FR	SA
			1	2	3	4
5	6	7	8	9	10	11
12	13	14	15	16	17	18
19	20	21	22	23	24	25
26	27	28	29	30	31	

JUNE

SU	MO	TU	WE	TH	FR	SA
						1
2	3	4	5	6	7	8
9	10	11	12	13	14	15
16	17	18	19	20	21	22
23	24	25	26	27	28	29
30						

JULY

SU	MO	TU	WE	TH	FR	SA
	1	2	3	4	5	6
7	8	9	10	11	12	13
14	15	16	17	18	19	20
21	22	23	24	25	26	27
28	29	30	31			

AUGUST

SU	MO	TU	WE	TH	FR	SA
				1	2	3
4	5	6	7	8	9	10
11	12	13	14	15	16	17
18	19	20	21	22	23	24
25	26	27	28	29	30	31

SEPTEMBER

SU	MO	TU	WE	TH	FR	SA
1	2	3	4	5	6	7
8	9	10	11	12	13	14
15	16	17	18	19	20	21
22	23	24	25	26	27	28
29	30					

OCTOBER

SU	MO	TU	WE	TH	FR	SA
		1	2	3	4	5
6	7	8	9	10	11	12
13	14	15	16	17	18	19
20	21	22	23	24	25	26
27	28	29	30	31		

NOVEMBER

SU	MO	TU	WE	TH	FR	SA
					1	2
3	4	5	6	7	8	9
10	11	12	13	14	15	16
17	18	19	20	21	22	23
24	25	26	27	28	29	30

DECEMBER

SU	MO	TU	WE	TH	FR	SA
1	2	3	4	5	6	7
8	9	10	11	12	13	14
15	16	17	18	19	20	21
22	23	24	25	26	27	28
29	30	31				

CALENDAR FOR 1862

JANUARY

SU	MO	TU	WE	TH	FR	SA
			1	2	3	4
5	6	7	8	9	10	11
12	13	14	15	16	17	18
19	20	21	22	23	24	25
26	27	28	29	30	31	

JULY

SU	MO	TU	WE	TH	FR	SA
		1	2	3	4	5
6	7	8	9	10	11	12
13	14	15	16	17	18	19
20	21	22	23	24	25	26
27	28	29	30	31		

FEBRUARY

SU	MO	TU	WE	TH	FR	SA
						1
2	3	4	5	6	7	8
9	10	11	12	13	14	15
16	17	18	19	20	21	22
23	24	25	26	27	28	

AUGUST

SU	MO	TU	WE	TH	FR	SA
					1	2
3	4	5	6	7	8	9
10	11	12	13	14	15	16
17	18	19	20	21	22	23
24	25	26	27	28	29	30
31						

MARCH

SU	MO	TU	WE	TH	FR	SA
						1
2	3	4	5	6	7	8
9	10	11	12	13	14	15
16	17	18	19	20	21	22
23	24	25	26	27	28	29
30	31					

SEPTEMBER

SU	MO	TU	WE	TH	FR	SA
	1	2	3	4	5	6
7	8	9	10	11	12	13
14	15	16	17	18	19	20
21	22	23	24	25	26	27
28	29	30				

APRIL

SU	MO	TU	WE	TH	FR	SA
		1	2	3	4	5
6	7	8	9	10	11	12
13	14	15	16	17	18	19
20	21	22	23	24	25	26
27	28	29	30			

OCTOBER

SU	MO	TU	WE	TH	FR	SA
			1	2	3	4
5	6	7	8	9	10	11
12	13	14	15	16	17	18
19	20	21	22	23	24	25
26	27	28	29	30	31	

MAY

SU	MO	TU	WE	TH	FR	SA
				1	2	3
4	5	6	7	8	9	10
11	12	13	14	15	16	17
18	19	20	21	22	23	24
25	26	27	28	29	30	31

NOVEMBER

SU	MO	TU	WE	TH	FR	SA
						1
2	3	4	5	6	7	8
9	10	11	12	13	14	15
16	17	18	19	20	21	22
23	24	25	26	27	28	29
30						

JUNE

SU	MO	TU	WE	TH	FR	SA
1	2	3	4	5	6	7
8	9	10	11	12	13	14
15	16	17	18	19	20	21
22	23	24	25	26	27	28
29	30					

DECEMBER

SU	MO	TU	WE	TH	FR	SA
	1	2	3	4	5	6
7	8	9	10	11	12	13
14	15	16	17	18	19	20
21	22	23	24	25	26	27
28	29	30	31			

CALENDAR FOR 1863

JANUARY

SU	MO	TU	WE	TH	FR	SA
				1	2	3
4	5	6	7	8	9	10
11	12	13	14	15	16	17
18	19	20	21	22	23	24
25	26	27	28	29	30	31

FEBRUARY

SU	MO	TU	WE	TH	FR	SA
1	2	3	4	5	6	7
8	9	10	11	12	13	14
15	16	17	18	19	20	21
22	23	24	25	26	27	28

MARCH

SU	MO	TU	WE	TH	FR	SA
1	2	3	4	5	6	7
8	9	10	11	12	13	14
15	16	17	18	19	20	21
22	23	24	25	26	27	28
29	30	31				

APRIL

SU	MO	TU	WE	TH	FR	SA
			1	2	3	4
5	6	7	8	9	10	11
12	13	14	15	16	17	18
19	20	21	22	23	24	25
26	27	28	29	30		

MAY

SU	MO	TU	WE	TH	FR	SA
					1	2
3	4	5	6	7	8	9
10	11	12	13	14	15	16
17	18	19	20	21	22	23
24	25	26	27	28	29	30
31						

JUNE

SU	MO	TU	WE	TH	FR	SA
	1	2	3	4	5	6
7	8	9	10	11	12	13
14	15	16	17	18	19	20
21	22	23	24	25	26	27
28	29	30				

JULY

SU	MO	TU	WE	TH	FR	SA
			1	2	3	4
5	6	7	8	9	10	11
12	13	14	15	16	17	18
19	20	21	22	23	24	25
26	27	28	29	30	31	

AUGUST

SU	MO	TU	WE	TH	FR	SA
						1
2	3	4	5	6	7	8
9	10	11	12	13	14	15
16	17	18	19	20	21	22
23	24	25	26	27	28	29
30	31					

SEPTEMBER

SU	MO	TU	WE	TH	FR	SA
		1	2	3	4	5
6	7	8	9	10	11	12
13	14	15	16	17	18	19
20	21	22	23	24	25	26
27	28	29	30			

OCTOBER

SU	MO	TU	WE	TH	FR	SA
				1	2	3
4	5	6	7	8	9	10
11	12	13	14	15	16	17
18	19	20	21	22	23	24
25	26	27	28	29	30	31

NOVEMBER

SU	MO	TU	WE	TH	FR	SA
1	2	3	4	5	6	7
8	9	10	11	12	13	14
15	16	17	18	19	20	21
22	23	24	25	26	27	28
29	30					

DECEMBER

SU	MO	TU	WE	TH	FR	SA
		1	2	3	4	5
6	7	8	9	10	11	12
13	14	15	16	17	18	19
20	21	22	23	24	25	26
27	28	29	30	31		

CALENDAR FOR 1864

JANUARY

SU	MO	TU	WE	TH	FR	SA
					1	2
3	4	5	6	7	8	9
10	11	12	13	14	15	16
17	18	19	20	21	22	23
24	25	26	27	28	29	30
31						

FEBRUARY

SU	MO	TU	WE	TH	FR	SA
	1	2	3	4	5	6
7	8	9	10	11	12	13
14	15	16	17	18	19	20
21	22	23	24	25	26	27
28	29					

MARCH

SU	MO	TU	WE	TH	FR	SA
		1	2	3	4	5
6	7	8	9	10	11	12
13	14	15	16	17	18	19
20	21	22	23	24	25	26
27	28	29	30	31		

APRIL

SU	MO	TU	WE	TH	FR	SA
					1	2
3	4	5	6	7	8	9
10	11	12	13	14	15	16
17	18	19	20	21	22	23
24	25	26	27	28	29	30

MAY

SU	MO	TU	WE	TH	FR	SA
1	2	3	4	5	6	7
8	9	10	11	12	13	14
15	16	17	18	19	20	21
22	23	24	25	26	27	28
29	30	31				

JUNE

SU	MO	TU	WE	TH	FR	SA
			1	2	3	4
5	6	7	8	9	10	11
12	13	14	15	16	17	18
19	20	21	22	23	24	25
26	27	28	29	30		

JULY

SU	MO	TU	WE	TH	FR	SA
					1	2
3	4	5	6	7	8	9
10	11	12	13	14	15	16
17	18	19	20	21	22	23
24	25	26	27	28	29	30
31						

AUGUST

SU	MO	TU	WE	TH	FR	SA
	1	2	3	4	5	6
7	8	9	10	11	12	13
14	15	16	17	18	19	20
21	22	23	24	25	26	27
28	29	30	31			

SEPTEMBER

SU	MO	TU	WE	TH	FR	SA
				1	2	3
4	5	6	7	8	9	10
11	12	13	14	15	16	17
18	19	20	21	22	23	24
25	26	27	28	29	30	

OCTOBER

SU	MO	TU	WE	TH	FR	SA
						1
2	3	4	5	6	7	8
9	10	11	12	13	14	15
16	17	18	19	20	21	22
23	24	25	26	27	28	29
30	31					

NOVEMBER

SU	MO	TU	WE	TH	FR	SA
		1	2	3	4	5
6	7	8	9	10	11	12
13	14	15	16	17	18	19
20	21	22	23	24	25	26
27	28	29	30			

DECEMBER

SU	MO	TU	WE	TH	FR	SA
				1	2	3
4	5	6	7	8	9	10
11	12	13	14	15	16	17
18	19	20	21	22	23	24
25	26	27	28	29	30	31

CALENDAR FOR 1865

JANUARY

SU	MO	TU	WE	TH	FR	SA
1	2	3	4	5	6	7
8	9	10	11	12	13	14
15	16	17	18	19	20	21
22	23	24	25	26	27	28
29	30	31				

APRIL

SU	MO	TU	WE	TH	FR	SA
						1
2	3	4	5	6	7	8
9	10	11	12	13	14	15
16	17	18	19	20	21	22
23	24	25	26	27	28	29
30						

FEBRUARY

SU	MO	TU	WE	TH	FR	SA
			1	2	3	4
5	6	7	8	9	10	11
12	13	14	15	16	17	18
19	20	21	22	23	24	25
26	27	28				

MAY

SU	MO	TU	WE	TH	FR	SA
	1	2	3	4	5	6
7	8	9	10	11	12	13
14	15	16	17	18	19	20
21	22	23	24	25	26	27
28	29	30	31			

MARCH

SU	MO	TU	WE	TH	FR	SA
			1	2	3	4
5	6	7	8	9	10	11
12	13	14	15	16	17	18
19	20	21	22	23	24	25
26	27	28	29	30	31	

JUNE

SU	MO	TU	WE	TH	FR	SA
				1	2	3
4	5	6	7	8	9	10
11	12	13	14	15	16	17
18	19	20	21	22	23	24
25	26	27	28	29	30	

NOTES

MARKS of reference have not been intruded into the narrative part of this book, because they would annoy the eye; and footnotes have not been used, because they would be interruptions to continuous reading. Few such interruptions would be welcomed except by avid students, or by readers habitually suspicious of unusual or unexpected incidents narrated by a memoirist. In the notes here supplied, the questions most likely to bother students and skeptics are, I trust, sufficiently answered. Mention of some books is unavoidable. References are made to the *Official Records of the Union and Confederate Armies* (cited as O.R.); the *General Orders Affecting the Volunteer Force* (cited as G.O.V.F.); the *Reports* of the Adjutant-General of the State of Maine (cited as A.G.S.M.), and other works named in these notes as bearing upon the subject-matter of the various chapters. Where no work is named, the information, if concerning family matters or correspondence, is from private material in my possession; if concerning more general matters, it is from common reference works or from correspondence with persons who did not supply exact references.

H.A.S.

BEGINNINGS

Page 1

Abner R. Small was born in Gardiner, Maine, May 1st, 1836, the second son of Abner Small and Mary Ann (Randall) Small. He was of the sixth generation of respectable and sometimes locally distinguished descendants of an early colonial settler and Indian trader, who had spelled the name Smale and pronounced it Smalley. The elder Abner was fond of company and the bottle, and made no fortune. The younger Abner wished very much to be a political cartoonist, and for this he had aptitudes, but he was set to commercial work instead. His going to war excepted, he served commerce faithfully, and hated it, all his life. His neighbors respected and enjoyed him. His companions of the war years loved him. On the last occasion of his attending a reunion of the 16th Maine, his old comrades lifted him to their shoulders and cheered him. He died at his home in Oakland, Maine, March 12th, 1910.

Page 1

Abner Small, of Gardiner, was commissioned lieutenant, 1st Infantry, 1st Brigade, 2d Division, Militia of Maine, to rank from August 18th, 1827; promoted captain June 4th, 1828. For many years he was commonly called Captain Small. He was born in Limington, October 22d, 1802, and died in Gardiner, November 17th, 1867.

Page 1

Readfield, Vienna, and Mount Vernon were, and are, townships in a farming country full of lakes and hills near Augusta, the capital, which is on the Kennebec River. Readfield Corner is a hamlet in Readfield township.

Page 2

Gardiner is about seven miles down the river from Augusta. The Small family moving from Gardiner to Mount Vernon shortly after Major Small's birth, he grew up in the latter place.

Page 3

George W. Batchelder, of Gardiner, served in the "Aroostook War" as brigadier-general, 1st Brigade, 2d Division, Militia of Maine, February 22d, 1839, to April 23d, 1839.

Page 4

The bombardment of Fort Sumter, at Charleston, South Carolina, by secessionists, was begun on April 12th, 1861. On April 15th, President Lincoln called for volunteers, and a requisition was made upon Maine for one regiment of infantry. The Maine Legislature, meeting in special session on April 22d, provided for the raising of ten regiments. The necessary act was approved on April 25th. Orders directing the raising of the first four regiments were issued by Governor Washburn on April 22d and 24th, in anticipation of the legislative enactment.

Page 4

Waterville is about eighteen miles up the river from Augusta. Waterville College is now Colby College. The West Village, or West Waterville, was set off from Waterville in 1873, and in 1883 its name was changed to Oakland.

Page 4

Henry N. Fairbanks was a lifelong friend of the memoirist's. They had first met in 1860.

Henry wrote, on May 3d, 1910, in a memorial tribute: "On the 26th day of April, 1861, Major Small and I left Oakland . . . by cars, and repaired to the recruiting office of Joshua Nye, . . . to sign the enlistment papers and take the oath. When this was done, Major Small said 'Amen.' So it was with him for the next four years . . ."

The date of enlistment is given differently by the memoirist. In his copy of the A.G.S.M., 1864–1865, Vol. I, p. 456, at the beginning of the biographical notice of himself, he wrote in the margin: "Enlisted Apr. 25, 1861."

Joshua Nye was treasurer of the Androscoggin & Kennebec Railroad (which, together with the Penobscot & Kennebec, became in 1862 the Maine Central). The general offices of this railroad were at Waterville.

Page 7

The 2d Maine, organized at Bangor, was the first regiment to leave the state. It left Bangor on May 14th, and Portland on May 15th.

Page 7

When the war began, Maine had a lot of militia on paper and almost none fit to take the field. The first six regiments of volunteers were recruited from the state's three territorial militia divisions, two from each. By an order dated May 4th, Governor Washburn directed the major-general of militia commanding the second territorial division to "order ten organized companies . . . into camp at Augusta, forthwith, and there complete a regimental organization by causing an election of officers."—A.G.S.M., 1861, Appendix A, p. 6. This regiment was to be the 3d Maine. Of its ten companies, only one was a company of active militia at the time of the passage of the Act of April 25th. That was Company A, formerly the Bath City Greys. The regiment was uniformed in grey, and armed, and equipped, at the expense of the state.

Page 8

According to the mode of regimental organization required by the Act of April 25th, companies elected their officers as soon as there were fifty men enrolled to a company, and the company officers subsequently elected the field officers of the regiment. The officers, after being elected, were commissioned by the governor.

Page 9

Israel Washburn, Jr., was governor of Maine in 1861 and 1862. He succeeded in office Lot M. Morrill, who was sent to the United States Senate to fill the place vacated by Hannibal Hamlin, elected Vice-President with Lincoln.

Page 9

Arthur Plumer, of Gardiner, was not, strictly speaking, a grandfather of the memoirist's (he had married, in 1821, the widow of Benjamin Randall, and it was a daughter of the Randalls that was the memoirist's mother); but he was held in warm affection by the young Abner Small. He died in Gardiner, June 26th, 1861, in the eighty-first year of his age. He had been an officer in the Militia of Maine: comissioned captain, 1st Regiment, 1st Brigade, 2d Division, to rank from April 2d, 1816; promoted lieutenant-colonel May 25th, 1820; colonel, September 7th, 1826; brigadier-general, 1st Brigade, 2d Division, August 20th, 1829.

Page 10

Captain Thomas Hight, of the 2d United States Dragoons, was mustering officer at the muster-in of seven of the ten regiments organized under the Act of April 25th. He was an Indianan.

Page 10

On August 3d, 1861, the dragoons, mounted riflemen, and cavalry were all organized into one arm, to be called cavalry. In consequence of this, the 1st Dragoons became the 1st Cavalry; the 2d Dragoons, the 2d Cavalry; the Mounted Riflemen, the 3d Cavalry; the 1st, 2d, and 3d Cavalry, respectively, the 4th, 5th, and 6th Cavalry.—Albert G. Brackett, *History of the United States Cavalry* (New York, 1865), pp. 218–219.

Page 10

Howard's order has been mentioned by another Maine officer, recalling how he took his regiment, the 7th Maine, from camp at Augusta:

"When the order came to break camp, it was a literal copy of the one used by Colonel O. O. Howard, a West Pointer, to take the 3d Maine out of Augusta. He had taken one used at West Point for some grand function of the corps of cadets, and it was longer than one of Grant's orders moving the army toward Richmond. I remember that the tent pegs were to be pulled in order at tap of drum, and the operation of taking care of them would take a week to learn."—Thomas W. Hyde, Brevet Brigadier-General of Volunteers, *Following the Greek Cross; or, Memories of the Sixth Army Corps* (Boston, 1894), p. 17.

Howard's order included the following:

"Then at the roll of the drum every man will proceed to the place assigned him, squads being under the charge of the Sergeants and Corporals, all will proceed at once to unfasten the cords, pull up the pegs and pile them in order by the side of each tent. The tent poles will be loosened but held steadily by two men holding each.

"Previous to striking tents, arms to be stacked on Company grounds and accouterments slung upon them. At the next tap of the drum, tents will all be lowered to the ground toward the west. Every man will forthwith give three cheers, without moving from his place."— A.G.S.M., 1861, Appendix A, pp. 23–24.

Page 10

John A. Andrew, governor of Massachusetts from 1861 to 1865, was a native of Maine and a graduate of Bowdoin College. It may be supposed that his greeting to the first Maine regiments passing through Boston was not merely a formal courtesy.

Page 11

News items about the 3d Maine at that time are in Moore's *Rebellion Record* (New York, 1861–1871), Vol. I, doc. 238, pp. 344–346. An item from the *National Intelligencer,* of June 9th, includes the remark that the members of the regiment are "men accustomed to muscular pursuits, and are of fine size for hard service." Another item, from the New York *Tribune,* of June 9th, includes mention that "the regiment is fully armed and equipped, and have tents and camp equipage. The uniform is Canada gray throughout."

Page 11

The Cooper Shop, formerly a shook factory, was used by the shop proprietors (William H. Cooper and Henry W. Pearce) and other citizens as a place for feeding soldiers passing through Philadelphia.— James Moore, M.D., *History of the Cooper Shop Volunteer Refreshment Saloon* (Philadelphia, 1866).

Page 11

The 6th Massachusetts, when marching through Baltimore, was assaulted by a mob. Four members of the regiment were killed and thirty-six were wounded.

Page 12

Meridian Hill was so called because it was the place from which the Washington meridian (the seventy-seventh west from Greenwich) was reckoned.

Page 12

The quotation from Howard is from his *Autobiography* (New York, 1908), Vol. I, pp. 133–134.

Page 13

The Capitol was completed, and topped with the statue of "Freedom Armed," while the war was being fought. The Washington Monument was then about one hundred and fifty feet high. Work on it had ceased in 1854, funds being exhausted and the project not being universally popular. Work was not resumed until 1879.

Page 15

Fort Ellsworth was so named to honor the memory of the young Colonel Ephraim E. Ellsworth, of the First Zouave Regiment, New York Militia. When his regiment participated in the occupation of Alexandria, in the morning of May 24th, he saw a secessionist flag flying above a hotel, the Marshall House. He pulled the flag down, and as he was taking it away he was shot and killed by one Jackson, the hotel proprietor.

Pages 15–16

The quotation from Howard is from the *Autobiography,* Vol. I, pp. 143–144.

Page 16

French Forrest was a naval officer with a long record of service. He had two sons. One, Dulany Forrest, a graduate of the United States Naval Academy, joined the secessionist cause and died before the war was ended; the other, Moreau Forrest, left the Naval Academy to enter the United States naval service in 1861 and died in 1866.

Page 16

John Brown, the abolitionist, with a few associates, made an attack on Harper's Ferry, Virginia, in the night of October 16th–17th, 1859, seized the arsenal, raided the premises of a few neighboring planters, and forcibly freed about thirty slaves. On October 18th, a detachment of marines under the command of Lieutenant-Colonel Robert E. Lee having arrived, Brown's force was overpowered. The abolitionist was tried under the laws of Virginia, was convicted of "treason, and conspiring and advising with slaves and other rebels, and murder in the first degree," and was hanged at Charlestown, Virginia (now in West Virginia), on December 2d, 1859.

BULL RUN AND AFTER

Page 19

The quotation is from McDowell's order.—O.R., Ser. I, Vol. II, p. 305.

Page 22

The quotation is from Howard's report.—O.R., Ser. I, Vol. II, p. 418.

Page 22

David Bates was taken prisoner, and died of his wounds while in the hands of the enemy.

Page 25

The Act of April 25th had "authorized and empowered the governor to accept the services of ten regiments, and caused them to be enlisted for two years unless sooner discharged. The 1st and 2d Regiments were thus enlisted; the former was mustered into the service of the United States for three months and the latter for two years. The 3d, 4th, 5th, and 6th Regiments were also thus enlisted, but subsequent orders from the War Department, requiring all State volunteers to be mustered into government service for three years, rendered an amendment necessary to our mode of enlistment. This consisted in signing a contract to serve for an additional year."—A.G.S.M., 1861, p. 6.

Page 26

Mrs. Sampson, the nurse, was the wife of Captain Charles A. L. Sampson, of Bath, commanding Company D. She went with the regiment from Maine to Virginia, and did welfare work among Maine soldiers until the end of the war.—A.G.S.M., 1864–1865, Vol. I, pp. 108–128.

Page 27

A visit of Vice-President Hamlin to the bedside of this sick soldier is recalled in Pullen's own words in Charles Eugene Hamlin, *The Life and Times of Hannibal Hamlin* (Cambridge, 1899), p. 446. Pullen is quoted as saying: "I had once been given up for dead."

Page 28

The quotation is from Scott's General Order No. 13, dated July 31st, 1861.—Brevet Major-General E. D. Townsend, *Anecdotes of the Civil War in the United States* (New York, 1884), p. 39.

Page 29

The key to the Bastille, which had been sent to Washington by Lafayette, was exhibited at Mount Vernon. It is still there.

Page 29

"On the 27th and 28th of August, a portion of the regiment under the command of Major Staples, had a brilliant skirmish with the enemy at Bailey's Cross Roads, and met with no loss."—A.G.S.M., 1861, p. 43. "The operations of the stove-pipe artillery, as it was called . . . The boys went into a meeting house, got a piece of stove-pipe, mounted it on a pair of wagon wheels that they obtained, and run it up a hill in sight of the enemy, whereupon the rebels commenced firing at it with their cannon; our boys abandoned their 'gun', after the first shot, but had the satisfaction of seeing the enemy waste twelve shot on it."— William E. S. Whitman and Charles H. True, *Maine in the War for the Union* (Lewiston, 1865), p. 63.

Page 31

Howard's farewell order included the following:

"May Heaven bless and guide your new Colonel in the performance of his duties, and enable him to add yet more to his well-earned laurels. To him your old Colonel entrusts you, and asks on your part the same promptness, diligence and regard towards him which have been shown in the past. Gen. Howard owes much of worldly notice and position to this regiment, and he trusts he will never tarnish the reputation given him by any neglect or miscarriage on his part.

"It is his duty and yours to face the enemy. By the help of God the enemy must be conquered. Forget not, then, daily to ask confidently for that help from on high."—*Maine in the War,* pp. 63–64.

The paragraph following in *Maine in the War* says:

"The regiment parted with Gen. Howard with feelings of the profoundest regret. He carried with him the love of the whole regiment, which ever afterwards felt inspired by the noble example of moral heroism which he left behind."

Against this, the memoirist wrote on the margin in his copy, "Bosh."

Page 32

Neal Dow, the prohibitionist, had drafted the Maine prohibitory law of 1851. As colonel commanding the 13th Maine, he served in Butler's New Orleans expedition. Promoted brigadier-general of volunteers, he commanded for a time the District of West Florida. After the war, he worked for the extension of prohibition, and through his exertions a prohibitory amendment was added to the Maine constitution in 1884.

Page 33

"Commanding officers of regiments will detail two commissioned officers, with four non-commissioned officers or privates, to report in person to the Superintendents of the Recruiting Service for their respective States, on the 1st day of January, 1862, or as soon thereafter as practicable. These officers and non-commissioned officers will be detailed for a tour of six months, and will be assigned as recruiting parties to rendezvous by the Superintendents . . ."—G.O.V.F., 1861, p. 55, G.O. No. 105, Par. III.

Page 33

Major John W. T. Gardiner, of the 2d United States Dragoons, was retired from active service on November 14th, 1861. By G.O. No. 105 (see above) he was appointed general superintendent of the volunteer recruiting service in Maine, and he entered upon the discharge of his duties on January 1st, 1862. In accordance with G.O. No. 140 (G.O.V.F., 1862, pp. 120–121) he was appointed special provost-marshal for Maine. He was a son of Robert Hallowell Gardiner, a principal founder of the city of Gardiner.

EDUCATION OF A REGIMENT

Page 35

In accordance with instructions from Washington, the volunteer recruiting service in Maine was discontinued on April 3d, 1862. On May 22d, pursuant to authority and request from the War Department, the raising of another regiment of infantry was ordered. This regiment was to be the 16th Maine. On June 6th, the volunteer recruiting service was restored.

Page 35

The memoirist was commissioned a first lieutenant in the 16th Maine, as from May 24th, without first being discharged from the 3d Maine; but this irregularity was rectified, later, by official correspondence.

Page 35

The adjutant-general of Maine was John L. Hodsdon. He served with conspicuous ability throughout the war.

Page 35

Emilus N. D. Small, the memoirist's younger brother, was first sergeant, Company A, 16th Maine, from muster-in, August 14th, 1862, until he was discharged for disability resulting from illness, March 2d, 1863. He was sergeant-major, 2d Maine Cavalry, from muster-in, December 11th, 1863, and second lieutenant, Company M, from March 1st, 1865, until muster-out, December 6th, 1865.

He was born in Mount Vernon, Maine, June 6th, 1842, and died in Oakland, Maine, February 8th, 1922.

These two brothers resembled each other strongly all their lives.

Page 36

". . . Adjutant Small took charge of the recruits as they came in and assigned them to their respective companies, generally placing an enlisted man as orderly in charge of the various squads. I enlisted in Presque Isle on June 16, 1862, and went to Augusta with fifteen or twenty other Aroostook men. When we reached the grounds Adjutant Small came forward to greet us, and selected myself as orderly to have charge of the men till further orders. That was my first introduction to Adjutant, afterwards Major Small, and on that occasion commenced a friendship that lasted during life. It was two months later before the regiment was fully recruited and ready to leave the state. During that two months I saw Adjutant Small every day and I noted his perfectly democratic spirit. He always greeted all, whether private, sergeant, or commissioned officer, with a cheerful 'Good morning', and very likely with some humorous remark, for he had an unfailing fund of humor which seemed to find expression under all circumstances. His cheerful spirit helped the whole regiment to undergo those fearful trials during the fall of 1862, when, without overcoats, tents or knapsacks, the regiment endured exposure, cold and deprivations . . .

"Who does not remember the trim little figure of Adjutant Small at dress parade, and the humorous way in which he used to read some of the verbose, high-sounding orders emanating from the headquarters of some general officer who wanted to exhibit his authority by unrolling yard after yard of red tape? He often brought a smile to the whole regiment, and even the stern features of the Colonel commanding have been known to relax somewhat. With all his cheerfulness he was a diligent and careful worker, and his papers and reports were so thorough and accurate that they attracted particular notice at headquarters."— Francis Wiggin, tribute to the memory of Major Small, *Thirty-fifth Annual Reunion of the 16th Maine Regimental Association Held at the National Soldiers Home, Togus, Wednesday, August 17, 1910* (Gardiner, 1910), pp. 15–16.

Page 37

James G. Blaine was at that time the chairman of the Republican Executive Committee, of Maine, and speaker of the Maine House of Representatives; John L. Stevens had preceded Blaine as chairman of the Republican Executive Committee, and had been associated with him in the publication of the *Kennebec Journal;* Nathan A. Farwell was a member of the Maine Senate; Lot M. Morrill was a United States senator from Maine.

Page 37

Governor Washburn's proclamation began by saying: "An additional number of troops is required by the exigency of the public service, and if raised immediately, it is believed by those who have the best means of knowledge, that the war will be brought to a speedy and glorious issue."—A.G.S.M., 1862, Appendix A, p. 30. The order referred to repeats the hopeful suggestion of getting the war over with: "Citizen soldiers! remember you have a country to save, and you are the men who can render most efficient aid in this holy and patriotic work. To render success speedy and certain, and to alleviate and abridge the calamities of war, the President of the United States has requested this call to be made."—A.G.S.M., 1862, Appendix A, pp. 6–7.

Page 47

Brigadier-General Seth Williams, a native of Maine, was adjutant-general of the Army of the Potomac.

Page 47

For Colonel Coulter the memoirist had much esteem, for reasons indicated in a recollection of him which he wrote as follows:

"Coulter was a favorite with us, because of his good nature and reckless daring. Apparently he knew no fear, and seemed equal to any demand made upon him. He was familiarly known throughout the corps as 'Dick' Coulter. While looking after the interests of his men, he would come into camp as if shot from a cannon, hat on the back of his head, coat buttoned up wrong or not buttoned at all; sometimes with a sword, but oftener without one; he would land in our midst with the familiarity of an old friend. This was a great relief to the men, who were so often under restraint in the presence of a commander wearing a 'Turn out the guard' expression, like Crawford, for instance. Coulter's first salutation, like that of the much-admired Warren, was 'Never mind the guard!' Love of display, or 'fuss and feathers', as he termed it, was foreign to the make-up of this intensely practical and eminently loyal officer.

"We could but love him for the tender sympathy which would persist in cropping out at every call. He did swear occasionally at a man for unmilitary deportment and dress, and for neglect of duty, but he did it in a way to make the culprit feel that a favor had been conferred upon him.

"Colonel Coulter never heard the opening gun of a battle without being 'sick at the stomach', as he remarked to me at the battle of Gettysburg; but there was not in the 1st Corps a better or braver fighter. He appointed me to his staff when he commanded the 1st Brigade, 2d Division, at Gettysburg; and his more than generous commendation of what services I rendered, and his uniform kindness, and anxious solicitude for both my comfort and my safety while I was a member of his military family, added the warmest affection to my admiration for him."

A tribute to Coulter at Gettysburg, from another hand, says:

"The history of Gettysburg yet remains to be written. So barren is the official record that a very gallant officer of the old First Corps said once that he often wondered if he had really been there, for he looked in vain at the official reports for any mention of his command, and yet Dick Coulter was never in action without leaving his mark."—Major Joseph G. Rosengarten, "General Reynolds' Last Battle," *The Annals of the War Written by Leading Participants North and South: Originally Published in the Philadelphia Weekly Times* (Philadelphia, 1879), p. 66.

Major Small also wrote of Coulter, elsewhere than in the recollection mentioned above:

"I am not sure, but I think it was in the second day's fight [May 6, 1864, battle of the Wilderness] that Colonel Coulter's dog was killed. She was the constant and devoted companion of the colonel in all the fights up to this time. Although Coulter's brigade had fought through the enemy's lines and was in a critical position, the colonel, on learning of his loss, made a detail from his regiment to dig a grave with their bayonets and bury the dog. He said that if he got killed he didn't wish to be ashamed to meet his old canine comrade."

For distinguished service in the field, Colonel Coulter received brevets of brigadier- and major-general of volunteers.

Page 47

"Those were glorious autumn days that followed the battle of Antietam. The camp of our division was in a walnut grove, on the farm of James Rowe, with the Potomac in full view. It was not easy to realize that the narrow, rocky stream rolling below was the same Potomac, of such majestic proportions, that we had crossed at Washington."— William Henry Locke, A.M., Chaplain, *The Story of the Regiment* [11th Pennsylvania] (Philadelphia, 1868), p. 135.

Page 49

Copies of the orders and requests for the return of supplies are in Major Small's history of his regiment, *The Sixteenth Maine* . . . (Portland, 1886), pp. 39–47.

Page 50

Dwight Maxfield, of Mount Vernon, was held in kindly remembrance by the memoirist. They had been boyhood friends. When Maxfield died, in 1884, Major Small wrote of him: "Dwight enlisted as a private in Company A, and was immediately detailed as adjutant's clerk. He proved himself a faithful assistant, and on the march and in campaigns his services were invaluable; he was always working, getting lists of the sick, of stragglers, of killed and wounded, and not forgetting to keep a record of 'bummers' for future use. After an engagement, or at the close of a long, tedious march, Dwight was always present with his rubber satchel, holding ink, paper, and pens, and all the necessary blanks for reports and returns. Through his faithfulness, the regiment won a reputation second to none in the 1st Corps for promptness in making 'reports in the field.' On February 26th, 1863, Dwight was appointed sergeant-major, which position he filled with credit to himself and to the regiment until he was discharged for disability, September 9th, 1863. He had been recommended for promotion by Colonel Tilden, who saw in him the qualities of a valuable officer, and the necessity which demanded his retirement was sincerely regretted by all of us."

Page 54

The 16th Maine was not alone in its misery. The historian of the 12th Massachusetts writes: "An extract from a letter written by one of the regiment about November 27 gives a correct idea of its condition during the winter campaign of 1862: 'We have not food enough to keep a bird alive: for forty-eight hours not a man in our mess has had a morsel, and I am confident that this is the state all through the division. Our clothing, too—some of the boys are not half clad, and our regiment is not an exception. While at Sharpsburgh ten requisitions for clothing were sent to Washington; and, after the tenth demand, some coats and pants were sent to us; but the men in the regiment today with suitable clothing are more easily counted than those without. There are very many men in the Twelfth who have not had a shirt on their backs for over six months; as many more are without shoes, and in this season of the year our boys are suffering greatly.' "—Lieutenant-Colonel Benjamin F. Cook, *History of the Twelfth Massachusetts Volunteers (Webster Regiment)* (Boston, 1882), p. 84.

Page 55

Surgeon Charles J. Nordquist, of the 83d New York (9th Regiment, New York State Militia), medical director of the 2d Division, 1st Corps, from November 11th, 1862, and medical inspector of the 1st Corps from September 20th, 1863, was well regarded by his own regiment. On May 27th, 1863, the second anniversary of the departure of the regiment from New York, there was formally presented to him, as a gift from the enlisted men, "a handsome gold watch, chain, and seal," value, $250.— George A. Hussey and William Todd, *History of the Ninth Regiment, N.Y.S.M.* (New York, 1889), pp. 255–256.

FREDERICKSBURG

The conspicuousness of the memoirist, as a mounted officer, may be understood from a letter written to him, June 7th, 1904, by a lifelong friend of his, Thomas S. Hopkins. In the 16th Maine, Hopkins was adjutant's clerk, after Dwight Maxfield. In later years, when he was practicing law in Washington, D.C., he used to return every summer to his boyhood home in Mount Vernon, Maine. He rarely saw Major Small, but occasionally wrote to him. The letter includes the following:

"I think of you so often, Abner. I can see you now almost as clearly as I did forty-two years ago, as you rode along the lines with Colonel Root on that fateful day at Fredericksburg, in December, 1862. We lay in the sunken road, with those terrifying shells screeching over us both ways. One or two of our boys had been torn and mangled. It was my first taste of war and I was horrified and frightened. I remember that as you and Colonel Root rode along, I gingerly climbed up and peeped through the rails and saw you looking as smiling and as fearless as if you were on dress parade. I remember that I wondered how in the world you could look so smiling, especially when you were on the wrong side of the fence and in a much more dangerous position than I. Honestly, I couldn't see anything to smile or laugh over. I realize now that probably you felt just as bad inside as did I, but that you had had more experience and had learned to control your feelings and realized that it was your duty to set a good example to the men. How well you did it, even you, with all that modesty that becomes you so, know very well."

Page 72

The quotations are from the official reports, O.R., Ser. I, Vol. XXI: Gibbon's report, pp. 480–481; Root's report, pp. 488–489.

Page 72

Colonel Root added, in his report: "Lieutenant Abner R. Small, 16th Maine, acting aide-de-camp, rendered me valuable and efficient service, and bore himself with a cool intrepidity worthy of his regiment."

Page 75

". . . Fletcher chapel, an unpretending frame building, thirty feet long and forty feet wide. The disproportion in its width was owing to an addition to one side of the main edifice, an afterthought, we were told, for the accommodation of the colored people, as the church was without the gallery usually appropriated to their use."—Locke, *op. cit.*, p. 171.

CHANCELLORSVILLE

The paper-collared regiment was the 13th Massachusetts. The history of that regiment says: "April 13. The division was reviewed today by its commander, Gen. John C. Robinson, and other distinguished officers. We were notified in advance that this was to be an unusual occasion, so the boys shined their buttons, blacked their boots, and last but not least, adorned themselves with paper collars purchased from the sutler. This prinking which the boys indulged in occasionally, just to remind them of days gone by, and which gave the regiment the sobriquet of 'Band-box guard', reached the ears of Colonel Coulter, of the Eleventh Pennsylvania, who was bound to have a little fun at the regiment's expense. Now it happened that 'Dick' Coulter was the owner of a brindle bulldog called 'Sally,' who was famous throughout the brigade for her intelligence, and had a habit of sticking close to the colonel's heels when not restrained. On this occasion she was decked with a white paper collar round her neck labeled '13', and a white glove fastened on each paw. During the whole of the ceremony 'Sally' trotted about in plain sight, a most ludicrous object, affording a deal of amusement to all who witnessed it. In spite of this ridicule the regiment made a fine appearance, and received the praise of General Reynolds, who liked neatness and orderly appearance in the soldier."—Charles E. Davis, Jr., *Three Years in the Army: The Story of the Thirteenth Massachusetts Volunteers from July 16, 1861, to August 1, 1864* (Boston, 1894), p. 199.

Page 83

Apparently, the band as now organized, and as reorganized in January, 1864, was officially the brigade band (see Small, *The Sixteenth Maine . . .*, pp. 99–100, 163–164). When the war began, a twenty-four-piece band was authorized for each volunteer regiment; but by General Orders No. 91, dated July 29, 1862, all concerned were advised that the provisions of 1861 for regimental bands were repealed and that thereafter only brigade bands, of sixteen pieces, would be authorized.—G.O.V.F., 1861, pp. 2, 13–14, 43; 1862, p. 79.

Page 83

Abner Coburn was governor of Maine in 1863. He was a dealer in land and timber, with an interest in politics and some experience in public office.

Page 84

Hooker's congratulatory order is in the O.R., Ser. I, Vol. XXV, p. 171.

Page 84

Some account of the damage done in Robinson's division by the Confederate artillery firing from beyond the river may be found in Davis, *op. cit.,* pp. 201–202. "In the two divisions exposed to the fire, eight or ten were killed and between forty and fifty were wounded" (p. 202).

Page 85

"Just as the reb batteries opened on the division, the commissary was issuing rations. The stampede among the teamsters can easily be imagined. They fled incontinent, abandoning everything, probably 'for lack of sufficient transportation.' After the division was withdrawn to the shelter of a ditch, a rumor that a barrel of whiskey was among the abandoned stores induced many exploring parties to defy the rebel batteries, and diligently search for the treasure. If found, it was never heard from."—Cook, *op. cit.,* p. 92.

Page 86

". . . the Wilderness on that night was a scene of appalling grandeur. The bursting shells had ignited the dry leaves, and the red flames, running up the tree trunks and enveloping the highest branches, made the whole country like an ocean of fire."—Locke, *op. cit.,* p. 197.

Page 87

Chancellorsville was one large brick house and its outbuildings, owned by a man named Chancellor.

Page 88

The paragraph beginning "Directly across the river" gives a too much compressed description of what the observer saw. A schedule of events and an interpretation are appended here in an attempt to show what he did see. It seems necessary to do this because, in all accounts of the battle generally available, the emphasis falls—naturally enough—on the actual movement of the conflict, which on the afternoon of May 3d was mainly influenced by Sedgwick's advance from Fredericksburg, and the situation on Hooker's right is neglected. So far as I am aware, the details assembled below have never before been thus exhibited. They show that a territory blank on most maps was pretty active.

[All references made below to O.R., Ser. I, Vol. XXV, Pts. I, II, omit the specification Ser. I. Abbreviations are: Bigelow = John Bigelow, Jr., *The Campaign of Chancellorsville* (New Haven, 1910); Cooke= John Esten Cooke, *Stonewall Jackson: A Military Biography* (New York, 1866); Dabney = R. L. Dabney, *The Life and Campaigns of Lieut.-Gen. Thomas J. Jackson* (New York, 1866); Dodge = Theodore A.

Dodge, *The Campaign of Chancellorsville* (Boston, 1881); Doubleday = Abner Doubleday, *Chancellorsville and Gettysburg* (New York, 1882); Hist. 3d Pa. Cav. = *History of the Third Pennsylvania Cavalry* (Philadelphia, 1905); McClellan = Henry B. McClellan, *The Life and Campaigns of Major-General J. E. B. Stuart* . . . (Boston and Richmond, 1885); von Borcke = Heros von Borcke, *Memoirs of the Confederate War* . . . (Edinburgh and London, 1866); Webb = Alexander S. Webb, "Meade at Chancellorsville," *Campaigns in Virginia, Maryland and Pennsylvania, 1862–1863* (Papers of the Military Historical Society of Massachusetts, Vol. III) (Boston, 1903).]

SCHEDULE OF EVENTS

Feb. 24th–25th.—Fitzhugh Lee, with Confederate cavalry, crosses the Rappahannock at Kelly's Ford and moves down to within a few miles of Falmouth, for the purpose of learning Hooker's position. (O.R., Vol. XXV, Pt. I, p. 25: Fitzhugh Lee's report. See also Bigelow, map 2, "Fitzhugh Lee's Route" marked in red.)

Apr. 27th–May 1st.—Hooker moves five of his seven corps upriver and assembles them at Chancellorsville. Kelly's Ford is used by three corps in crossing the Rappahannock, and Ely's Ford is used by one and Germanna Ford by two in crossing the Rapidan, Confederate cavalry pickets at these and other fords being driven off. (O.R., Vol. XXV, Pt. I, pp. 197–199.)

May 2d.—Afternoon. A squadron of the 6th N. Y. Cav. is on picket at Ely's Ford. (O.R., Vol. XXV, Pt. I, p. 781.)

May 2d.—5–7:15 P.M. (Bigelow, pp. 295–308), Jackson with his corps, constituting a wing of the Confederate army, having moved around to the Federal right, attacks and drives in Howard's (11th) Corps (O.R., Vol. XXV, Pt. I, pp. 798–799) until, as darkness falls, he is stopped. He has intended to get between the Federal forces and the rivers to their rear, thus blocking their way of retreat, and he now intends, as soon as he can resume his offensive, to continue with this plan; but he does not know, as the night advances, that Reynolds is moving in on his left. (Bigelow, pp. 316–317, 340, n. 4; Cooke, p. 419; Dabney, pp. 699–700; McClellan, commenting on Dabney, pp. 251–253.)

May 2d.—(About 7:30 P.M.: Bigelow, p. 308) Stuart takes "some cavalry and infantry" (1st and 2d Va. Cav. and 16th No. Ca. Inf., numbering together, says Bigelow [p. 322], about 1000 men; the infantry alone numbering about 1000, says von Borcke [Vol. II, p. 228]) "to hold the Ely's Ford road" (O.R., Vol. XXV, Pt. I, p. 887: Stuart's report).

May 2d.—10:30 P.M. (O.R., Vol. XXV, Pt. I, p. 1076), Averell's division of cavalry (Federal)—3400 sabers and 6 guns (O.R., Vol. XXV, Pt. I, p. 1074)—reaches Ely's Ford from the direction of Rapidan Station, and pitches camp. The squadron of the 6th N. Y. Cav. lately on picket at Ely's Ford has fallen back toward United States Ford (Bigelow, p. 322).

May 2d.—11:30 P.M. (O.R., Vol. XXV, Pt. I, p. 1076), Averell's camp is fired on by the 16th No. Ca., which then starts back to rejoin its brigade (O.R., Vol. XXV, Pt. I, p. 937). Meanwhile, Stuart himself rides back to assume command of the Confederate left, succeeding Jackson, wounded (O.R., Vol., XXV, Pt. I, p. 887), and arrives about midnight (Bigelow, p. 339).

May 2d–3d.—Reynolds, with the 1st Corps (Federal), ordered up by Hooker, crosses the Rappahannock at United States Ford and takes up a position on the Union right (O.R., Vol. XXV, Pt. I, pp. 254–255; see Bigelow, maps 22 and 24). Robinson's division (2d Div., 1st Corps) takes up a position "on and covering the Hunting Creek road, arriving at that point at 1 o'clock on Sunday morning" (O.R., Vol. XXV, Pt. I, p. 276). Root's brigade (1st Brig., 2d Div., 1st Corps) takes up a position "on the right of the army. The pickets became engaged in a noisy skirmish with the enemy, and sent in several prisoners who stated that our right would be attacked in the morning" (O.R., Vol. XXV, Pt. I, p. 279: Root's report). Apropos of the prisoners' statement, see Dabney (pp. 699–700): "Jackson proposed . . . to move still farther to his left, during the night" [in order to attack again the next morning]. (See also Cooke, p. 419.)

May 3d.—"At 3 A.M. the 16 No. Ca. rejoined its brigade from Ely's Ford. The cavalry, under Fitzhugh Lee, was in observation between Ely's Ford and the left of Stuart's infantry" (Bigelow, p. 340).

May 3d.—Stuart, attacking in the morning, "departed from the plan of General Jackson, by extending his right rather than his left" (Dabney, p. 700; see also O.R., Vol. XXV, Pt. I, pp. 887–888: Stuart's report).

May 3d.—"Early Sunday [=this] morning," reports Gen. Rowley, commanding 1st Brig., 3d Div. (Doubleday's), 1st Corps, "sharpshooters were sent out to ascertain if the enemy were appearing on our front. An hour or two later five companies were sent to the front to do picket duty. The first picket line was formed on the left of that established by Gen. Robinson's division [2d Div.]. They were not on their posts long before skirmishing began between our pickets and those of the enemy, which continued steadily during the entire day, the result of which was our line was advanced several hundred yards, and upward of 100 prisoners were taken by the pickets of this brigade alone, besides some 15 or 20 killed and wounded. The loss on our side was 1 killed, 12 wounded, and 36 missing" (O.R., Vol. XXV, Pt. I, p. 290: Rowley's report).

May 3d.—"9 to 9:30 A.M. . . . Meade had been hoping for orders or permission to strike a blow at Stuart's left. By his own order, Colonel Webb of his staff had ridden to the left of Stuart's line, and seen it moving forward across his front. He went with Webb to Hooker's tent, and urged that he and Reynolds be allowed to attack the enemy's left, . . . stating what Webb had seen. Reynolds also besought Hooker for permission to attack, but Hooker, renouncing what offensive designs he may have entertained, positively refused to allow it" (Bigelow, p. 364. See also O.R., Vol. XXV, Pt. I, p. 508; Webb, pp. 222, 231; Doubleday, pp. 53–54; Dodge, pp. 156–157).

May 3d.—"About 1 P.M." Averell's cavalry division, moving from Ely's Ford, enters the Union lines and crosses to United States Ford. Nothing is seen of Fitzhugh Lee's cavalry. (Hist. 3d Pa. Cav., pp. 231 and 234.)

May 3d.—Beckham's horse artillery—8 pieces (O.R., Vol. XXV, Pt. I, pp. 1048–1049: Beckham's report; Bigelow, p. 245)—"was placed in position to the left of the Plank road, to guard against a reported attempt of the enemy to turn our flank from the direction of the Ely's Ford road," and "remained here until ordered to join General Fitz. Lee, and moved with his brigade toward Ely's Ford, near which place we stayed until [after the battle] we took up the march for Orange Court House" (O.R., Vol. XXV, Pt. I, p. 1050: Beckham's report). Fitz. Lee already had 2 other pieces of Stuart's horse artillery (Bigelow, p. 245).

May 3d.—J. C. Wiggins and N. Henry Camp, Federal lieutenants and acting signal officers, "spent this day reconnoitering as far as possible, reporting to General Reynolds; the densely wooded character of the country rendering this station of observation a very unsatisfactory one" (O.R., Vol. XXV, Pt. I, p. 233).

May 3d.—This day, about 100 prisoners were taken and sent in by Robinson's pickets (O.R., Vol. XXV, Pt. I, p. 277: Robinson's report).

May 3d.—At 4:30 P.M., Robinson's order for a reconnaissance is written, in obedience to which Adjutant Small, 16th Me. Inf. (1st Brig. [Root's], 2d Div. [Robinson's], 1st Corps [Reynolds']), rides out toward Ely's Ford from Root's position (see Bigelow, map 24; also O.R., Atlas, Pl. XLI, type map 1, and Pl. XCIII, type map 2) all the way to a point of observation on the Rapidan just below Ely's Ford, arriving at dusk ("at that season about quarter past seven," Dodge, p. 96). On starting back, he finds his way barred by a Confederate picket line, rides through it, and is fired on. Since he notes that the weapons used are carbines, it appears that the pickets are dismounted cavalrymen. He brings back to Gen. Reynolds news that he has seen Confederate troops with artillery moving away from the Union front and "in the direction of Fredericksburg."

May 3d.—The squadron of the 6th N. Y. Cav. which has been picketing Ely's Ford reports to its brigade commander. "They had been completely cut off from our army, and had to fight their way through the enemy's skirmishers to our lines, losing several men and horses. They only came in by direction of the field officer in command of our outposts on that line." (O.R., Vol. XXV, Pt. I, p. 782; Bigelow, p. 380.)

May 3d–4th.—Col. Harrison Allen, commanding 151st Pa. Inf. (1st Brig., 3d Div. [Doubleday's], 1st Corps), reports: "During the 3d and 4th we took 61 prisoners and killed 12 of the enemy" (O.R., Vol. XXV, Pt. I, p. 295).

May 4th.—Lieutenants Wiggins and Camp "tried again [i.e., attempted to reconnoiter] in front of General Robinson's command, taking our glasses and going outside of our lines, but nothing satisfactory could be discovered" (O.R., Vol. XXV, Pt. I, p. 233).

May 4th.—Col. Root, at the invitation of Gen. Reynolds, accompanies the general on a reconnaissance "to the right and front of our position, developing the enemy's pickets in close proximity to our own" (O.R., Vol. XXV, Pt. I, p. 279: Root's report).

May 4th.—By an order written at 11:30 A.M., Hooker directs Reynolds to make a reconnaissance "for the purpose of ascertaining the best route for him to take should it be necessary for him to advance to the Chancellorsville and Germanna Bridge road" (O.R., Vol. XXV, Pt. II, p. 413).

May 4th.—Gen. Robinson takes the 12th and 13th Mass. Inf. and a section of Hall's battery (2d Me.) "to make a reconnaissance on the road leading to Ely's Ford. . . . After proceeding about three miles, I received the fire of the enemy's skirmishers to the left of the road, and had some of my skirmishers wounded. I proceeded cautiously to the forks of the road, when, becoming satisfied the enemy was in force on the left, I directed the command to return to camp" (O.R., Vol. XXV, Pt. I, p. 277: Robinson's report).

May 4th.—By an order written at 4:15 P.M., Hooker directs Reynolds "to send a sufficient force to penetrate as far as the Plank road, through Chancellorsville, up Hunting Run, of sufficient strength to drive in the enemy's skirmishers if they have any" (O.R., Vol. XXV, Pt. II, p. 413).

May 4th.—Col. Roy Stone, commanding 2d Brig., 3d Div. (Doubleday's), 1st Corps, reports: "At 6 P.M. I was ordered to reconnoiter with my brigade the Ridge road leading south from General Robinson's left, to ascertain the enemy's position and whether it was held in force. . . . [A mile out] I found the enemy in force in front and to the left" (O.R., Vol. XXV, Pt. I, p. 296).

INTERPRETATION

Lee was intrenched south of the Rappahannock River, and the only way to assail him was by turning his position. Hooker, who had been encamped north of the river, moved five of his corps northwesterly, put two of them over the Rappahannock, and three, farther up, over both the Rappahannock and the Rapidan, and thus turned Lee's left and brought him out of his trenches; but, instead of pressing on so as to get clear of the Wilderness and fight Lee in the more open country nearer Fredericksburg, he then halted at Chancellorsville, and the initiative passed to Lee. Jackson, whose corps formed a wing of Lee's army, proposed to take it beyond Hooker's right and then turn and attack. Lee agreed. The attack was made, and was stopped only with nightfall and the fatal wounding of Jackson. Next morning, Stuart, succeeding to the command of Jackson's corps, made a new attack, not farther to the left as Jackson had originally intended to do, but toward his right so as to join forces again with Lee.

The territory beyond Jackson's, now Stuart's, left continued to be of interest to the Federals, however, because (1) Lee, if contemplating a new move against the Federal rear and communications, could only make it by attacking farther to his left than Jackson had done, or by repeating in reverse what Hooker had done—that is, move a force first up and across the rivers, and then down on the northerly side; (2) Hooker, who now had Reynolds' and Meade's corps, could attack with them from his right, falling upon Stuart's left.

The foregoing would presumably have been in the mind of any "intelligent officer" of Reynolds' corps on the afternoon of May 3d; and fresh in his remembrance would be Fitzhugh Lee's cavalry dash of February 24th and 25th. If the enemy had once used this route, why not again? Such a movement, the purpose of which would be to move *toward* Fredericksburg, must necessarily begin in a direction *away from* Fredericksburg. The direct road from Chancellorsville to Kelly's Ford on the Rappahannock crossed the Rapidan at Ely's Ford. Hence, Adjutant Small's natural objective was a point from which he might observe Ely's Ford; and when he says he saw troops moving *toward* Fredericksburg, he is speaking correctly, although at the moment of observation he sees them moving in just the opposite direction.

Now, what troops did Adjutant Small see? And why were they there? The "Schedule of Events" preceding this "Interpretation" makes abundantly plain that there were Confederates near Reynolds' corps front throughout both May 3d and May 4th; the picket line of Doubleday's division captured a hundred of them and killed or wounded fifteen or twenty, and Robinson's picket line sent in a hundred prisoners more. In the official Federal reports the prisoners are not specified as cavalrymen, and it is therefore to be assumed that they were infantrymen. In the official Confederate reports no particular force is named as operating in this territory; but operations that were no more than duties, and that did not bring on an engagement, often passed without mention in the reports made in the later years of the war.

There were also Confederate troops near Ely's Ford. The territory between Jackson's, later Stuart's, left and the fords of the Rapidan required to be closely watched; the Confederate flank could not be left unguarded against a possible surprise attack from the woods.

At night, May 2d, Stuart had some troops, both infantry and cavalry, at Ely's Ford. May 3d, his cavalry, at most a few hundred troopers under Fitzhugh Lee, was "in observation" between Ely's Ford and his left. In the earlier part of the afternoon, May 3d, Averell's large cavalry force came in from Ely's Ford; and Fitz. Lee then drew his smaller force out of the way. Where? The nearest places that would give him room to turn in, and water for his horses and men, were the farm clearings near the fords next upriver from Ely's. And for how long? Averell had "3400 sabers and 6 guns" to move along a narrow forest road; it would take some time. It was in this interval, in all probability, and at the farm clearings, that Beckham with his eight pieces of artillery joined Fitz. Lee.

Now, it is reasonable to suppose that as soon as Averell had moved within the Federal lines and left the territory clear, Fitz. Lee again posted his forces there "in observation." His approach to Ely's Ford could be glimpsed by an observer situated as Adjutant Small was; and if he sent patrols to cover the roads leading from the Rapidan River toward Kelly's Ford on the Rappahannock—as would be militarily advisable: for if Averell had come from that direction with a large force, might not more be coming?—then Adjutant Small saw indeed two columns moving "in the direction of Fredericksburg." The campfires he saw were doubtless those of some of Fitz. Lee's troops—of an advance guard "directly across the river" at the far side of Ely's Ford, and of the main body "from one to three miles to the left" at the near side of the fords next upriver from Ely's; and the burning buildings were perhaps old shacks by the river, or bonfires, blazing where soldiers were drying themselves after a dip in the stream, or lighted for the purpose of giving the impression that the south bank of the river was more strongly occupied than it actually was.

Fitz. Lee's resumption of control over the territory near Ely's Ford would of course drive away the squadron of the 6th New York Cavalry which had been picketing the ford; and it would be through Fitz. Lee's new picket line that Adjutant Small made his dash for the Union lines. The next day, May 4th, the Confederates certainly were still there; Robinson himself, going out with two regiments of infantry and a section of a battery, became satisfied that "the enemy was in force" near the forks of the Ely's Ford road, at the very place, "about 3 miles" out, where Adjutant Small had found a picket line barring his way.

Major Small wrote, in his history of his regiment, that the force he saw was "withdrawing to fall upon Sedgwick"; but the specific purpose thus given was a misinterpretation from reading done after the event and before the publication of those sources, later made available to all, which might have assisted him to refresh his memory more accurately. Actually, by the time he started on his reconnaissance, Lee had sent McLaws' division and Mahone's brigade of Anderson's division against Sedgwick, and the fighting near Salem Church was already begun. (Sedgwick, left behind when Hooker moved around Lee's left, on May 3d took by assault the heights behind Fredericksburg and came on toward Hooker until stopped by the troops sent against him by Lee.)

On May 10th, a few days after the battle, Adjutant Small wrote to friends at home a letter in which he mentioned the reconnaissance and said: "Had a fine time and came near being 'gobbled up' by the devils, who discovered my presence. However, I had been gone two or three hours and obtained all the intelligence I was after." This indicates that, at the time, he knew distinctly what he was after. When he wrote the history of his regiment, twenty years later (it was published in 1886), he did not have for the refreshment of his memory the volume of the *Official Records* which deals with the battle (Vol. XXV, Pts. I, II, and III, all published in 1889), nor the maps of the battle included in the *Atlas* accompanying the *Official Records* (the two volumes of the *Atlas* were published in 1891–1895). Bigelow's *Campaign of Chancellorsville,* with its detailed analysis and many maps, was published in 1910, the year of Major Small's death; he did not see it.

Page 92

[As the division moved back toward the river] "of all the thousands of men who had marched over that ground, and the hundreds of wagons and artillery that were going and coming night and day for a week past, nothing was to be seen. The fire that blazed so furiously in the midnight of Saturday, had burned far into the woods, leaving the road-side lined with charred and smouldering tree trunks, while here and there a noble oak, growing among its meaner kind, and more tenacious of life than they, presented in that early morning a heart still glowing with fire."—Locke, *op. cit.,* p. 204.

Page 93

"Not far from the camp of the Eleventh was another of those Virginia mansions, resembling in its generous dimensions, as in its internal finish and outward beauty of grounds, the residence of Major Fitzhugh. The proprietor was in the South, and for two years the fields had been uncultivated, and the garden and lawn suffered to grow wild with weeds, save the little attention given to them by a family of miserably poor white retainers living on a part of the estate.

"In two days after our arrival, if one had made a tour through the encampments of the First Corps lying nearest this mansion, he might have found distributed here and there, as additions either ornamental or useful, almost everything that could be carried from the forsaken house. The heavy panelled doors were transformed into camp bedsteads of the most approved style, or made to serve the meaner purpose of a tent floor. In one of our company streets, cool and airy quarters were constructed of its venetian shutters; and though all the glass had been broken from the windows, members of another company, not to be outdone by the inventive genius of their neighbors, carried away the empty sash, of which they built quarters still more cool and airy."— Locke, *op. cit.,* pp. 207–208.

Page 97

The orders of Hooker and Meade are in the O.R., Ser. I, Vol. XXVII, Pt. II, pp. 373–374.

The battery mentioned here was, apparently, Cooper's Battery B, 1st Pennsylvania Light Artillery, one of the five batteries composing the artillery brigade of the 1st Corps. In *Maine at Gettysburg: Report of Maine Commissioners: Prepared by the Executive Committee* (Portland, 1898), p. 45, a map of the "successive positions of the 16th Maine Infantry" shows Stevens' 5th Maine Battery north of the seminary; but in the same book, p. 83, an account of the services of Stevens' battery says that Captain Stevens "took his second position on the right of Cooper's Battery B, 1st Pennsylvania; Cooper was next to the seminary building and Stevens was next to Cooper. It was about 2 P.M. when this movement was made. At this hour the 16th Maine had already moved from the entrenchments at the seminary and was facing or about to face the onset of Rodes's right."

Pages 99–101

Colonel Alfred J. Sellers, of Philadelphia, formerly major of the 90th Pennsylvania, having read Major Small's history of the 16th Maine, wrote to the author on November 2d, 1891, for information about the movements and positions of the regiments of Robinson's division in the first day's fight. On December 23d, 1891, Major Small replied, in part, as follows:

"MY DEAR COMRADE:

"Your kind letter with enquiries deserved an earlier answer. I waited to attend a meeting of the executive committee of the 16th [Maine], hoping to confirm some of my impressions and recollections.

"We [the 16th Maine] are to occupy a place in the forthcoming 'History of Maine Troops at Gettysburg' [*Maine at Gettysburg*, Portland, 1898], and have prepared a digest. I found that after twenty-five years, men who July 1st, 1863, occupied the same half-acre and helped make history, differ most essentially in all that most concerned us as a regiment—except in the quantity of rations, and the quality of our foes. That half-acre should be portable, and I would like to have every old soldier take turns in placing it geographically. By the time the last man settled it into position, there would be seven lines of rebels around it—and on it, were there room. Pardon me for so much apparent nonsense, but I found myself one of the number [trying to contribute material for the digest] at the meeting.

"The formation of our brigade was as you have it [Colonel Sellers had drawn a sketch map in his letter] for a short time only. As I recollect it, the 16th [Maine] occupied the same ground where now stands the 88th [Pennsylvania] monument. (Our colonel says No.) Our last position as a forlorn hope was broken on the Mummasburg road, by order of Division A.D.C., and almost immediately afterwards repeated to Colonel Tilden by General Robinson in person, who years after confirms it in an autograph letter to Colonel Tilden . . .

"I feel positive that our brigade crossed the Mummasburg road for about five minutes. I do not recollect about your brigade, except that they fought like devils. The 13th Mass. are way off in their position, but if they are satisfied, I am. Recollect that no five men of us can place the five regiments of the 2d Brigade in position occupied at the same moment. The changes were so frequent and rapid that it is utterly impossible (today), hence the variance in opinion.

"After all, what matters it whether we were on either side the wall, the fence, or the road—whether one regiment led or another? The facts are patent, that we were all—Penn., N. Y., Mass., and Maine—there on an acre or two of ground, and fought like hell so long as we could, and saved the division. I don't care if our little shaft is surrounded and overshadowed by a thousand monuments: our interests were and are identical . . .

"P.S. Regiments in our brigade much of the time acted independently, i.e., by direct orders from the division commander (as at Gettysburg).

"See 'War of the Rebellion' [*Official Records*], Ser. I, Vol. 27, Gettysburg. I did not have this when telling the story of the 16th [that is, when writing the history of that regiment], or I should have made the work more full and 'official.'

"You will notice that General Robinson complains to General Meade, and expresses his mortification and disappointment that the 2d Division (his) did not receive the credit belonging to it. The 16th [Maine] could with reason express the same sentiments to General Robinson for failing to give this regiment credit, officially, although he did it later in letters to General Tilden—but too late to get [it] its place in history."

General Robinson's complaint to General Meade, under date of November 15th, 1863, is in the O.R., Ser. I, Vol. XXVII, Pt. I, p. 291.

Page 101

The "rebel repulse earlier in the day" was the repulse of O'Neal's brigade by Baxter's.—O.R., Ser. I, Vol. XXVII, Pt. I, pp. 307, 592.

Page 102

Incidents of the capture have been recorded by several members of the regiment.

Lieutenant Francis Wiggin wrote, for *Maine at Gettysburg* (p. 44): "The two Confederate battle lines, closing together, struck the regiment simultaneously. Ewell's men appeared upon the north side of the cut and Hill's upon the south side so nearly at the same time that both lines, with levelled muskets, claimed the prisoners. Colonel Tilden fell to Ewell's share."

Major Small wrote, for the same book (p. 46): "Summoned to surrender, Colonel Tilden plunged his sword into the ground and broke it short off at the hilt, and directed the destruction of the colors."

Colonel Tilden, in a letter to Major Small, in reference to this, wrote (on December 30th, 1896): "I was ordered to surrender and lay down my sword by a Johnnie with his musket levelled at my head; but instead of laying it down, plunged it in the ground as stated. As to its being broken, I am unable to state definitely. I know I attempted to break it."

Lieutenant Wiggin, in a letter to General Charles Hamlin, chairman of the executive committee of the Maine Gettysburg Commission, wrote (on November 5th, 1896): "When capture seemed inevitable, with the consent of Colonel Tilden the staff of the flag was broken and the flag itself torn up and concealed about the persons of the survivors of the Sixteenth. I have a piece of the flag in my possession now; so has Colonel Tilden, and many other members of the regiment."

The report of Captain James A. Hopkins, commanding the 45th North Carolina, of Daniel's brigade, Rodes's division, Ewell's corps, says: "We also captured a very fine flag-staff and tassels; the remains of what had been a fine Yankee flag were lying in different places."—O.R., Ser. I, Vol. XXVII, Pt. II, p. 575. This may refer to the flag-staff and colors of the 16th Maine.

Sergeant Luther Bradford, one of the captured members of the 16th Maine, wrote in 188– an account of his experiences as a prisoner. His account includes the following:

"After being taken a prisoner, I was sent to the rear with a few others of our regiment. When we got back to where the 1st Division of our corps fought in the forenoon, we were allowed to go over the field and pick up the wounded. . . . Just before dark, we were called together and started towards the rear again and I should think that they marched us four or five miles. By this time it had become dark, and we were filed off into a field and allowed to lie down, but the officer in charge would not allow the prisoners any fires to make coffee over, so we had to get along with dry hard-bread. . . .

"After daylight the next morning we turned around and marched back to the battlefield of our regiment the day before; there we were allowed to go about on the field and pick up any of our men that we might find wounded. . . . We found many of our regiment dead. . . . We were taken back about a mile west from the seminary, where we found a squad of prisoners under guard. We were put in with them, making about thirteen hundred in all. On the afternoon of the 3d we were paroled and started for Carlisle under a flag of truce with an escort of rebel cavalry and mounted infantry.

"We marched that night until near midnight before we made any halt. At daylight on the 4th we started again. A little after noon we met a large force of Pennsylvania State Militia on their way to Gettysburg. The rebel officer in command of our escort had a consultation with the officer in command of the militia, called his men together, turned towards Gettysburg and left us. We went to Carlisle; from there to Harrisburg; from there we were sent to Westchester, where we went into camp, and rations and clothing were issued. We were kept there about six weeks; then we were returned to our regiments. The 16th was at Rappahannock Station when we joined it."

Colonel Tilden is handsomely mentioned by General Pickett, who would have paroled the prisoners placed under his charge but was not permitted to do so.—*The Heart of a Soldier as Revealed in the Intimate Letters of Genl. George E. Pickett, C.S.A.* (New York, 1913), p. 111.

Page 103

Doubleday himself seems to have felt that he had earned the command of the 1st Corps, and that Meade had given it to Newton, instead, because Howard had sent Meade a "very misleading dispatch" misrepresenting the state of affairs on the field before Meade got there. See Howard's report to Meade, dated 5 P.M., July 1st, 1863 (O.R., Ser. I, Vol. XXVII, Pt. I, p. 696; also Hancock's report to Meade, dated 5:25 P.M.: "Howard says that Doubleday's command gave way" (O.R., Ser. I, Vol. XXVII, Pt. I, p. 366). The matter is discussed in Abner Doubleday, *Chancellorsville and Gettysburg* (New York, 1882), pp. 134–135, 137–138, 151, 154, and is referred to in George Meade, *Life and Letters of George Gordon Meade* . . . (New York, 1913), Vol. II, Appendix Y. Howard does not mention it in his *Autobiography*.

Page 103

Colonel Coulter, as commander of the 1st Brigade, 2d Division, 1st Corps, at Gettysburg, succeeding the wounded General Paul, wrote in his official report: "Three officers of General Paul's staff being reported among the missing, I selected Adjt. A. R. Small, Sixteenth Maine, as acting assistant adjutant-general, and Lieutenant Howe, of the Thirteenth Massachusetts, as aide-de-camp, of whom I desire to make special mention for assistance rendered me."—O.R., Ser. I, Vol. XXVII, Pt. I, pp. 294–295.

Page 104

Lieutenant Fred H. Beecher had been wounded severely in the knee at Fredericksburg. When on the point of rejoining his regiment, at the expiration of his leave of absence, he had been thrown from his carriage, and the wounded knee had been injured so severely as to require an extension of his leave. Although lame and unfit for duty, he rejoined his company in season to be in the Gettysburg battle; and was again wounded in the same knee (by the explosion of the shell here mentioned), and was carried from the field. After the war, he was a lieutenant in the 3d Infantry, regular army. Detailed as second in command to assist Major Forsyth in the latter's expedition against the Cheyenne Indians, in the fall of 1868, he was killed in the battle fought in the bed of the Arickaree River; and the little island defended by Major Forsyth and his men was named Beecher's Island, in honor of his memory. He was a nephew of Henry Ward Beecher.—Small, *The Sixteenth Maine* . . . , p. 244; also Cyrus Townsend Brady, *Indian Fights and Fighters* (New York, 1904), pp. 77, 88.

Page 104

As of an incident occurring on July 3 (apparently in error for the incident of July 2, here described), the historian of the 13th Massachusetts writes: ". . . we [Robinson's division] were ordered to hasten to the support of the Second Corps, now engaged in repulsing Pickett's charge. We ran along the crest of the hill amid a continued shower of rebel shell, while the noise was increased by musketry-firing and the shouting and yelling of troops on both sides. . . . During the movement, an incident happened to show the hard luck that followed a gallant regiment. The Sixteenth Maine, during the first day's fight, was assigned the very difficult duty of holding on and delaying, if possible, the advance of the enemy until the rest of the division could get to the rear; and it did its work bravely and with great credit to itself, its colonel and most of the men being taken prisoners in the endeavor. The remnant of about twenty men that escaped were just ahead of us as we double-quicked along the ridge. Suddenly a Whitworth shell from one of the enemy's batteries exploded in their midst, and it seemed to us, as we hurried on over their mangled bodies, that every man must have been killed. Our entire division at this time, consisting of eleven regiments, numbered only about nine hundred men, and we felt sorry to see the remnant of this excellent regiment so completely wiped out."—Davis, *op. cit.*, p. 236.

Page 106

Of Colonel Lyle as commander of the brigade, the memoirist has written elsewhere: "I had the pleasure of serving on the staff of both commanders [Colonels Lyle and Coulter]. Colonel Lyle was an intelligent and brave officer, a modest and unassuming gentleman, who was generally liked by his associates. He handled his regiment well, but as brigade commander he sometimes became confused and lost his head in action."

Page 111

"Our present encampment is in sight of the handsome town of Middleburg. The citizens of the place showed their utter contempt for us by retiring to their houses and closing every door and window. Not a white person was to be seen, and but for the negroes that met us on the street corners, we might have thought the town uninhabited.

"Another reason for the unusual quiet of Middleburg has just been discovered. Between one and two hundred rebel wounded from the field of Gettysburg are quartered in the town, and it was very desirable that they should remain undiscovered by the prying and curious Yankees. Liberal supplies of stores, stolen from Maryland and Pennsylvania, were also left for their subsistence. General Newton has very properly ordered this supply to be considerably lessened."—Locke, *op. cit.*, p. 261.

Page 117

Captain John S. Mosby, operating with an irregular mounted force that would assemble at his call and disperse after making a raid, was a minor but troublesome opponent of the Union armies in northern Virginia. On the present occasion, it appears, Mosby himself was elsewhere, and the raiding party was led by "a Captain Turner" [Lieutenant William T. Turner].—O.R., Ser. I, Vol. XXIX, Pt. I, p. 659, report of Brigadier-General David McM. Gregg, commanding 2d Division, Cavalry Corps.

Page 118

The incident of Captain Meade's fall is mentioned by his father, General Meade, in a letter dated December 3d, 1863, which dismisses his hurts as nothing serious.—*Life and Letters*, Vol. II, p. 159.

Page 119

Another incident of the sheep hunt is given in the history of the 13th Massachusetts: "A sheep was seen running along outside of our skirmish line, when it was fired upon and wounded. An adventurous member of Company E ran out for it, but a Johnnie on the rebel skirmish line covered him with his gun, shouting, 'Divide, Yank!' which was agreed to. The sheep was then split in halves, each taking his portion, returning to their places amid shouts of laughter from both sides."—Davis, *op. cit.*, p. 289.

Page 126

General Newton's farewell order is in the O.R., Ser. I, Vol. XXXIII, p. 735.

Page 129

"During the crossing of the Rapidan, the stations of observation upon Stony, Pony, and Garnett's Mountains were occupied by parties watching the movements of the enemy upon the south bank of the river."—O.R., Ser. I, Vol. XXXVI, Pt. I, p. 283, report of Major Benjamin F. Fisher, chief signal officer, Army of the Potomac. There is no mention of Cedar Mountain by that name; but Garnett's Mountain is a knob that rises perhaps half a mile to the southwest of the ridge that forms the height of Cedar Mountain proper, and it is doubtless to this knob that the memoirist refers. The view of the Confederate camps was probably better from Garnett's Mountain than from the other heights mentioned by Major Fisher. General Meade, in a letter to his wife, mentions the signal station on Pony Mountain as a place from which, by means of the telescope there, a good view could be had of the enemy's camps (*Life and Letters,* Vol. II, p. 185); and Pony Mountain was by several miles farther than Garnett's from the Confederate position.

Page 130

"On the eighth [of April] we were reviewed by General Grant. . . . We waited in line but a short time when an officer was seen approaching at a gallop, completely outstripping the members of his staff, who found it impossible to keep pace with him, so great was the speed. He made a complete circuit of the regiment, looking every man square in the face, returning our salute as he passed along, continuing [at] the same rapid gait to each camp of the brigade until the work was completed. It was performed so quickly that we hardly realized that it was done."— Davis, *op. cit.,* p. 315.

Page 130

The spring day, the wild flowers, and the view seem generally to have been noticed. See, for example, George R. Agassiz, ed., *Meade's Headquarters, 1863–1865: Letters of Colonel Theodore Lyman from the Wilderness to Appomattox* (Boston, 1922), p. 87; Morris Schaff, *The Battle of the Wilderness* (Boston, 1910), pp. 83–84.

Major Small's campaign diary has two sets of entries for the two days, the 13th and 14th of May. Apparently, one set refers to the movements of the regiment, the other to his own. The personal entries are the following:

"13th. Went to rear to get rest and sleep. Heavy cannonading.

"14th. Marched with train to park two miles southwest of Fredericksburg. Sent letters to Father and J.M."

The single entry for May 15th includes, in parentheses, the personal entry: "Adjt. rejoined last night."

Page 142

A "brass" battery was of smooth-bore 12-pounders, which generally were made of bronze, cast solid and then bored. The plain exterior of the barrel when burnished looked bright and "brassy."

Page 144

Bull's Church may be found on the maps under the name of St. Margaret's Church. "May 22. At 11 A.M. we started for Bull's Church, about ten miles. The day was hot and sultry and the roads dusty. The only fun we had was making puns on the name of the church. It was also known as St. Margaret's Church. We were under the impression that St. Margaret was generally attended by a dog, so we were unable to understand the significance of calling it Bull's Church."—Davis, *op. cit.*, p. 346.

Page 145

The words commonly sung to the tune of "Old Hundredth" were those of the familiar doxology: "Praise God, from whom all blessings flow; praise Him, all creatures here below; . . ."

Page 153

The words sung to the music of "Pleyel's Hymn" may have included, from the lines composed by the Reverend Joseph Swain, the following:

> "Brethren, while we sojourn here,
> Fight we must, but should not fear; . . ."

Page 155

"In this assault I lost my sergeant-major, killed, 28 men wounded, Adjt. Small, 3 line officers, and 33 men taken prisoners."—Report of Colonel Charles W. Tilden, commanding 16th Maine, of operations August 18th–19th, 1864: O.R., Ser. I, Vol. XLII, Pt. I, p. 508.

Through the celebrated Rose tunnel, one hundred and nine captives escaped from Libby Prison in the night of February 9th–10th, 1864. Fifty-nine got away, forty-eight were recaptured, and two lost their lives by drowning.—Frank E. Moran, "Colonel Rose's Tunnel at Libby Prison," *Century Magazine,* March, 1888, pp. 770–790.

Page 162

Jefferson Davis was returning from the farther South, whither he had gone to see what could be done against Sherman. Early in the morning of Tuesday, October 4th, he arrived at Columbia, South Carolina. He was entertained there at the home of Brigadier-General James Chestnut.—*Jefferson Davis, Constitutionalist: His Letters, Papers, and Speeches* (Jackson, 1923), Vol. VI, p. 349. Mrs. Chesnut's diary shows that Mrs. Davis did not accompany Mr. Davis on this journey.—Mary Boykin Chesnut, *A Diary from Dixie* (New York, 1906), pp. 328–329, 377. General Beauregard, having conferred with Davis at Augusta, Georgia, on October 3d, went the next day to Milledgeville; so he could not have been on the train with Davis.—Alfred Roman, *The Military Operations of General Beauregard* (New York, 1884), p. 280.

Davis had made speeches at Dexter, Augusta, Belfast, and Portland, Maine, in the summer of 1858, and the memoirist may have seen and heard him then.

Page 171

For a view through a prisoner's eyes, see "Morning Toilette, Union Officers' Prison (Top Floor), Danville, Va., Winter, '64–5," a drawing made on the spot by Lieut. Henry VanderWeyde, A.D.C., 1st Div., 6th Corps, as reproduced in George Haven Putnam, *A Prisoner of War in Virginia, 1864–5* (New York, 1912), facing p. 40.

Page 173

An account of the first visit paid to the prisoners by the Reverend Charles K. Hall is in one of the "Extracts from a Rebel Prison Diary" which Major Small wrote, in later years, for the Waterville *Mail,* a newspaper now extinct. The clergyman was brought to the prison and introduced by the editor of the Danville *Register.* The account continues:

"I thought the presence of these loving missionaries inopportune, as 'twas just at 'dinner time,' when the kitchen department was in full blast; and the din increased rather than subsided when the little dried-up specimen of a rebel editor introduced the Rev. Dr. Hall. . . . Dr.

Hall mounted a bread-box and waited for no lull, but at once read from the Bible: 'I was an hungered and ye gave me no meat; I was thirsty and ye gave me no drink; was sick and in prison, and ye visited me not.' The true significance of these words had been forced upon him of late, and he was constrained to ask himself if he had knowledge of prisoners close at hand—of their needs—that they were starving for spiritual food. Gen. Hayes here interrupted the reverend gentleman, and suggested that material substances would prove more acceptable just now. 'Feed the body first, and then your remarks will be better appreciated.' And then followed just such 'observations' as one would naturally expect. The Dr. was meekness personified, yet sustained by a manly sense of his position. He proposed, if this lecture was acceptable, to visit us twice a week. Today he would choose for the subject of his remarks, 'Charity.' In ten minutes all noise subsided, and for forty minutes the closest attention was given to the most eloquent man I had ever heard speak. When he closed, the majority of officers were gathered around him and loath to have him leave!"

Page 182   # CONCLUSIONS

For mention of Major Small in the grand review, see Joshua Lawrence Chamberlain, Brevet Major-General U.S. Volunteers, *The Passing of the Armies: An Account of the Final Campaign of the Army of the Potomac, Based Upon Personal Reminiscences of the Fifth Army Corps* (New York, 1915), Chap. IX, "The Last Review," pp. 347–348.

Page 195

Warren was relieved from duty by Sheridan in the midst of the final campaign, Sheridan having authorization from Grant. The matter is discussed in U. S. Grant, *Personal Memoirs* (New York, 1886), Vol. II, pp. 436–445; *Personal Memoirs of P. H. Sheridan* (New York, 1888), Vol. II, Chap. VI; Chamberlain, *The Passing of the Armies,* Chaps. II–IV; Emerson Gifford Taylor, *Gouverneur Kemble Warren* (Boston, 1932), Chaps. X–XI.

THE DIARY

Friday, August 19, 1864
Petersburg, Va.

Captured on 18th with Capt. Conley, Lieuts. Broughton, Chapman.

Confined in lockup (negro prison) with enlisted men until 11 A.M., 19th.

Moved to island in Appomattox River.

Sold watch for $150, Confederate scrip.

Watkins, scout, gave me $10.

While in Petersburg, I gave Lieut. Chapman $20, Lieut. [name erased: *Kane,*] $10. Wrote to Col. T[ilden].[1]

Saturday 20
Libby Prison, Richmond, Va.

Took rooms at this hotel this P.M., 8:30 o'clock.

Food furnished us for first time since capture—bacon, one-third pound; coarse corn-bread three inches square—at 9 P.M.

Capt. Lord and Lieut. Fitch with eighty-five commissioned officers from 3d Division joined us this P.M.

Formed in messes of twelve. Our mess designated "No. 6."[2] Northeastern corner of west room, second story.

Officers chosen: secretary, A. R. Small, Adjt., 16th Me.; treasurer, Lieut. Charles W. Hanson, 39th Mass.; commissary of subsistence, Lieut. W. H. Chapman, 16th Me.

Contributions were made and money passed to treasurer for purchase of "luxuries" for mess.

Wrote to J[ulia]. M[aria]. F[airbanks].[3]

Sunday, August 21, 1864
Services at 7 P.M. by Chaplain C. B. Keyes, 9th N.Y. Cavalry.

---

[1] Superior figures refer to notes on pp. 297–304.

A.M. Sunshine   MONDAY 22   P.M. Showery

Breakfast at 12 M.

Sent out by sergeant for $40 in "luxuries"—flour-bread, $1 [*per*] loaf.

Gave Lieut. Keene [Kane], 1st Conn. Cavalry, $10; Capt. Conley, $30.

Had but 50 cents when captured. Sold my watch for $150 on the 18th.

Chaplain C. B. Keyes, 9th N.Y. Cavalry, after a psalm and reading of chapter in Bible, made a few very appropriate remarks cheering to the captives, last evening.

Chaplain Keyes and Surgeon —— leave us for flag-of-truce boat.

Reprimanded and threatened with punishment by Maj. Turner[4] for "making a fuss," said fuss being the prayer meeting Sunday evening.

A.M. Cloudy   TUESDAY 23   P.M. Very pleasant

Quite unwell yesterday. Feel better this morning.

We received, of the articles sent for yesterday, flour-bread only.

I am much surprised at the exhibition of selfishness by some of the officers, who cling to the maxim, "Look out for Number One."

Capt. Conley and I made a backgammon board and checkers. Loud singing prohibited.[5]

Present at roll-call, 132 commissioned officers.

Bill of fare for dinner: bean soup and bugs; corn-bread and water; dessert, water.

WEDNESDAY 24

A.M. Warm and pleasant

Received on requisition of 23d thirteen loaves of bread for mess.

Mess No. 6 subscribes for paper and receives first number of "Enquirer"[6] at 40 cents [*per*] number. News quite encouraging. There seems to be good reason for an early and general exchange of prisoners.

Received addition to mess, of Lieut. D. [E.] R. Sage, 144th Ohio.

Breakfast at usual hour: bread and bacon. Yesterday 'twas bacon and bread.

Capt. [*Carswell*] McClellan received heaps of luxuries from his brother [*Maj. Henry B. McClellan*] in Confederate Army.

Money market dull.

Thursday 25

A.M. Warm and pleasant   P.M. Sunshine

Received on requisition [*of the*] 24th thirteen loaves [*of*] bread.

Received tobacco, $4.

"Prices current"[7]—tobacco, one-pound bale, $3.50 to $4; pipe and stem, 50 cents; onions, dozen, $3; bread, loaf, $1; cards, pack, $10; tomatoes, quart, $2; apples, 25 cents apiece.

Bought tooth-brush, $2.50.

Rebel Lieut.-Col. visited Capt. ——; was received very cordially.

I admire Gen. Hayes.

[Words erased.]

Tables to seat fifty brought in today.

Dinner at the fashionable hour of 4 o'clock: bean slosh and corn-bread; relished well.

Adjt. —— [*Latouche*] of Libby thinks exchange distant.

Friday 26

A.M. Warm and pleasant

Some thief stole my Confederate cap.[8]

Note: Notice many noble traits of character among officers, but regret the fact that selfishness is predominant.

SATURDAY 27

Reading matter distributed.

Present at roll-call, 143.

Seventy-nine officers from 2d Corps took rooms at Libby.

Commenced [*reading*] history of New York, "Knicker-bocker."[9]

Sunny   SUNDAY, AUGUST 28, 1864   Sunny

Three officers add[itiona]l.

Finished reading "Knickerbocker."

Sunny   MONDAY 29   Sunny

Present [*at roll-call*], 224.

Wrote to Mother.

Lieut. W. H. Chapman, 16th Me., sent to general hospital, sick.

Commenced reading "The Cross and the Crown."[10]

Sunny, cool   TUESDAY 30   Sunny

"C. S. Military Prison,

"S[pecial] Order—   "Aug[t] 30, 1864.

"No Federal officers will be allowed after this date to put their blankets on the floor during the day. Each officer failing to comply with this order will have his blanket taken from him and be otherwise punished.

"By order of T. P. TURNER, Maj. Comdg."

A.M. Pleasant   WEDNESDAY 31   P.M. Pleasant

Cold nights.

Finished "Cross and Crown." Commenced "Athelings."[11]

Pleasant, cool   THURSDAY, SEPTEMBER 1, 1864   Cloudy

Maj. Goff, Virg. Cavalry, and Capt. McClellan,[12] [?and] surgeons, left by flag-of-truce boat.

Breakfast, 12 M. Bill of fare "as usual."

Turner offers to exchange Confederate [*currency*] for greenbacks,[13] 2 to 1. Confederate Government pays 6 to 1.

Capt. Poor [Cook], 9th Colored Troops, added to mess.

Pleasant all day   FRIDAY 2

Paid into treasury last dollar.

Unwell all day.

Finished "Athelings." Commenced "Henry Smeaton."[14]

Slight rain   SATURDAY 3   Sunny

Sick.

Received sixteen apples, for $5, for mess.

[Words erased.]

Very pleasant   SUNDAY 4

Sermon by Chaplain Fowler, N.Y. Vols., Colored Troops.

Finished reading "Henry Smeaton."

Wrote to J[ulia]. M[aria]. F[airbanks].

Very warm all day   MONDAY 5

Thunder shower at 9 P.M.

Showers   TUESDAY 6

Received two loaves bread, self; two bales tobacco, mess.

Paid into treasury $7.

Confirmation of fall of Atlanta.[15]

Nights quite cold.

A.M. Pleasant but cool WEDNESDAY 7   P.M. Ditto

Fresh beef issued instead of bacon—an agreeable change.

Prospects for an exchange about middle of October.

Lieut. Barker received $110 for watch.

[Words erased.]

A.M. Rainy   Thursday 8   P.M. Rainy

Capt. G. W. Goler, 6th N.Y. Cavalry, assigned to Mess No. 6.
Walked two miles before breakfast.[16]
Read "Wildflower."[17]

A.M. Cloudy   Friday 9   P.M. Pleasant

Wheat-bread issued in lieu of corn[-*bread*].
Walked one mile before breakfast.
[Words erased.]
Capt. H[?utchins] and Lieut. [?*C. H.*] C[?hapman] say they
will starve before they will pawn their watches. Wonder if the
sacrifice would [*be*] greater than that of Barker and Fitch, who
keep them in bread.

Pleasant   Saturday 10   Showery

Large fire in Manchester.
Flag-of-truce boat arrived 9th.
Received $60 Confederate for $10 U.S. [*currency*], of ———.
[Words erased.]
Warm night.

Pleasant   Sunday, September 11, 1864   Showery

Flag-of-truce boat expected hourly.
[Words written as follows, but crossed out:] Wrote to B. F.
Otis—deposit money in state treasury.

Showers and cool   Monday 12

Capt. Sloan, surgeons, and others left by flag-of-truce boat.
Sent letter to Col. Tilden by boat.
Gave address of Father to Chaplain Fowler, who promises to
write and inform [*him*] of my condition.
Butler's letter[18] to Col. Auld [Commissioner Ould] published
in "Examiner";[19] an unanswerable argument, it seems.

Prospects of an exchange dull.

Very cool night.

Cool and clear   TUESDAY 13

Ration of meat decreases.

Canvas shades put in windows, adding much to comfort of room.[20] [Words erased.]

Weather moderated.

Pleasant   WEDNESDAY 14

"Enquirer" says Commissioner Auld [Ould] will not notice Butler's communication on exchange. Therefore all hopes of an exchange seem vain.

Bread ration decreases in size; of poor quality. Meat ration grows visibly less.

Euchre: Conley and Hanson, 16; Barker and Small, 17.

Cloudy but pleasant   THURSDAY 15   Pleasant

Rice served for dinner instead of beans—an agreeable change. Br. bor^d [word illegible: ?money] and ex^d 70. L. sold wa 12–84. Lt. Sa. bor^d 20 – 120 – fur^d ms. tr.[21]

Lieut. W. H. Chapman returned from hospital.

Pleasant   FRIDAY 16

Fifteen or twenty deserters from U.S. Army said to have taken the oath of allegiance to Confederate Government.

Surgeon from 5th Corps takes room at Libby.

Formed in four ranks and [abbreviation illegible: ?re^d] one hour this evening for punishment—waste of tallow.

Very fine   SATURDAY 17

Bacon issued in lieu of beef. Beans short; twelve rations.[22]

Paid $1 for week's subscription to "Enquirer." The mess do not care to continue the subscription.

Cloudy   SUNDAY, SEPTEMBER 18, 1864   Pleasant
    Flag-of-truce boat expected.
    Wrote to B. F. Otis.

Cloudy   MONDAY 19 Pleasant   Cloudy
    Roll-call by name.
    Commenced "Dream Life," by D.G.M.[23]
    Rice issued in lieu of beans.
    Lieut. Sage sent to hospital.
    Twelve cavalry officers admitted.
    Capt. Cook assigned to Mess [No.] 7.
    Cool night.

Cloudy, cool   TUESDAY 20   Cloudy but pleasant
    Flag-of-truce boat arrived.
    Three officers from Lynchburg.

Cloudy   WEDNESDAY 21   Cloudy
    Breakfast, 3:30 P.M. Dinner, ditto.
    Heavy rain during night.

Rainy, cloudy   THURSDAY 22   Cloudy
    Have we an impostor among us? One who professes to have
ascended the ladder which Jacob saw in his dream, and yet knoweth not the name and possesseth not knowledge of the third
round, "Charity"?[24] [Words erased.]

Rainy   FRIDAY 23   Rainy
                    [No entry]

Cloudy but pleasant   SATURDAY 24
    About forty commissioned officers left Libby this A.M.;
mostly from hospital.

Symbolical: ragged, lousy and half-starved sentinel with crutch, obliged to pause when he "looks up."

Cold night.

Cold and clear   SUNDAY, SEPTEMBER 25, 1864

Shadows lengthen.

Regular afternoon entertainment outside: colored individual repelling onslaught of Libby pups. Manager and proprietor of pups, [?*Dick*] T[?urner] and Adjutant Latouse [Latouche].

Night cold.

Clear, very pleasant   MONDAY 26

[No entry]

Clear and pleasant   TUESDAY 27

Lieut. Fitch sent to hospital.

Have we a selfish man among us? Aye! A hog, who dwelleth within himself and liveth much off others. [Words erased.]

Clear and pleasant   WEDNESDAY 28

Have we a noble, generous soul among us? A man? Aye! In Gen. Hayes, who has the respect of all men.

Very pleasant   THURSDAY 29

Heavy and rapid cannonading in direct of D.B. Much ex Gen. tu ou Ala bell rung. C an [*or,* C arr] [?d] t B ar. Cit all st to fr.[25]

About fifteen c o o col t ar[d] and put in c.[26]

[*Lieut.*] Broughton played sick and went to hospital.[27]

Cloudy   FRIDAY 30   Cloudy

"Whig"[28] the only paper published this A.M.

The Confederates are much troubled and there is hurrying to and fro.

Heavy firing heard in direction of Drury's [=*Drewry's*] Bluff.[29]

Rainy   SATURDAY, OCTOBER 1, 1864

Coming events cast their shadows before. What is coming, an exchange or a change?

Rainy   SUNDAY 2

3 A.M., ordered to "pack up"—minus blankets, plates and cups; were marched across the James; and took a train of box cars at Manchester for the South, destination unknown.

Haversacks with "three days' rations" were given us: three square inches corn-bread and ten or twelve ounces meat.

On the road, officers disposed of watches, rings, hats and caps for seemingly fabulous sums in bluebacks.[30]

Sunshine and rainy   MONDAY 3   Rainy

Remained Sunday night at Clover Station;[31] slept in car.
Breakfast on corn-bread.
Apples bought at $1 and $2 per dozen.
Capt. Kinslee [Kinsley] sold meerschaum pipe for $200, and gave me $50 for use of mess, in case we become separated.

Sunshine and clouds   TUESDAY 4   Very warm and pleasant

Arrived at Greensboro, N.C., 3:30 o'clock [P.M.]. Bivouacked in pine grove. Kind treatment received from citizens and North Carolina troops. Found friends who proved to be "brothers"[32] and furnished me with food. J. B. Hobson, 1st N.C. Sharpshooters, gave me nice warm bread and bacon.

Fine   WEDNESDAY 5

Breakfast of steak and biscuits by a "brother."
Condemned hard-bread issued, and cakes[33] for officers.
Arrived at Salisbury[34] at dark. Lodged in fourth story of cotton factory. Attempt by scoundrelly deserters in third story to enter hall and rob officers, failed.
Quite unwell.

Cloudy, rainy   THURSDAY 6   Cloudy

Through influence of Gen. Hayes, officers moved from quarters in hall and now occupy log houses in yard.

Messes Nos. 1, 8, 18 and 6 in "No. 2," very warm and comfortable quarters.

"Found" dipper, knife and fork. A "brother" gave me a bunk, quilt and blanket, and table.

Capt. Conley and I bunk together.

Have use of four acres of ground; an improvement on Libby.

More prisoners arrived.

Very fine all day   FRIDAY 7   and warm

[Words erased.]

More prisoners arrived.

Pleasant   SATURDAY 8

Present, 6917 prisoners of war.

Deserters from U.S. Army in bad repute.[35] Our men will not allow them over [a] certain line. A number were obliged to run the gauntlet of kicks, cuffs etc., this A.M.

Pleasant but cool SUNDAY, OCTOBER 9, 1864

39th Mass. and 16th Me. have bunks.[36]

Services by chaplain.

Someone says: "Restraint from *ill* is the *best* kind of *freedom*."

Very cold night.

Very pleasant   MONDAY 10

Hugh C[letters illegible]y [Conway] detached as orderly.[37]

Sixty-seven commissioned officers arrived during the night. Among them was Capt. Thomas J. C. [C. J.] Bailey, 17[th U.S.] Infantry, and Capt. Dean, 31st Me.

Hear that Col. Tilden was killed the 20th![38]

No soup.

Night very cold.

TUESDAY 11

Breakfast, 7 A.M., bread; extra side-dish of rice soup.

Adjt. of Post introduced a citizen to Gen. Hayes, and he was received with a quiet dignity truly admirable.

Capt. Conley sold his gold M[asonic] pin for $30 Confed. No soup.

Received of Sergt. J. H. Frain $5 [U.S.]; paid $5 [U.S.] to sutler for cotton shirt.

Very pleasant   WEDNESDAY 12

Five enlisted men reported to have died in the grounds last night. This proves to be worse than Belle Isle.[39]

Enlisted men receive one-half loaf bread per day and water insufficient to quench thirst.

Two enlisted men died last night on grounds.

Enlisted men are assured that they will be paroled soon; told, no doubt, to keep them quiet.

Very pleasant   THURSDAY 13

Five enlisted men said to have died last night.

Breakfast, bread and meat, 7 A.M. Supper, 1:30 [P.M.], rice soup. Our rations are very good, and, if served regularly, are sufficient to keep the officers in good health.

Pleasant all day   FRIDAY 14

Two enlisted men died last night.

Breakfast, 8 A.M. Saved ration over.

Authorities make many fair promises and assure us of as good treatment as Confederate prisoners receive in U.S.

Rumor that men are to be paroled within ten days. Poh!

Very pleasant   SATURDAY 15

Three enlisted men died last night.

From gamblers and extortioners, from incarnations of selfishness, from bugs in beans and various worms, from strong stench and lice, from Dick Turner[40] and other filth: good Lord, deliver us!

"Think not of the morrow, for sufficient unto this day is the evil thereof."

SUNDAY, OCTOBER 16, 1864

Lieut. Davis shot dead by guard.[41]
Eight enlisted men died last night.
Services by chaplain.
[Words erased.]

Very warm and pleasant   MONDAY 17

Six enlisted men died last night.
Sorghum issued this morning in lieu of meat.
[Words erased.]

Very pleasant   TUESDAY 18   Signs of rain

Sorghum issued instead of meat.
P t e d b g^d in com^n of Lieut. Gardner.[42]
Diligent inquiry by officials for Lieut. G.
Lieut. G. cannot be found.
Cool and damp night.

Warm and pleasant   WEDNESDAY 19

Report of capture of Petersburg, sixty-five guns.[43]
Sheridan [in con]junc[tion with] Grant.[44]
Five hundred enlisted men arrived from Danville.[45]
Meat issued.
Left Salisbury at 5 P.M. for Danville.

Cold and cloudy   THURSDAY 20

Arrived at Danville at 10 P.M.
Sixteen commissioned officers missing; escaped from train.
Took rooms at Prison No. 3, in second and third story. Mess

No. 6 in upper room, which is much the warmest; tinned roof draws the sun.

Our room is like Libby, only more so. Very uninviting. Our fare [*is*] such as I imagine State's Prison convicts live upon; to wit, coarse corn-and-cob bread and much water at 7 or 8 or 9 A.M.; boiled beef at 12 M.; very poor and very thin black bean soup at 2, 3 or 4 P.M.

Have felt very unwell all day; severe cold and dizziness.

Pleasant   FRIDAY 21   Pleasant

Enjoyed a lengthy conversation with Capt. Stewart on the subject of religion. [*The*] Capt. is a firm Calvinist and predestinarian, of good sense and well informed, but [*he*] fails to convince me in his theory. Seems as though I should be very unhappy did I believe [*in*] it. Having a strong desire to be a consistent Christian, I find much comfort in Christ's sermon on the mount and in [*the*] 13th, 14th and 15th chapters [*of*] John; and [*I*] feel chilled when Capt. Stewart tells me that God foreordained individuals to salvation before they were born. Seems as though I had nothing to base a hope upon. I believe the Capt. to be a good man. Possibly I may not understand him.

Our condition as prisoners and officers is humiliating enough without our becoming aware of the presence among us of thieves and villainous scoundrels in U.S. uniform, individuals disgracing not only the Government they represent and the position they hold, but humanity itself. A man of any morals or sensibilities cannot but be thoroughly and perceptibly disgusted with his associates who steal the meagre ration of a brother officer while he sleeps, steal the blanket from a sentry, buy bread under a false name in the night, cheat the sutler of $28, try to buy whiskey by a lie. The true character of man is here exhibited: selfishness in its meanest and most disgusting aspect. [Words erased.]

Gen. Hayes quite unwell.

Cloudy and cold   SATURDAY 22   Raw day
                           [No entry]

SUNDAY, OCTOBER 23, 1864
Wrote to Mother and Julia.
Very fine and appropriate remarks by chaplain.

Cloudy   MONDAY 24   Fair
                           [No entry]

Very fine all day   TUESDAY 25
     Quite unwell this night.
     Hugh and I boiled a little rice which we brought from Salisbury. Gave the Gen. [*Hayes*] a plateful, and he insisted on presenting me with a piece of butter to eat on two nice white biscuit and sweet potato; also a pickle; all of which I divided around. They were indeed luxuries and the sweetest morsels I ever tasted. [Words erased.]

Cloudy   WEDNESDAY 26
     Poor molasses issued at 12 M. in lieu of meat.

Pleasant during   THURSDAY 27   the day
     [Words erased.]
     Heavy rain during night.

Cloudy   FRIDAY 28   Fair
     The Confederates, having compassion on our bowels (or being short of corn cobs), improve the corn-bread by adding one part flour!
     "Moral" much improved; "physical" obliged to assume a horizontal position and practice self-denial: that is, deprive my stomach of its legitimate rations.

Had a very interesting conversation with Chaplain Emerson on predestination. He explained the theory as taught by Calvinists, but does not subscribe to it, being a good, wholesome N[ew] E[ngland] Methodist.

Pleasant   SATURDAY 29

Many rumors of an exchange. Hope very strong among many, without foundation. Doubtless January, 1865, will see us exchanged. Do not anticipate a release without anticipating a certain passage in Scripture: "Put not your trust in Princes." I cannot believe [*that*] the Administration which is so solicitous of the welfare of 150 colored soldiers[46] will forget the 8000 sufferers at Salisbury. It is hoped that politics will be secondary.

Quite unwell all day.

Very pleasant   SUNDAY 30   Fine atmosphere

"Physical" much improved; had a rice broth for breakfast.

Feel mighty hungry; hungry all the time. Dreamed of home last night. Of home! Luxuries are always appreciated most when lost to us. The better portions of a farmer's swill-pail would indeed be luxuries [*here*]. The most valuable "friendship" to a man in prison is that bought with money or obligation.

Services by Chaplain Emerson, who says [*that*], being indebted to the Confederates for nothing, we have no right to sink our "moral" to a level with our surroundings.

[Words erased.]

Quite unwell.

Very pleasant   MONDAY 31

Again are our carnal desires remembered and our stomachs much astonished with a ration of corn-and-flour bread.

Capt. John Daley [Daly], 104th N.Y., tried by "vig[ilance] com[mittee]" for insulting Col. Sprague with abusive and obscene language.[47]

Guard cheated out of $10 by a thug in U.S. uniform.

Sights which I don't like to see: "Eagles" and "Leaves"[148] squatting on the ground and blowing a splinter fire under a pint dipper full of boiling corn-bread or "mush."

"Many a one digs his grave with his teeth." No chance for it in "No. 3" [Prison No. 3].

Pleasant   TUESDAY, NOVEMBER 1, 1864

Unwell.

A most detestable soup was issued today: beeves' head, lights, liver, feet and paunch all boiled in. A part of the paunch with hay on it was taken from a pailful! [Words erased.]

Judging from the tone of conversation of officers, I am of the belief that we had better be exchanged by January, 1865. If we are forgotten by an Administration we have perilled our lives to sustain, what will follow?

"All's well that ends well." I've seen the last of my bread, and now where is the application?

Rainy   WEDNESDAY 2

"Human sympathy!" What a humbug! Have been sick for ten days, and, being prohibited the use of my rations in order to be cured, gave them away. I have lived on three spoonfuls of rice a day, boiled in a quart of water. My God, what should I have done, had I not had the rice!

I never suffered so with hunger before; and yet there are men (?) who lie near me with plenty of money and an abundance to eat. Capt. [name erased], —st Me., with plenty of money and haversack full of apples, sits beside me eating a dish of boiled bread and butter, turns round and asks me "how I am, this morning," when he knows I am almost starved and suffering for a little of his abundance! That is sympathy!

Hugh, my servant, tried to buy a few biscuits of an officer who had five dozen, but he wanted them all for his own use.

Hugh earns a few dollars washing clothes, and offers to buy me something to eat.

How long, oh, how long!

Assuredly, the way to a man's heart is through his stomach. I feel much more charity since I put away a heap of rice.

Money may be the root of all evil, but oh, for a few golden sorrows!

Capt. Stewart (I knew he was a Christian) just gave me $5. Thank God for all His mercies!

I am much better today.

Double meat ration today! We consider it a mistake.

Rainy   THURSDAY 3

Rumors of an exchange.

Reported that slaves who had been returned to their masters were being got together by Government for an exchange. [Words erased.]

Cloudy   FRIDAY 4

Feel quite well, with a heart full of thankfulness to our Father for His merciful kindness.

Breakfast on corn-bread and cod.

[Words erased.]

Cold, fair   SATURDAY 5

Last night, about 2 A.M., sentinel discovered hole leading under prison and sounded alarm.[49] Roll-call: all present. Money and watches taken from officers.

P.M. Money restored, 1 [$1] Confederate for 1 [$1] U.S.

Capt. Bailey joined mess.

Seventy commissioned officers arrived. Among them is Gen. Duffea [Duffié].

Hostages ordered away, Manning from Maine[50] among them; sent to Richmond and placed in cells.

I am sick and hungry and can borrow no money, hire no money, beg no money; neither can I find the virtue called charity. [Words erased.]

Cold, fair   SUNDAY, NOVEMBER 6, 1864

Breakfast, 8 A.M.; corn-bread and salt cod.

Ice made last night, one-eighth inch.

Services by chaplain, 2:30 P.M.

Messes Nos. 1, 8, 18 and 22 purchased [a] cook-stove and set it up this A.M. I must own that my mouth waters for some of the luxuries brought in. 'Tis hard to relish dry corn-bread and water and salt fish while one's neighbor is eating sweet potatoes and butter, boiled lamb, etc. Ah, money, money!

Cloudy   MONDAY 7

Codfish issued.

Arrival of three officers from Salisbury.

Three hundred enlisted men have taken the oath of allegiance [to the Confederate Government]. The loyal boys stripped the U.S. uniform from some of them.

Capt. James Dean, 31st Me., sent to hospital; sore throat.

Present, 387 commissioned officers.

> "Though in the paths of death I tread
> With gloomy horror overspread,
> My steadfast heart shall fear no ill:
> For thou, O Lord, art with me still."

Man has no friend in man. God alone is man's friend. He alone can save.

Had a very pleasant dream of home last night.

Cloudy   TUESDAY 8   Rain

Codfish issued.

Votes cast for President and Vice-President at 10 A.M. Lincoln and Johnson, 267; McClellan, 91. Electioneering quite brisk all the morning. Much useless discussion, as usual.

'Tis said that Lieut. [name erased], 52d N.Y., took the oath of allegiance to the Confederate Government yesterday—a loss of one on the copperhead ticket.

Our halls are 38 × 80 feet; upper room has —— men,[51] giving 15¾ square feet per man.

Reported that Lieut.-Col. Smith (son of Gov. Smith)[52] takes command of military prisons. It is believed our condition will be perceptibly improved under him.

Capt. Boyce [Boice] of New Jersey[53] gave me reason to call him a commissioned hog, a traitor, and a scoundrel (under certain circumstances by himself allowed). [Words erased.]

It requires a well trained and balanced mind to endure such a degrading life as this without a murmur. To study such human nature as stays here, and [to] bear with it, requires Christian fortitude—more than I possess.

Cloudy   WEDNESDAY 9   Rain

Again is the heart and stomach of the captive made glad by wheat-bread. Our bowels yearn for the flesh-pots of Egypt.

Confederates can't prevent "happy anticipations" or pleasant dreams of retaliation.

'Tis said that "nations weep for fallen heroes." Wonder where the Government keeps her museum for pocket-handkerchiefs?

[Words erased.]

No meat today.

Rainy   THURSDAY 10

Breakfast, 8 A.M.: corn-bread and water.

I am faint from hunger and compelled to lie down. Should my friends at home hear of this, they wouldn't believe it. I think if the Com[missioner] of Exchange were compelled to live on our rations, an exchange would be made at once. God grant that our Government be human and relieve us from indignities and suffering; us, but more especially the enlisted men at Salisbury.

An officer stole a pair of boots last night and sold them to the guard for $10; second ins[*tance of this*].

Meat issued.

I am unhappy today, for I have not been good or kind. It is so very hard to go hungry while those who were fed by my money in Libby are now having luxuries and offer me not a morsel. I am glad that they have been fortunate in obtaining the money, but [*I*] feel hurt at the selfishness of human nature. I always thought that there was more brotherly love among men.

P.M. Lieut. Hanson just gave me $10, saying 'twas in return for my kindness to him in Libby when he had no money, [*and*] that I could have more soon. Thank God that human nature is redeemed! I was very glad to receive the money, but happy that Lieut. Hanson had not disappointed me in his character; happier than I've been for days.

Fair   FRIDAY 11

And one day nearer the end, one day nearer home, one day nearer eternity.

Great excitement over an item in Richmond "Enquirer" stating that arrangements had [*been*] made for an exchange of all prisoners in the Southern and Gulf Departments, which fact led the editor to believe that a general exchange would follow soon.

Capt. Bailey received $25 for watch, promise of butter, etc.

Enlisted men ordered away from No. 3 in answer to petition of some officers in second room, who were disgusted with speculating carried on by Lieut.-Col. M—— and others through the enlisted men. Hugh, although a good fellow, was obliged to go with the others. I had $8 and gave him $5. Capt. Bailey gave him $5.

Capts. Bailey and Conley sleep under my quilt with me; a scant covering, yet we are quite comfortable. We share all we possess. Capt. Bailey is a generous and kind-hearted man, and much liked. I think he is a true friend to one he loves. Capt.

Conley makes the most of everything and complains not at anything.

'Tis 11 o'clock and I have finished cooking a dipper of rice for our breakfast by holding the dish against the stove. A few are collected around the stove to keep warm, not having blankets to sleep under. The night is the only quiet we have, and then 'tis only comparatively so, for the snoring and grunting can't be beaten. Occasionally a deep oath or a loud curse will be heard because someone's bones ache, someone is cold, or one has pulled the coverlid off from his mate. The conversation around the stove is peculiarly interesting at times, showing to good advantage the gross ignorance of officers in the U.S. A[rmy]. The principal topic of conversation is victuals. We can't keep our minds from this all-important subject of food. Have had a good smoke and now will go to bed—go to bed!

Cloudy   SATURDAY 12

Hear that Lincoln is elected, that [*a majority of the*] 5th Army Corps went [i.e., *voted for*] McClellan, that 10,000 letters have arrived for us!

Breakfast, 8 A.M.: corn-bread and water; side-dish of rice for three.

Have we a thief among us? Lieut. —— accuses Lieut. ——, Heavy Artillery, of stealing his knife and selling the same to guard. Guard identifies the Lieut.

Purchased five pounds rice and one pound butter, one quart sorghum.

Capt. Bailey places money in my hands for disposal, to be shared with [*by*] him, Capt. Conley and myself.

Cold   SUNDAY, NOVEMBER 13, 1864   Fair

Rumor that all prisoners captured prior to August 18th will be exchanged within two weeks. Glorious news, but not reliable, as it came through [name erased].

'Twas intensely cold last night. I was compelled to walk the floor to keep warm.

Fair   MONDAY 14

Learn from Richmond paper that Lincoln received 208 electoral votes, and McClellan 29; that 1,000,000 men had been called for![54]

Meat issued today.

Letters not yet distributed.

Lieut. Chapman and I bet with Capts. Bailey and Conley a good supper (wines and liquor excluded) that we would spend New Year's Day in the Rebel States.

Cloudy   TUESDAY 15

A number of officers who love their stomachs have sold their uniform coats and appear out in "grey." One officer tried to sell his shoulder straps!

The guard carry on a brisk and profitable business with officers having money; supply them during the night with all kinds of meats and vegetables and bread, etc., at enormous prices. Rice, [sold] outside at 40 cents, they sell for $1.50 to $2 per pound; biscuit, $3.50 to $4 per dozen; bacon, $6 to $9 per pound.

Capt. Boyce [Boice], N.J. Cavalry, joined mess.

Fair   WEDNESDAY 16   Cloudy

Like every day, an irregular program of cooking, swearing, eating and smoking. We lie down to get up and get up to lie down. Propensity for stealing continues strong in a few scoundrels. Lice continue to increase.

Our mess [took its turn] on police duty; swept up filth and emptied spittoons.

The last of grease! Butter expired today at 12 M. Was buried in our stomachs amid the ruins of broken corn. We parted with it in tears and sighed an appropriate adieu.

"Money is no object, but time is everything," for it eats our butter, wastes our rice, wears out our clothes and covers us with vermin.

Col. Smith visited prison today and complimented us by saying that "you officers are ten times dirtier than the men," referring to rooms.

Cloudy   THURSDAY 17

Troubled much with "vapours" for the first time since I was captured.

About thirty small sticks of wood are issued to each room, giving two sticks to each mess, which is used in the yard and cookstove for cooking small pots of rice, etc., saving enough to kindle a coal fire, which lasts through the night and sometimes through the following day. Supply of coal certainly is insufficient to warm the room.

There are various kinds of "fixtures." We have some here; one in particular, a long-haired specimen of mortality [as] full of conceit as he is of lice and filth, with a countenance about as expressive as a stick, loose-built in body as in morals, exhibits his dirty phiz and unwashed hands daily from 3 A.M. to 12 Midnight on a pail in rear of stove, always there, and never tires of asking for a "chaw of terbarker." [Words erased.]

Our condition is humiliating, degrading and almost unbearable. Many are the bitter curses which hourly arise for the Confederacy.

"Nary red"[55] on which to lay my hands.

"Let not your heart be troubled. Ye believe in God, believe also in me," A. Lincoln.

Cloudy   FRIDAY 18   Rain

One more long, long weary day in thought has passed away.

"I am the way, the truth, and the life."

"If ye love me, keep my commandments."

Rainy   SATURDAY 19

Letters for commissioned officers to letter H arrived and distributed. Capt. Conley received three; not one, I.

Remainder of letters distributed. Capt. Lord received two; Lieut. Chapman, one; none, I.

Meat issued.

Lieut.-Col. Smith, commander of post, expresses it as his opinion that a general exchange will take place soon. Bah!

Rainy   SUNDAY, NOVEMBER 20, 1864

Sermon by Chaplain Emerson.

Wrote to Mother.

Flour-bread issued. Meat issued.

"If ye shall ask anything in my name, I will do it."

"Deliver me."

Rainy   MONDAY 21

Sorghum issued in lieu of meat—and a damned poor substitute [it is].

Made a pudding of rice, corn-bread and sorghum, which we find very palatable.

Third day of the storm; dark and dreary enough.

Very cold night.

Cold and cloudy   TUESDAY 22

Breakfast of corn-bread and water.

Supper, one pint of bean-water.

Very cold   WEDNESDAY 23

Fight between Capt. Harris, H.L. Cavalry, and Lieut. McGraw of Col. Rallston's [Raulston's] regiment.

"Greater love hath no man than this, that a man lay down his life for his friends." Say "country" instead of "friends."

Night very cold; and much suffering.

Cold and clear   THURSDAY 24

Thanksgiving Day in [*a*] Dixie prison. [Words erased.]

This should be a day of "humiliation, fasting and prayer, and of public thanksgiving"—so our governor says, in Maine. Did he mean to include us? And why not? Haven't we much to be thankful for: relieved of all business and so kindly cared for? Even our doors are guarded at the expense of J. Davis & Co., that none may disturb us while we worship. Lewd women are kept from our sight, that our minds may not be carnally inclined. All intoxicating drinks are prohibited, that we may not appear unseemly. [Words erased.] A Christianizing system, this. Why, we fast every day in the week, and poor old Job could not have been more deeply humiliated.

Governor Cony, we fast, we are humiliated, and we are deeply thankful that we have our being, that we are not starved to death, or shot down like brutes as were poor Davis and others at Salisbury by an idiotic sentry. We wish you knew this.

The sun rose and made bright a clear and very cold morning, and we easily imagine the happiness it shines upon in our Northern homes; upon peace and plenty, tables groaning with every luxury for those who have not [*lifted*], neither will they lift a hand to protect the land yielding them this abundance.

The sun that makes cheerful [*our*] New England homes sends through grated and smoky windows a few sallow rays, revealing the miserable, squalid and poverty-striken inmates of Prison No. 3, half-stripped and shivering while they remove the vermin that collected on their rags during the night.

The coal fire has expired, and real suffering calls from many [*of the prisoners*] deep curses and bitter lamentations at their miserable condition. Some few walked the floor all night. Others, favored with blankets, are growling because they haven't more, and many damns and curses are heaped upon the tired walker because he stumbles over some half-awakened cuss.

Later. Many are telling their happy dreams of home, of big turkeys and plum puddings, and build up bright hopes of a Christmas with those they love. Eight o'clock, and we are politely informed through our chief commissary that breakfast has come. Many are the inquiries and guesses as to the kind: "Is it corn?" "Is it wheat?" "Oh, I hope 'tis flour-bread!" After roll-call the twelve-ounce [*ration of*] coarse corn-bread is dealt out, and this with cold water is our "Thanksgiving breakfast," which we hastily swallow that we may enjoy the luxury of a smoke. Our "terbarker" seems to hold out yet.

Much to our surprise we are furnished with meat, and this is our "Thanksgiving dinner." They open their hearts and issue bean soup also, and this is our "Thanksgiving supper." The Massachusetts or left wing of our mess, having raised money by disposing of rings, etc., astonished their stomachs with a vegetable soup. The Maine wing are damned hungry at 4 P.M.

5 P.M. Capt. Bailey raises $35 Confederate by sale of ring, on the strength of which I borrow a pint of rice, buy a pint of molasses; and at 7 o'clock we eat our "Thanksgiving" and go to bed.

How the money comes in! Sold a 50-cent U.S. scrip (all I had when captured) for $3.

A happy Thanksgiving for our Chaplain Emerson: he left this morning for Richmond for exchange.

"Better is little with fear of the Lord than a great treasure and trouble therewith."

Salisb[ur]y makes a monu[men]t of shame and of the cruelty of man to man.

Cold and clear   FRIDAY 25

For the third time we are supplied with wheat-bread.

Capt. Hutchins sent to hospital.

Maj. Burns [Byrne] addressed a communication to Col. Smith in reference to boxes for officers, whether they would be received and delivered to officers by the Confederate authorities.

The same was forwarded by Col. Smith to Gen. Gardiner, who forwarded the same for information to Col. Ould, Commissioner of Exchange. Returned to Col. Hooper endorsed: "Boxes will be received from the U.S. for Federal officers (prisoners of war) and delivered. The size and weight have not been limited, but the boxes had better be as compact as possible; not too large."

'Tis said during the fight between Capt. Harris and Lieut. McGraw that Col. R—— said, "Don't part them; let them fight it out." This same colonel remarked to Col. S—— that "Euclid" was one of our oldest and best English writers! Also that "Casey's Tactics" were a combination and revision of tactics used in [the] time of Julius Caesar!

Cold and clear   SATURDAY 26

Exchange stock has an upward tendency.
Perhaps some folks like this life. *I don't.*

Cloudy   SUNDAY, NOVEMBER 27, 1864

Breakfast, 8 A.M.: corn-bread.
Dinner, 3 P.M.: meat; dessert, meat-and-vegetable soup concocted by [a] number of [our] mess.
"Whatsoever ye shall ask the Father in my name, He will give it you."

Warmer and pleasant   MONDAY 28

Seven of our mess went under guard to River Dan and washed.
Wonder if the word "exchange" can be found in rebel dictionaries.
Shook hands with Capt. Boyce [Boice] on a better acquaintance.

Warmer and pleasant   TUESDAY 29

Wheat-bread issued.

Pleasant   WEDNESDAY 30

Hungry. "Take no thought what shall we eat, what shall we drink. Your heavenly Father knoweth that ye have need of all these things."

Gen. Hayes sent to Confederate hospital.

Warm   THURSDAY, DECEMBER 1, 1864

Capt. Carroll, [5th] Maryland, shot through the hand by guard, ball coming up through floor, having been fired at an officer on second floor who accidentally spilled some water on window sill while standing near it.[56] This is the [words erased].

Warm   FRIDAY 2   Rainy

Exchange stock firm. Good news from Sherman.[57]

Cloudy   SATURDAY 3   Rain

Capt. Boyce [Boice] sent to Richmond, probably as a hostage,[58] at 6 A.M. Left [his] haversack, canteen to Capt. Bailey, and ten pounds [of] rice for "us," to be divided between five persons. The quart cup and canteen are very acceptable. Since we came to Prison No. 3, we have been minus plates and knives and forks; are obliged to eat meat from [our] hands as we sit on the floor. Our soup we eat with wooden spoons from tin cups. Many have not even cups.

One of the guards offers 11 to 1 for greenbacks. He says he has made $1000 Confederate since he came here, and he wants to get U.S. money as he intends to go through the lines [at] the first opportunity, with many others.

An intelligent Reb says the Confederacy will go under in six months; such is the [word illegible: ?opinion] outside.

Wheat-bread issued.

Wrote to Uncle Sedgwick, urging him to see Gilbreth, Morrill, and Blaine and effect my exchange.

Warm   SUNDAY, DECEMBER, 4, 1864   Fair

[No entry]

Warm   MONDAY 5   Fair

The "N[ew] I[ssue]"[59] to relieve the "O[ld] G[uard]"[60] arrived
this A.M., numbering about 300 conscripts, old and young, of
all sizes and description[s], in all styles of garb; boys of 14 and
[word illegible] of 60, to keep in bondage "we'uns" until that
o— s——— Stanton deems it practicable to release us.[61]

[Another entry under the same date says: "New Issue" arrived about 600 strong to relieve the "Old Guard," who leave
for the front tomorrow.]

The "Old Issue" have been very jubilant (outwardly) over
their "call,"[62] and deeming their "election"[63] sure, some thirty deserted last night and are now en route for the "New Jerusalem"[64]
by the shortest cut, with a pocket full of greenbacks purchased
of "we'uns" for $8 to $11 Confederate for $1 [U.S.].

S t m t d, t n a w d t d j t f o, s a t a a t f.[65] Secondly, Confederate officer visited the Yanks today; said he was "puty [pretty]
drunk," and I thought he was. Off. D and G w o l f l n — b o d —
and t w and f — s "w w def f sh s l, and t t t fut l w a s a t 'N I' a?"[66]

Have a sense of fullness peculiarly delightful and gratifying
to the material portion of Abner R. Our mess made a nice dinner
from a stew made of meat, rice and onions, thickened with bread.

Federal Congress assembles today. We anxiously await the
coming of the President's Message, expecting his views regard-
ing a general exchange of prisoners. Our only hope of release
from this most degrading life is in the people and through their
Representatives in Congress. God grant that the dictates of humanity will bring about the desired object at once and release
the enlisted men.

Wheat-bread issued.

Trade with guard stopped.

Warm   TUESDAY 6   Fair

Exchange stock remains firm.

The stomach has no ears.

Sufficient unto this day is the evil thereof.

Some rain   WEDNESDAY 7

Exchange stock dull.

Capt. Bailey sold canteen for five pounds [of] rice.

Enlisted men arrived from East Tennessee.

Sentry very much demoralized, heartsick of war, feels for family. Says there are three classes in the South: landowners and slaveholders, middle class able to hire slaves, and the poorer class despised by all; caste strictly observed; no advantages of education except to those able to hire a private tutor. He gets $17 Confederate per month and receives nothing. Is over 50.

Crisis exp[ected] by all the "Old Guard." Boys are full of terror, and fear the Yanks.

Cold, fair   THURSDAY 8

We lie down to get up, and get up to lie down; long for night, long for day.

Feel quite unwell; lungs very sore; used croton oil.

Capt. Newton brought me a plate of pot pie, a luxury indeed.

No sleep for pain.

Six commissioned officers and 125 enlisted men arrived from East Tennessee.

Hailstorm   FRIDAY 9

Last night was forty-eight hours long!

No sleep last night.

Flour-bread issued.

Commenced storming, hail and sleet, 10 A.M.

[Words erased.]

"New Issue" relieved by citizen militia of Danville, and ordered to Staunton Bridge to repel a raiding party from Grant.[66]

Rain and snow   SATURDAY 10

Col. Rallstone [Raulston], [*24th*] N.Y. [*Cavalry*], shot in bowels by guard during the attempt of about 100 officers to break [*prison*] and escape; the unfortunate termination of a quixotic movement. Col. R[aulston] takes the blame all on himself.[67]

Warmer, cloudy SUNDAY, DECEMBER 11, 1864

Message of Abraham Lincoln received in Richmond "Whig." [Words erased.]

Exchange stock dull.

Twenty-three commissioned officers, recaptured on Tennessee line, arrived today. Escaped from Columbia, S.C.,[68] and after traveling over 400 miles and enduring great suffering, were captured on Tennessee line. Maj. Mattocks, [*1*]7th Me.,[69] Lieut. Hunt, 5th [Me.] Battery, and Capt. Litchfield, 4th Me., among the number.

Thirty [*commissioned officers*] via Richmond arrived today.

Cold, clear   MONDAY 12

Present at roll-call, 420 commissioned officers; 444 in hospital and prison.

Cloudy   TUESDAY 13

Sixth day since I applied croton oil to lungs. The blisters are still drawing.

Commenced reading "Diana of Meridor."[70]

I am very weak; growing so gradually; probably from lack of nourishment. Our rations are but just enough to keep soul and body together. I dread to go up and down stairs.

Warm, fair   WEDNESDAY 14

Intensely hungry.

Warm, cloudy   THURSDAY 15

Col. Rallstone [Raulston] died in the night.

Capt. Dean, 31st Me., with thirteen others, returned from hospital.

How are you, exchange?

Gen. Hayes returned from hospital.

Warm, cloudy   FRIDAY 16

Capt. Lord received of Gen. Hayes $50 Confederate.

Col. Smith told Maj. Ruggles that he had just received a letter stating that we should be kept here until exchanged. When?

Warm   SATURDAY 17
                      [No entry]

Warm, fair   SUNDAY, DECEMBER 18, 1864

Four months ago I was captured. Four months of suffering and starvation. Witnessed dress parade[71] and couldn't help feeling sad when I thought of my regiment, of its depletion.

Boiled potatoes issued instead of meat.

Warm, rain   MONDAY 19

Exchange stock fluctuating.

Cool, cloudy   TUESDAY 20

Exchange stock has an upward tendency, owing to Col. Smith's statement that of the 6000 prisoners to be exchanged 1200 would be taken from this post; proportion of officers, 150.

Wrote to Col. S——.

Potatoes issued, eight to a man; eight very small.

Cool, rain   WEDNESDAY 21

Capt. Bailey received of Gen. Hayes $40; Capt. Lord, $50; for benefit of and to be paid by mess of five, $1 to $3.50 in U.S. currency.

Cool and clear   THURSDAY 22

Report that 1200 prisoners [*are*] to be exchanged, one officer to ten enlisted men, within twelve days, confirmed by sergeant and officer of the day. We are all elated and expect to leave this time, sure.

Meat [*issued*].

Cold and clear   FRIDAY 23

Report that Hood has been badly whipped; lost forty pieces [*of*] artillery.[72]

Clear   SATURDAY 24

Capt. H. C. Newton sent to hospital.

Meat [*issued*].

Cloudy   SUNDAY, DECEMBER 25, 1864

Capt. Conley received his shoes from Corporal Turner; both for one foot!

Present, 2 brigadier-generals, 4 colonels, 8 lieutenant-colonels, 16 majors, 86 captains and 328 lieutenants.

Rainy   MONDAY 26

Received three boxes of hard-bread, three and one-half pieces per man, in lieu of meat.

Sold [*my*] boots for shoes and $100.

Officer of the guard reports Savannah fallen; that the garrison escaped; 7000 prisoners taken.[73]

[Tuesday, December 27, to Saturday, December 31, inclusive, no entries]

SUNDAY, JANUARY 1, 1865

Exchange looks as distant as ever.

[Monday, January 2, to Sunday, January 8, inclusive, no entries]

MONDAY 9

[*From*] December 27th to January 8th [*I*] have been quite unwell.

Our hopes have been raised that we should soon be exchanged, as Richmond papers stated that Maj. [Col.] Mulford was expected at Richmond last week to complete arrangements. Baltimore "American" stated that [Col.] Mulford would go to Richmond authorized to negotiate a cartel, etc.

TUESDAY 10

Learn that Maj. [Col.] Mulford has arrived and is now in session with Cols. Ould and Hatch [Commissioner Ould and Capt. Hatch] at Richmond. Will they agree? We are doomed to years of captivity and suffering.

WEDNESDAY 11

Capt. Bailey sent to hospital.

THURSDAY 12

Exchange stock firm.
Report that Butler has been relieved.[74]

FRIDAY 13

All impatiently waiting for result of negotiations for exchange.
Exchange stock firm.

[Saturday, January 14, to Monday, January 16, inclusive,
no entries]

TUESDAY 17

Meat has been issued but once for nineteen days. This is the fourth day we have lived on corn-bread and water.

WEDNESDAY 18

Meat issued.

THURSDAY 19

Corn-mush issued.

FRIDAY 20

Meat [*issued*].

No intelligence yet from the Commissioner of Exchange.

SATURDAY 21

Meal gruel issued.

SUNDAY, JANUARY 22, 1865

Rumor of Col. Mulford's movements still published. Chances for exchange still good.

MONDAY 23

Gen. Hayes loaned me $40 unasked.

[*Corn-*]mush [*issued*].

Col. Hartshn [Hartshorne] and Maj. Horton exchanged.

TUESDAY 24

Corn-bread [*issued*].

Received two letters from home, one from Mother, one from Emma, dated October 3d and 12th.

Private boxes arrived.

Enlisted men died: 170 O [October] 130 N [November] 140 D [December] from 1450.

Wrote to Mother.

WEDNESDAY 25

Gen. Hayes and Lieut. Lucas [Lucore] exchanged.

THURSDAY 26

Capt. Lord received of Gen. Hayes $100.

[Friday, January 27, and Saturday, January 28, no entries]

SUNDAY, JANUARY 29, 1865

Capt. Newton returned from hospital.

Peace commission sent to W[ashington]?[75]

MONDAY 30
[No entry]

TUESDAY 31

Report that exchange [*has been*] left in hands of Grant.[76]
Sermon by Hope and "Charity."

WEDNESDAY, FEBRUARY 1, 1865

Exchange stock declining.
Capt. Conley sold pipe for $75.
Capt. Conley received of B. F. Leighton and contributed to
mess, $50.

THURSDAY 2

Whole matter of exchange left to the supervision of Gen.
Grant (23d ult.).[77]

[Friday, February 3, and Saturday, February 4, no entries]

SUNDAY 5

Capt. Gregg received a letter today from Salisbury, stating
that the deaths among our men at Salisbury since October 15th
number 3000! Over one-third of [*the*] prisoners (8999); mortality at the rate of thirty per day. This information is deemed
reliable, coming from a member of Capt. G[regg's] Co[mpany]
detailed as clerk at headquarters, having access to the records.[78]

MONDAY 6

Meat has been issued since December 15th: on December
15th, 25th and 29th, January 18th and 20th; beans, two times
since January 1st. [*The*] principal and only food issued [*is*] corn-
bread at 9 A.M., and occasionally meal gruel.
    Selections made of officers to distribute clothing said to have
arrived at Richmond: Capt. Stewart, Capt. Porter and Maj.
Horan [Haurand] to go to Salisbury; Cols. Prey, Sprague and

Carl [Cols. Prey and Carle and Lieutenant-Colonel Sprague] to distribute at Danville.

TUESDAY 7

Richmond papers contain encouraging news relative to exchange. Exchange stock firm.

WEDNESDAY 8

Woolen mill burned last night.

THURSDAY 9

Store burned last night.

Lieut.-Col Hooper writes to [Capt.] Granger that Gen. Hayes has direct communication with Gen. Grant, who assures him that the exchange of prisoners will go on as rapidly as possible.

Potatoes issued. Money all gone.

FRIDAY 10

Maj. Ruggles, paymaster, U.S. A[rmy], died in hospital.

Clothing, etc., and private boxes arrived.

SATURDAY 11

Northern letters received with money in drafts, [*bills of*] exchange on London.

Received letter from Aunt Emma, [*dated*] January 27th.

Clothing issued to enlisted men and private boxes delivered.

SUNDAY, FEBRUARY 12, 1865

Sermon by Dr. Hall[79] from 2 Timothy: 1–12.[80] Very fine.

MONDAY 13

[No entry]

TUESDAY 14

19 [9?] commissioned officers sent to Richmond—Cols. 1, Capts. 4, Lieuts. 4—for exchange. Northern papers state that general exchange has been agreed upon.

WEDNESDAY 15

The welcome intelligence has at last arrived. We leave for Richmond for exchange on Friday and Saturday. Three cheers were given, and a tiger.

THURSDAY 16

Two hundred leave 17th alph^y rr. [Two hundred commissioned officers, to be taken alphabetically commencing with the letter "A," are to leave by railroad.] Ordered to be in readiness to leave for Richmond at 6 A.M. 17th.[81]

No sleep tonight, either.

FRIDAY 17

All [? *left at one time*].
Left Danville 12 midnight.

SATURDAY 18

Arrived Richmond 2 P.M. Quartered in Libby. Capt. Conley and I slept in the same place as in September last.

SUNDAY, FEBRUARY 19, 1865

Libby. Enjoyed the luxury of hot coffee milked and sugared, the first for six months. Corn-bread and corned beef issued at 9 A.M. Ration smaller than ever: two ounces.

Signed parole.

MONDAY 20

[No entry]

TUESDAY 21

About eighty officers left this morning with sick from hospital.

We go tomorrow morning.

WEDNESDAY 22

Left the Southern hell at 8 A.M. Placed our feet on God's soil near Cox's Landing [*at*] 10 A.M. Got sight of Stars and Stripes at Aiken's Landing at 11:30 [A.M.] Left Aiken's Landing in [*the steamer*] "George Leary" at 1:30 P.M.[82] Ham, white bread, and coffee issued; [*also*] a half-ration [*of*] whiskey.

THURSDAY 23

Arrived Annapolis 7 A.M. Quartered at Building 6, Co. K, Room 2, Naval School Barracks.

FRIDAY 24

Received of Maj. Wilson, U.S. A[rmy]. paymaster, $233 for months of December and January.

CASH ACCOUNT

DATE (1864)		[DOLLARS CENTS]
Aug. 25	1 pipe and stem: clay	.50
	1 tooth-brush	2.50
	1 pack cards	12.00
	1 loaf bread	1.00
Sept. 12	4 loaves bread	4.00
13	5 loaves bread	5.00
	18 onions	5.00
	20 peaches	5.00
	1 loaf bread	1.00
Sept. 16	2 loaves bread	2.00
17	4 loaves bread	4.00
19	2 loaves bread	2.00
20	2 loaves bread	2.00
		$46.00
Contributed to mess	. . . .	40.00
		$86.00

CASH ACCOUNT

DATE (1864)	REC'D	PAID
Aug. 18 Present from Watkins . . . $ 10.00		
Sold watch 150.00		
20 Gave Lieut. Chapman . . .		20.00
Gave Lieut. Kane		10.00
Gave friend [*Capt. Conley*] .		30.00
Contributed to mess and paid		
into treasury, Lieut. Hanson		20.00
27 Ditto		20.00
29 Ditto		20.00
31 Ditto		10.00
Ditto		20.00
Sept. 1 Ditto		10.00
6 [Received from] Lieut. French,		
94 N.Y. Vols., and gave him		
an order on B. F. Otis, $20,		
U.S. c[urrency] 130.00		
Col. Hooper (for exchanged		
$20)		130.00
Capt. Roath (107th Pa.) . . 7.00		
Tobacco and bread		7.00
Capt. X 1.00		
10 Capt. X		1.00
Col. Hooper 130.00		
11 Capt. Roath		7.00
Capt. Newton 7.00		
Capt. Newton		7.00
Lieut. Hanson		10.00
Friend [*Capt. Conley*] . . .		10.00
17 Capt. Cook		5.00
Totals $435.00		337.00

DATE (1864)		REC'D	PAID
Brought forward . . .	$435.00	337.00
Sept. 20	Capt. Black	10.00	
23	Capt. Black		10.00
Sept.	Sundries while in Libby . .		46.00
	Contributed to mess . . .		40.00
Oct. 2	Capt. Kinsley	50.00	
	Friend [*Capt. Conley*] . . .		10.00
2, 3	Food on road		20.00
4	"Etceteras"		20.00
11	Sergt. Frain, $5 [exchanged for] ($25)	25.00	
	Sutler, for shirt		25.00
13	Two pumpkin pies [bought] of guard		4.00
	Tobacco		4.00
	One plug tobacco		3.00
15	Capt. Conley	5.00	
	Sweet potatoes		4.00
17	Five apples		1.00
Nov. 3	Capt. Stewart	5.00	
	Tobacco		1.00
	Rice		3.00
	Salt		1.00
	Capt. Bailey	10.00	
	One dozen biscuits . . .		4.00
	One pint chestnuts . . .		2.00
	One pint sorghum . . .		5.00
10	Lieut. Hanson	10.00	
	Tobacco		2.00
11	Hugh Conway		5.00
	Nine apples		3.00
Totals	$550.00	550.00

DATE (1864)		REC'D	PAID
	Brought forward . . .	$550.00	550.00
Nov. 12	Capt. Bailey	20.00	
13	Five pounds rice		10.00
	One quart sorghum . . .		10.00
14	One pint sorghum	5.00	
	Salt		1.00
	Soap		1.00
24	Salt		2.00
25	Paper		1.00
	Capt. Bailey	35.00	
	Sorghum		8.00
	Ten pounds rice		20.00
	Paper and envelopes . . .		2.00
26	Flour		5.00
Dec. 1	Capt. Newton	5.00	
	One cake soap		2.50
3	Two papers tobacco . . .		2.00
	One plug tobacco		.50
8	Capt. Bailey, sale of canteen .	10.00	
	Five pounds rice		10.00
20	Capt. Lord (from Gen. Hayes)	50.00	
	Capt. Bailey	40.00	
	Rice and flour		10.00
	Tobacco		4.50
	Paper and envelopes . . .		5.00
	Ten pounds flour		18.00
	Ten pounds rice		20.00
	Rice		6.00
	Five pounds salt		2.50
24	One-half pound bacon . . .		5.50
	Five pounds flour		9.00
	Totals	$715.00	705.50

DATE (1864)	REC'D	PAID
Brought forward . . .	$715.00	705.50
Dec. 26 Adjt. Small, sale of boots . .	100.00	
Six spools thread		4.00
28 Ten pounds flour		20.00
Ten pounds rice		20.00
One-quarter pound pepper .		7.00
Capt. Kinsley		10.00
Col. Hartshorne		10.00
Capt. Stewart		5.00
One pint sorghum		5.00
Soap		.50
Tobacco		4.00
(1865)		
Jan. 4 Bacon		2.00
Onions		1.00
Salt		1.00
Five pounds rice		10.00
Five pounds flour		10.00
11 Adjt. Small (from Capt. Cook)	10.00	
Turnips and potatoes . . .		2.00
Salt		1.60
Tobacco		5.00
17 Adjt. Small, sale of [word il-legible]	10.00	
18 Tobacco		2.50
Rice		4.65
Capt. Trull (for tobacco) . .		1.00
Tobacco		3.00
24 Adjt. Small (from Gen. Hayes)	40.00	
Five pounds rice		10.00
Two pounds meal		3.00
Totals	$875.00	847.75

DATE (1865)			REC'D	PAID
	Brought forward . . .		$875.00	847.75
Jan.	24	Lieut. Hanson (for tobacco) .		2.00
	25	Two dozen apples		5.00
		One quart sorghum . . .		11.25
		Adjt. Small (for tobacco) . .		5.00
	26	Capt. Lord (from Gen. Hayes)	100.00	
		Two dozen apples		5.00
		Four quarts beans		12.00
		One quart sorghum . . .		11.25
		One pound pork		10.75
		Tobacco		2.50
		Five pounds flour		15.00
	30	Capt. Conley	50.00	
		Pork		14.00
	31	Capt. Conley	50.00	
		Five pounds flour		15.00
		Beans		7.50
Feb.	1	One piece soap		2.00
		One-half pound bacon . . .		5.00
		Seven pounds rice		14.00
	2	Four pounds dried apples @		
		$2.25		9.00
		One paper smoking tobacco .		2.00
		One pound pork		12.00
		One quart sorghum . . .		15.00
		White bread		7.00
		Fifteen onions		10.00
		Four plugs tobacco		2.00
		Four quarts beans @ $2.00 .		8.00
	4	Cut tobacco		1.50
	5	Capt. Conley	2.00	
		Totals	$1077.00	1051.50

DATE (1865)	REC'D	PAID
Brought forward . .	$1077.00	1051.50
Feb. 5 Five pounds flour		15.00
6 One-half peck potatoes . .		5.00
Two turnips		2.00
7 Thread		4.00
13 Capt. Conley	40.00	
Tobacco		2.00
Two dozen apples		5.50
Five pounds rice		10.00
One-half peck potatoes . .		7.00
Salt		2.00
Soap		1.75
14 Two pounds flour @ $3.60 .		7.20
15 Capt. Conley	50.00	
16 One-fourth pound pepper . .		5.00
Capt. Conley		10.00
Capt. Lord		10.00
Bread		20.00
17 Adjt. Mathews	5.00	
20 Capt. Lord	10.00	
Col. Hartshorne	20.00	
21 Capt. Conley	10.00	
Capt. Conley		10.00
Tobacco		20.00
Gave hostage belonging to 94[*th N.Y.* ?]		20.00
	$1212.00	1207.95

NOTES TO THE DIARY

[1] Colonel Charles W. Tilden, 16th Maine, captured on August 19th, escaped, and rejoined his regiment on the morning of the 22d.

"A correspondent of the New York *Herald* thus describes the experience of Colonel Tilden:

" 'Having on a light-colored and broad-brimmed Kossuth hat and a rubber overcoat was unquestionably his salvation. The fact that it rained nearly all the time he was a prisoner gave no look of strangeness or ground of suspicion in his wearing a rubber coat, while his broad-brimmed beaver gave him the air and tone of a true Southerner "to the manor born." At all events, he walked through the streets and public places of Petersburgh, picking up much valuable information, which he has since imparted to the commanding general. When he first struck the rebel lines, with a view to get through them, he was fortunate enough, in his place of concealment and observation, to hear a rebel soldier remark to another, "The Yanks will have hard work getting through our three lines of battle here, but below, where there is only a thin skirmish line, it ain't so safe, I reckon." The Colonel thought he would take a look after that thin skirmish line, and he found it. The heavy storm and dense darkness of the night enabled him to get through the line. He did not get through any too quick, for two shots were fired at him while between the enemy's skirmish line and ours. He came upon the pickets of his own brigade—a piece of good fortune, pleasing, agreeable, and quite as remarkable as agreeable.'

"The correspondent omitted to compliment Lieutenant Davies in seconding all the Colonel's movements."—A. R. Small, *The Sixteenth Maine Regiment in the War of the Rebellion, 1861–1865* (Portland, 1886), pp. 202–203.

[2] The members of Mess No. 6 at the time of its organization, August 20th, 1864, were the following officers from two regiments of the 1st Brigade, 3d Division, 5th Corps.

16th Maine	*39th Massachusetts*
Capt. John D. Conley	Capt. Frederick R. Kinsley
Capt. Joseph O. Lord	Capt. John Hutchins
1st Lieut. and Adjt. A. R. Small	1st Lieut. Charles W. Hanson
1st Lieut. William H. Broughton	1st Lieut. Luke R. Tidd
2d Lieut. Wilmot H. Chapman	2d Lieut. George A. Barker
2d Lieut. Atwood Fitch	2d Lieut. Charles H. Chapman

[3] Julia Maria Fairbanks, of Wayne, Maine, whom the diarist married on April 8th, 1865.

[4] Major Thomas P. Turner, commanding the Confederate military prisons at Richmond, Virginia.

[5] "In the Libby the prisoners were not allowed to remind the chivalry that John Brown's soul was marching on, or to suggest that the body of Jeff Davis would yet hang from a sour apple tree."—Henry S. Burrage, "Reminiscences of Prison Life at Danville, Va.," *War Papers Read before the Commandery of the State of Maine, Military Order of the Loyal Legion of the United States,* Vol. III (Portland, 1908), p. 155.

[6] Richmond *Enquirer.*

[7] Prices in Confederate currency.

[8] A cap acquired by the diarist after he was captured. His hat, and other articles, had been taken from him.

[9] *Diedrich Knickerbocker's History of New York,* by Washington Irving.

[10] *The Cross and Crown: A Poem,* by Joseph H. Martin.

[11] *The Athelings,* by Mrs. Margaret Oliphant; a novel.

[12] Captain McClellan can hardly have left by the flag-of-truce boat at this time; according to the prison record, he was captured August 18th, 1864, received at Libby Prison August 20th, sent to Salisbury October 2d, returned to Libby Prison February 18th, 1865, and paroled February 22d.

[13] United States currency.

[14] *Henry Smeaton: A Jacobite Story of the Reign of George the First,* by G. P. R. James; a novel.

[15] Sherman had taken possession of Atlanta on September 2d.

[16] Paced the floor that distance.

[17] *Wildflower,* by the author of *The House of Elmore* (Frederick William Robinson); a novel.

[18] This letter of General Butler's to Judge Ould, the Confederate agent of exchange, may be found in the *Official Records,* Ser. II, Vol. VII, pp. 678–691.

[19] Richmond *Examiner.*

[20] "There was little or no glass in the windows, and the old bagging which had been nailed up to keep out the cold and wind only partially fufilled that duty."—Henry S. Burrage, "My Capture and What Came of It," *War Papers Read before the Commandery of the State of Maine, Military Order of the Loyal Legion of the United States,* Vol. I (Portland, 1898), p. 7.

[21] Perhaps meaning: Lieutenant Broughton borrowed a certain sum of money in United States currency and exchanged it for $70 in Confederate currency; Captain Lord sold his watch for $12 in United States currency and exchanged the $12 for $84 in Confederate currency; Lieutenant Sage borrowed $20 in United States currency, exchanged it for $120 in Confederate currency, and furnished the mess treasury.

[22] Twelve rations issued, three fewer than the number of officers then in Mess No. 6.

[23] *Dream Life: A Fable of the Seasons,* by Ik. Marvel (Donald G. Mitchell).

[24] ". . . that theological ladder which Jacob, in his vision, saw, reaching from earth to heaven—the three principal rounds of which are denominated Faith, Hope and Charity; which admonish us to have faith in God, hope of immortality, and charity for all mankind."—Monitorial work of the first degree of symbolic masonry. The diarist was a Freemason.

[25] Perhaps meaning: Heavy and rapid cannonading in the direction of Drewry's Bluff. Much excitement. General turn-out. Alarm bell rung. (Next sentence problematical; something about Butler's army?) Citizens all start towards front.

Troops of the 18th Corps, General Ord commanding, of Butler's Army of the James, took by assault on this day the Confederate fortification known as Fort Harrison, north of the James River, roughly opposite to Drewry's Bluff on the south side of the river, and only six or seven miles distant from the listening prisoners in Richmond. Fort Harrison was part of the continuous outer line of the defenses of Richmond, and its capture by the Federals occasioned much anxiety among the Confederates. Richmond citizens turned out to help stop the thrust against the Southern capital.

[26] Perhaps meaning: About fifteen commissioned officers of colored troops arrived and were put in cells.

In accordance with Davis' proclamation of December 24th, 1862, captured Federal officers of negro troops were not treated as prisoners of war, but as felons.

[27] Perhaps Lieutenant Broughton thought that, in the event of a Federal advance on Richmond, he would stand a better chance of escaping from the prison hospital than from the prison proper.

[28] Richmond *Whig*.

[29] Confederate troops made unsuccessful attempts to recapture Fort Harrison.

[30] Confederate currency.

[31] Clover, Halifax County, Virginia, near the northern border of North Carolina.

[32] Freemasons.

[33] Cakes of rice-bread.

[34] The destination of the prisoners was the Confederate military prison at Salisbury, North Carolina.

[35] Some deserters from the Union armies were held prisoners at Salisbury. They were suspected of being spies.

[36] Prisoners belonging to these regiments, members of Mess No. 6, had bunks to sleep in.

[37] Private Hugh Conway, Company I, 16th Maine, a prisoner, was permitted to act as the diarist's orderly.

[38] Colonel Charles W. Tilden, 16th Maine, was very much alive. See note 1 above.

[39] The Belle Isle prison camp, in the James River at Richmond, had a reputation for high mortality among the prisoners, enlisted men, confined there.

[40] Richard R. Turner, inspector (or turnkey) at Libby Prison, Richmond.

[41] 2d Lieutenant John Davis, 155th New York. See the *Official Records*, Ser. II, Vol. VIII, p. 958, charge against John H. Gee, "late keeper of the rebel military prison at Salisbury," that Major Gee was responsible, by reason of his orders to the prison guards, for the death of Lieutenant Davis: "murder, in violation of the laws of war." Major Gee was acquitted of the charge.

[42] Perhaps meaning: Plan to escape discovered by guard in communication of Lieutenant Gardner.

[43] Petersburg did not fall into the possession of the Army of the Potomac until April 3d, 1865.

[44] Sheridan defeated Early at Cedar Creek on this day.

[45] From the Confederate military prisons at Danville, Virginia.

[46] On October 29th, 1864, Major Turner reported to Captain Hatch, assistant agent of exchange, that one hundred and forty-eight negro soldiers, in all, had been delivered at the prisons under his charge.—*Official Records*, Ser. II, Vol. VII, pp. 987–988.

[47] See Homer B. Sprague, *Lights and Shadows in Confederate Prisons: A Personal Experience, 1864–5* (New York, 1915), p. 88.

[48] Colonels and majors. The reference is to the insignia on their shoulder straps.

[49] Prisoners had dug a tunnel from the prison cellar to beneath a walk along which marched one of the sentries. "The engineering failed in precision," the tunnel approached too close to the surface of the ground, and the sentry fell through.—George Haven Putnam, *A Prisoner of War in Virginia, 1864–5* (ed. 3, New York, 1914), pp. 55–60.

[50] It is virtually certain that this was 1st Lieutenant William C. Manning, 2d Massachusetts Cavalry. I cannot find that any Manning from Maine was then a prisoner at Danville.

[51] Calculation from the figures here supplied gives one hundred and ninety-three men.

[52] The only Smith commanding Confederate military prisons was the one then in command of the prisons at Danville. The rumor and the Smith mentioned by the diarist seem not to have materialized.

[53] Captain Daniel R. Boice, 3d New Jersey Cavalry. They seem to have made up their quarrel; see entries of Tuesday, November 15th, and Monday, November 28th.

[54] Lincoln actually received 212 electoral votes, McClellan 21. A call for 300,000 additional troops was made on December 19th, 1864.

[55] Not one red copper; no money.

[56] Captain John Carroll, 5th Maryland, was sent from Prison No. 3 to the hospital December 1st, 1864, with a gunshot wound in his left hand, and was returned to prison quarters January 29th, 1865.

[57] Sherman was marching from Atlanta to the sea, and opposition to him was ineffectual.

[58] Captain Boice and Lieutenant W. D. Hoff, 15th West Virginia Infantry, were held as hostages in close confinement in a cell under Libby Prison in retaliation for the allegedly improper treatment of two Southerners held by the civil authorities in Western Virginia. See the *Official Records,* Ser. II, Vol. VII, pp. 1227–1228; Vol. VIII, pp. 129–130. For an account of imprisonment in a Libby cell, as a hostage, see John W. Phillips [Lieutenant-Colonel, 18th Pennsylvania Cavalry], "Experiences in Libby Prison," *War Papers and Personal Reminiscences, 1861–1865, Read before the Commandery of the State of Missouri, Military Order of the Loyal Legion of the United States,* Vol. I (St. Louis, 1892), pp. 62–65.

[59] The latest draft of Confederate conscripts; men from this.

[60] The soldiers that had been guarding the prisoners at Danville.

[61] Secretary of War Stanton thought that it would not be profitable to exchange able-bodied Confederates for prison-weakened Federal officers and men; or so some of the prisoners believed. See Albert D.

Richardson, *The Secret Service, the Field, the Dungeon, and the Escape* (Hartford, Connecticut, 1865), p. 457; George Haven Putnam, *op. cit.*, p. 89.

[62] Their call to active service.

[63] The certainty of service on the fighting line.

[64] The North.

[65] These abbreviations can be made to yield sentences; but the result, at best, is guesswork.

[66] Grant being desirous of having the railroad broken up near Gordonsville and Charlottesville, Sheridan on December 19th sent Torbert with two divisions of cavalry through Ashby's Gap in the direction of Gordonsville, while Custer moved toward Staunton with the purpose of attracting the attention of the Confederates from Torbert's column.

[67] See Putnam, *op. cit.*, pp. 50–55.

[68] The Confederate military prison at Columbia, South Carolina.

[69] For accounts of Major Mattocks' escape and recapture, see *Report of the Adjutant General of the State of Maine for the Years 1864 and 1865*, Vol. I, pp. 414–416; Charles P. Mattocks, "In Six Prisons," *War Papers Read before the Commandery of the State of Maine, Military Order of the Loyal Legion of the United States*, Vol. I (Portland, 1898), pp. 161–180.

[70] *Diana of Meridor*, by Alexandre Dumas, *père;* a novel.

[71] Saw from a prison window a dress parade of the guard. See Burrage, "Reminiscences" (as cited), pp. 51–52.

[72] Hood was defeated by Thomas at Nashville, Tennessee, on December 15th and 16th. He counted his loss in artillery at fifty-four pieces.

[73] Sherman entered Savannah, Georgia, on December 21st. The Confederate troops there, under Hardee, had left the city the day before.

[74] General Butler was relieved from command of the Department of Virginia and North Carolina (which meant, chiefly, the Army of the James; also a part in the conduct of exchange) on January 7th, 1865.

[75] The Confederate peace commissioners presented themselves on the Union lines around Petersburg January 31st; Grant received them at his headquarters at City Point the same day, and a few days later sent them to Hampton Roads, where Lincoln received them. They did not go to Washington.

[76] The subject of exchange was placed in the hands of Grant on October 15th, 1864.

[77] See note 76.

[78] See the *Official Records,* Ser. II, Vol. VII, p. 1222, report (dated

December 14th, 1864) of J. A. Fuqua, captain and assistant command-ant of post, of the average number of prisoners daily, and the average number of deaths among the Federal prisoners at this post, from October 12th, 1864, to December 12th, 1864: daily average of prisoners, 8200; daily average of deaths, 22. See also the *Official Records,* Ser. II, Vol. VIII, p. 254, report (dated February 1st, 1865) certified by Major Gee as a correct copy of the prison journal: total prisoners, October 5th, 1864, to February 1st, 1865, 10,321; largest number at hand at one time, November 6th, 1864, 8740; hospital report—died, from October 5th to October 31st, 1864, 224; in November, 761; in December, 858; in January, 748; total, 2591; burial-sergeant's report—from October 21st to October 31st, 1864, 193; in November, 917; in December, 1081; in January, 940; total, 3131; discrepancy, 540.

[79] Charles K. Hall, a Methodist clergyman of Danville.

[80] This text includes the exhortation, "Thou therefore endure hard-ness, as a good soldier of Jesus Christ," and the saying, "If we suffer, we shall also reign with Him; if we deny Him, he also will deny us."

[81] The plan of sending the officers to Richmond in two groups, at different times of the day, was abandoned. All were sent together, late Friday night. They left the prison at 10 P.M.—See Burrage, "Reminis-cences" (as cited), pp. 57–60.

[82] The paroled prisoners, taken from Richmond by boat down the James River, were put ashore on the north bank at Cox's Landing, where the river began to make a wide meander. A short march, or am-bulance ride, across the neck of the bend brought them again to the north bank of the river at Aiken's Landing, where they were taken aboard a Federal boat for the journey to Annapolis, Maryland. The scene at Cox's Landing when the diarist and his companions were put ashore there has been described by an eyewitness as follows:

"Wednesday last, Feb. 22d, was the anniversary of Washington's birthday, and a special order from the Hdqrs. of the Union army made it a general holiday. It was a rainy day. About nine o'clock in the fore-noon Quarter-Master Morrison and myself started off on horseback for Cox's landing on the James river, where the exchange of prisoners takes place every day at ten o'clock. We visited several points, and ar-rived at the landing a few moments before the rebel flag-of-truce boat, and watched its approach. It had the Confederate flag flying at the stern, and was towing a barge filled with our sick soldiers, the boat itself being a dirty affair. In a few moments more, six hundred of our men, half of them commissioned officers, including two Brigadier Generals, were on the shore; and those of them who could walk immediately started for Aiken's landing, at some distance below, where our flag-of-truce boat lay. The rest filled a long line of ambulances, and fully two hours were consumed before they were all transferred to our own boat. Such a looking set of men I never saw before, and hope never to see again. Hatless, shirtless, shoeless, wrapped in old bed-quilts of as many hues as Joseph's coat; their feet wound with rags, and many of them barefoot (and the wintry, ice-cold mud six inches deep), their clothing in tatters, their hair long and matted, dirty and unshaven, and all look-ing as pale and thin as though wasted with consumption or fever. Many were carried on board our boat on stretchers, too weak and sick to stand. . . . Just before our boat moved off, the Naval Band on one of our gunboats struck up the 'Star Spangled Banner', and the poor ema-ciated fellows tried to cheer. They were too weak to give a very loud one, but I never heard a more impressive cheer in my life."—Quotation from "a letter written at the front on Feb. 25, 1865," in S. Millett Thomp-son, *Thirteenth Regiment of New Hampshire Volunteer Infantry in the War of the Rebellion, 1861–1865: A Diary Covering Three Years and a Day* (Boston, 1888), pp. 535–536. The letter was written by 1st Lieu-tenant Royal B. Prescott, 13th New Hampshire.

INDEX

Accotink Run, slow crossing of, 18

Aiken's Landing, paroled prisoners at, 178, 288, 288 n.

Alexandria, Virginia, 13, 14, 25, 27

"All quiet along the Potomac," 26 ff.

Andrew, Governor John A., of Massachusetts, 10, 10 n.

Annapolis, paroled prisoners at, 178, 288

Antietam battlefield, 47, 110

Apple orchard near Petersburg, 152

Appomattox Court House, 180

Atlanta, fall of, 253, 253 n.

Atwood, Captain Eleazer W., 16th Maine, 195–196

Augusta, Maine, 7 ff., 112 ff., 182, 183

Averell's cavalry division, 88 n.

Ayer, Captain John, 16th Maine, 52, 57, 70

Ayres's division, 154

Bailey, Captain Thomas C. J., 17th United States Infantry, 112, 170, 175, 259, 266, 269, 270, 271, 275, 277, 279, 281, 283, 291, 292

Balkam, Chaplain Uriah, 16th Maine, 124, 127, 128, 129, 142, 189, 201

Baltimore, 9, 11

Baltimore *American*, 283

Band, 83, 93, 121–123, 123, 126, 153

Baptisms in the Potomac, 47–48

Barker, Lieutenant George A., 39th Massachusetts, 161, 249 n., 253, 255

Barker, Levi, 16th Maine, 71

Barney, Henry W., 3d Maine, 113–114

Batchelder, General George W., 3, 3 n.

Bates, David, 3d Maine, 22, 22 n.

Bates, Colonel James L., 12th Massachusetts, 72

Bath, Maine, 113, 114

Battle, experience of, 184

Baxter, General Henry, 126, 180

Baxter's brigade, 93, 98, 100, 101 n., 180

Bayard, General George D., 54

Beans, 196–197

Beauregard, General Pierre G. T., 17, 162, 162 n.

Beckham's artillery, 88 n.

Beecher, Lieutenant Fred H., 16th Maine, 104, 104 n.

Belcher, Captain Samuel C., 16th Maine, 136

Belle Isle, 160, 260, 260 n.

Belle Plain, 82

Ben, cook, 59, 76, 77

Benson, George T., 3d Maine, 4

Berlin, Maryland, 53, 110

Birney's division, 67

Black, Captain Samuel V., 97th Pennsylvania, 291

Blaine, James G., 9, 37, 37 n., 277

Blaisdell, George L., 3d Maine, 26

"Bloody Angle," 139, 141

"Bluebacks," 162, 258

Boice, Captain Daniel R., 3d New Jersey Cavalry, 170, 268, 268 n., 271, 276, 277, 277 n.

Boston, 10, 112

Bowdoin College, 10

Boyle, Barney, 16th Maine, 138

Bradford, Luther, 16th Maine, 124, 138; quoted, 102 n.

Bravery, mystery of, 70, 185

Brooks's division, 84

Broughton, Lieutenant William H., 16th Maine, 161, 170, 249, 249 n., 255 n., 257, 257 n.

Brown, John, 16, 16 n., 17

Browne, Junius Henri, New York *Tribune* correspondent, 202

Brunswick, Maine, 10, 116

Bull Run, battle of, 20 ff., 94; campaign, 18 ff.; retreat from, 23 ff.; second battle of, 42

Bull's Church (St. Margaret's Church), 144, 144 n.

Bullen, Chaplain George, 16th Maine, 48

Burnside, General Ambrose E., 57, 77, 78, 79, 130

Burnside's corps, 142

Burrage, Captain Henry S., 36th Massachusetts, 174; quoted, 250 n., 255 n.

Burt, Sergeant Edwin, 3d Maine, 8; lieutenant, 3d Maine, 21

Bush Hill, near Alexandria, 15, 25

Bushwhackers, 110

Butler, General Benjamin F., 254, 254 n., 255, 283, 283 n.

Butler's army, 161, 257 n.

Byrne, Major John, 155th New York, 275

Camp Keyes, Augusta, Maine, 112

Camp Parole, Annapolis, 179

Carle, Colonel James, 191st Pennsylvania, 151, 286

Carle's brigade, 151

Carroll, Captain John, 5th Maryland, 277, 277 n.

Casey, General Silas, 41

Cedar Mountain, 129, 129 n., 201

Centreville, Virginia, 19 ff., 94

Chadwick, Francis E., 3d Maine, 5

Chamberlain, General Joshua L., 195

Chancellorsville, Virginia, 87, 87 n.; battle of, 84 ff.; campaign, 83–93; reconnaissance made by Adjutant Small, 87–89, 88 n.

Chapel, at Mitchell's Station, 125

Chaplains: take down fence, 50; in eloquence and flight, 85; in general, 189–190

Chapman, Lieutenant Charles H., 39th Massachusetts, 161, 249 n., 254

Chapman, Lieutenant Wilmot H., 16th Maine, 110, 161, 249, 249 n., 252, 255, 271, 273, 290; quoted, 55

Chenery, George W., 16th Maine, 198

Church, Chaplain Andrew J., 3d Maine, 32

Clermont, home of Commodore French Forrest, damaged, 16; used as a hospital, 26

Clover, Virginia, 162, 258, 258 n.

Coburn, Governor Abner, of Maine, 83, 83 n.

Cold Harbor, 148, 149

Conley, Captain John D., 16th Maine, 110, 116, 129, 130, 161, 162, 164, 165, 170, 172, 173, 177, 201, 249, 249 n., 250, 255, 259, 260, 269, 270, 271, 273, 282, 285, 290, 291, 294, 295

Conway, Hugh, 16th Maine, 168, 259, 259 n., 263, 265, 266, 269

Cony, Governor Samuel, of Maine, 183, 274

Cook, Chaplain Philos G., 94th New York, 189

Cook, Captain William, 9th United States Colored Troops, 161, 253, 256, 290, 293

Cooper Shop Volunteer Refreshment Saloon, 11, 11 n.

Cooper's battery, 99 n.

Copp, William H., 3d Maine, 5

Coulter, Colonel Richard, 11th Pennsylvania, 47, 47 n., 48, 50, 51, 82 n., 102, 103, 104, 105–106, 109, 136, 138, 195; quoted, 103 n.

Coulter's brigade, 47, 51, 103, 104, 105, 107, 109, 139

Cox's Landing, paroled prisoners at, 178, 287, 288 n.

[Crane, Stephen], 185

Crawford, General Samuel W., 149, 154

Crawford's division, 131, 139, 149, 150, 154

Crediford, Oliver, 16th Maine, 71

Crowell, Baxter, 3d Maine, 23

Custer's brigade, 146

Cutler, General Lysander, 139–140

Cutler's division, 139, 146

Daly, Captain John, 104th New York, 264, 264 n.

Danville, Virginia, military prison at, 168 ff., 261 ff., 286, 287

Davies, Lieutenant Edward F., 16th Maine, 118, 249 n.

Davis, Jefferson, 162, 162 n., 163

Davis, Mrs. Jefferson, 162, 162 n., 163

Davis, Lieutenant John, 155th New York, 167, 261, 261 n., 274

Davis, Colonel Phineas S., 39th Massachusetts, 152

Day, Lieutenant John R., 3d Maine, 7
Dean, Captain James, 31st Maine, 259, 267, 281
Deering, Lieutenant George A., 16th Maine, 100
Deserters, 112 ff., 258, 259, 259 n.
Desiccated vegetables, 197
Dexter, Henry E., 16th Maine, 35
Doubleday, General Abner, 102, 103, 103 n.
Doubleday's division, 62, 68
Douglas, Stephen A., 10
Dow, Colonel Neal, 13th Maine, 32, 32 n.
Drill, 191
Drummer boy, straggler, 144
Duffié, General Alfred N., 177, 266
Dunbar, Walter, 16th Maine, 191
Dunnells, Joseph, 16th Maine, 110
Duryée's brigade, 57
Dust, 191
Dyer, George F., 16th Maine, 191

Edwards, Lieutenant George W., 16th Maine, 70
Emerson, Chaplain Joseph C., 7th New Hampshire, 174, 176, 264, 273, 275

Fairbanks, Henry N., 3d Maine, 4; quoted, 4 n.
Fairbanks, Julia Maria, 249, 249 n., 253, 263
Fairbanks, Robinson, 16th Maine, 136, 138
Farnham, Lieutenant Augustus B., 2d Maine, 7; major, 16th Maine, 39, 40, 45, 73, 74; lieutenant-colonel, 16th Maine, 80–81, 94, 111, 119, 120, 121, 124, 126, 127, 140, 147, 149, 157, 180
Farwell, Nathan A., 37, 37 n.
Fence rails, 200
Fessenden, Mrs., 124
First Corps, consolidated with Fifth, 125, 126
Fitch, Lieutenant Atwood, 16th Maine, 161, 170, 249, 249 n., 254, 257
Fletcher's Chapel, camp of 16th Maine near, 75 ff., 75 n., 78

Foraging, 51–52, 53, 55–56, 78, 197
Forrest, Commodore French, 16–17, 16 n.; quoted, 16–17
Fort Cass, 41
Fort Corcoran, 43
Fort Craig, 43
Fort Davis, 152
Fort De Kalb, 43
Fort Ellsworth, 15, 15 n.
Fort Harrison, attack on, 161–162, 257 n.
Fort McHenry, 9
Fort Mahone, 153
Fort Preble, deserters taken to, 115, 116
Fort Sedgwick, 153
Fort Tillinghast, 41, 44
Fort Woodbury, 41, 42
Foss, James C., 16th Maine, 140
Fowler, Chaplain [? J.H.], [? 33d United States Colored Troops], 174, 253, 254
Fowler, Lieutenant Nathan, 16th Maine, 136
Frain, John H., 16th Maine, 260, 291
Franklin, General William B., 62
Franklin's grand division, 61, 62, 69
Fredericksburg, Virginia, 60, 61, 141, 180; battle of, 60 ff.; campaign, 59–72
French, Lieutenant George F., 94th New York, 290
Fuqua, Captain John A., assistant commandant, military prison at Salisbury, North Carolina, quoted, 285 n.

Gardiner, Maine, 2, 2 n.
Gardiner, Major John W. T., superintendent, volunteer recruiting service, Maine, 33–34, 33 n., 35, 39, 40; and special provost marshal, Maine, 114, 115
Gardner, Lieutenant William C., 13th Connecticut, 167–168, 168, 261, 261 n.
Gardner, General William M., 276
Gee, Major John H., commanding military prison at Salisbury, North Carolina, 165, 169, 261 n., 285 n.
George, servant, 182
Gettysburg, battle of, 98 ff.; campaign, 94–109

Gibbon, General John, 55, 57, 64, 66, 67, 80, 103; quoted, 72

Gilbreth, Major Benjamin H., military storekeeper, ordnance, at Kennebec Arsenal, 277

Goff, Major Nathan, Jr., 4th West Virginia Cavalry, 252

Goler, Captain George W., 6th New York Cavalry, 161, 170, 254

Gordon, General John B., 201

Grand review, 181–182

Granger, Captain Warren, Jr., 100th New York, 286

Grant, General Ulysses S., 125, 130, 130 n., 131, 134, 147, 180, 195, 261, 280, 280 n., 285, 285 n., 286

Greensboro, North Carolina, 162, 164, 258

Gregg, Captain Henry H., 13th Pennsylvania Cavalry, 285

Griffin's division, 131; corps, 181

Griffith, Major David A., 88th Pennsylvania, 72

Growlers, 188

Grumblers, 189

Hall, Charles K., clergyman, 173, 173 n., 177, 286, 286 n.

Hall, Captain James A., 2d Maine Battery, 65, 67, 72

Hall's battery, 64, 65, 67, 72, 91

Halleck, General Henry W., 182

Hancock, General Winfield S., 102, 126

Hancock's corps, 102, 137, 181

Hanscom, Lieutenant Nathaniel, 3d Maine, 6

Hanson, Lieutenant Charles W., 39th Massachusetts, 161, 249, 249 n., 255, 269, 290, 291, 294

Harris, Captain Ethan T., 3d New Jersey Cavalry, 174, 273, 276

Hartshorne, Colonel William R., 190th Pennsylvania, 284, 293, 295

Hartsuff, General George L., 47

Hartsuff's brigade, 44, 47

Haskell, Frank W., 3d Maine, 4, 5

Hatch, Lieutenant William A., 3d Maine, 6

Hatch, Captain William H., assistant Confederate States agent of exchange, 264 n., 283

Hathaway, shirtmaker of Waterville, Maine, 5, 6

Haurand, Major August, 4th New York Cavalry, 285

Hayes, General Joseph, 165, 167, 174, 177, 251, 257, 260, 262, 263, 277, 281, 284, 286, 292, 293, 294

Heintzelman, Colonel Samuel P., 17th United States Infantry, 14–15; brigadier-general, 15

Heintzelman's division, 15, 20

Herrick, Lieutenant Henry P., 16th Maine, 70

Hesseltine, Captain Frank S., 3d Maine, 4, 5, 6, 27, 29, 32

Heth's division, 107

Hight, Captain Thomas, 2d United States Dragoons, 10

Hobson, J. B., 1st Battalion, North Carolina Sharpshooters, 163, 202, 258

Hodsdon, Adjutant-General John L., of Maine, 35, 35 n., 37, 37 n.

Hoff, Lieutenant William D., 15th West Virginia, 277 n.

Honey, 55, 198

Hood, General John B., 282, 282 n.

Hooker, General Joseph, 79, 80, 81, 86, 89, 97, 130, 134

Hooker's corps, 44

Hooper, Lieutenant-Colonel Charles H., 24th Massachusetts, 161, 276, 286, 290

Hopkins, Captain James A., 45th North Carolina, quoted, 102 n.

Hopkins, Thomas M., 16th Maine, 35, 64; quoted, 64 n.

Horton, Major Everett S., 58th Massachusetts, 284

Hospital "bummers," 187–188

Hospitals: field, near Sudley Church, 21; 3d Maine, at Clermont, 26–27; improvised military, in Alexandria, 27; division, at Smoketown, 49; field, near Fredericksburg, 68; field, near Gettysburg, 107–108; camp, 186–187

Howard, Colonel Oliver O., 3d Maine, 8, 8 n., 9, 10, 10 n., 11, 12, 13, 14, 15, 30, 31, 31 n., 32, 195; commanding brigade, 15, 16, 20, 21, 22, 24, 25, 26, 30; promoted brigadier-general, 31; major-general, 103 n.; quoted, 12, 15–16, 22

Howard's brigade, 20, 21, 22, 23, 25, 30; corps, 86, 100, 102

Humphreys' corps, 181

Hunt, Lieutenant Charles O., 5th Maine Battery, 280

Hunter's division, 19, 20

Hutchins, Captain Charles K., 16th Maine, 36, 37, 70

Hutchins, Captain John, 39th Massachusetts, 161, 249 n., 254, 275

Hutchinson, George L., 3d Maine, 115, 116

Hyde, Major Thomas W., 7th Maine, quoted, 10 n.

Jenkins, Robert, 108

Jenkins, Will, Confederate soldier, 107–108

"John Brown's Body," 86, 196, 250 n.

Johnson, Andrew, 175, 181, 182, 267

Kane, Lieutenant James H., 1st Connecticut Cavalry, 249, 250, 290

Kelly's Ford, camp of 16th Maine at, 119–121

Kennebec Arsenal, 8

Keyes, Chaplain Charles B., 9th New York Cavalry, 249, 250

Kinsley, Captain Frederick R., 39th Massachusetts, 161, 162, 249 n., 258, 291, 293

Latouche, Lieutenant John, adjutant, Libby Prison, 251, 257

Leavitt, Major Arch D., 16th Maine, 81, 96, 109, 110, 119, 121, 126, 127, 140, 149

Lee, General Robert E., 116, 134, 180

Lee's [Fitzhugh] cavalry, 88 n.

Leighton, Benjamin F., 285

Leonard, Chaplain Henry C., 3d Maine, 32

Leonard, Colonel Samuel H., 13th Massachusetts, 93, 94, 100, 124, 126, 135

Leonard's brigade, 68, 124, 132, 133–134

Libby Prison, 126, 146, 157–158, 159 ff., 170, 178, 180, 249 ff., 259, 262, 269, 287

Lincoln, Abraham, 50, 50–51, 82, 84, 175, 182, 267, 270, 271, 271 n., 272, 280

Litchfield, Captain Julius B., 4th Maine, 280

Lockwood, General Henry H., 147, 148

Lockwood's division, 147, 148

Lord, Lieutenant Joseph O., 16th Maine, 109; captain, 16th Maine, 161, 170, 178, 249, 249 n., 255 n., 273, 281, 284, 292, 294, 295

Lowe, Charles W., 3d Maine, 6, 8, 24

Lowell, Lieutenant Oliver H., 16th Maine, 50, 58; captain, 16th Maine, 102, 124–125

Lucore, Lieutenant Moses W., 190th Pennsylvania, 284

Lyle, Colonel Peter C., 90th Pennsylvania, 67, 106, 106 n., 109, 120, 133–134, 139

Lyle's brigade, 62, 63, 66, 68, 109, 120, 134, 135, 138, 139, 140, 141, 143, 147, 150, 152, 154

McClellan, Captain Carswell, assistant adjutant-general, 4th Division, 5th Corps, Army of the Potomac, 251, 252, 252 n.

McClellan, General George B., 25, 26, 43, 48, 50, 51, 53, 57, 130, 146, 175, 267, 270, 271, 271 n.

McClellan, Major Henry B., assistant adjutant-general and chief of staff, cavalry corps, Army of Northern Virginia, 251

McClellan's army, 26, 42, 44, 46, 48

McCoy, Colonel Thomas F., 107th Pennsylvania, 120

McDowell, General Irvin, 15, 16, 17, 19, 20, 23, 25; quoted, 19

McDowell's army, 15, 25, 26

McFadden, Michael, 3d Maine, 29

McGraw, Lieutenant Michael L., 24th
    New York Cavalry, 174, 273, 276
Mahone, General William, 156
Maine troops: artillery—*2d Battery*
    (Hall's), 1st Mounted, 63, 64, 65, 67,
    72, 91; *5th Battery* (Stevens'), 1st
    Mounted, 99 n.; *1st Regiment,*
    Heavy, and its record loss in one en-
    gagement near Spotsylvania, 143; in-
    fantry—*2d Regiment,* leaving home,
    7, 7 n.; at Washington, 12; *3d Regi-
    ment,* recruited, 4, 4 n.; organized,
    7 n., 8, 8 n.; leaving Maine, 10, 10
    n.; at Boston, 10; at New York, 11,
    11 n.; at Baltimore, 11; at Washing-
    ton, 11; at Meridian Hill, Washing-
    ton, 12–14; near Alexandria, 14–18;
    in advance on Manassas, 18–21; in
    Bull Run battle, 21–23; in retreat, 23–
    25; again near Alexandria, 25–33;
    in Fredericksburg battle, 67; Com-
    pany E, 42; G, 4, 5, 6, 7, 28; H, 4,
    6, 7, 28, 42; I, 42; K, 42; *4th Regi-
    ment,* near Alexandria, 15, 16; in Bull
    Run battle, 21; after Bull Run, 25;
    assigned to Sedgwick's brigade, 30;
    5th Regiment, near Alexandria, 15,
    16; in Bull Run battle, 21, 22; after
    Bull Run, 25; *13th Regiment,* being
    raised, 32; *16th Regiment,* being
    raised, 35, 35 n., 35–40; organized,
    40; leaving Maine, 41; in defenses
    of Washington, 41–43; in Antietam
    campaign, 44–47; near Sharpsburg,
    47–52; marching south, 52–54;
    called "Blanket Brigade," 49, 49 n.,
    54; near Rappahannock Station, 54–
    57; in Fredericksburg campaign, 57–
    72; in Fredericksburg battle, 63–72;
    in camp near Fletcher's Chapel, 72–
    77; in "Mud March," 77–79; in
    camp again, 79–82; in Chancellors-
    ville campaign, 82–93; in Chancel-
    lorsville battle, 86–87, 91–92; in camp
    near White Oak Church, 93; in Get-
    tysburg campaign, 94–109; in Get-
    tysburg battle, 98–107, 99–101 n., 99
    n., 101 n., 102 n., 104 n.; marching south

again, 109–111; in marches known as
    the "Culpeper-Centreville Express,"
    116; in camp near Liberty, 116; in pur-
    suit of some of Mosby's men, 117;
    in Mine Run campaign, 117–119; in
    camp near Kelly's Ford, 119–121; again
    on the march, 121; in camp near
    Mitchell's Station, 121–127; in Wil-
    derness-Petersburg campaign, 130–
    151; in trenches at Petersburg, 151–
    154; in Weldon Railroad battle,
    154–155; in camp near Black's and
    White's Station, 180; on return
    march through Virginia, 180–181; in
    grand review at Washington, 181–
    182; return of, to Maine, 182–183;
    last march of, as a regiment, 183;
    make-up and reputation of, 199; *20th
    Regiment,* at Mine Run, 119
Major, Mrs., 127
Manassas, advance on, 18 ff.
Manchester, Virginia, 157, 160, 162, 180,
    254, 258
Manchester, William, Jr., 16th Maine,
    136, 138
Manning, Lieutenant William C., 2d
    Massachusetts Cavalry, 266, 266 n.
Mansfield, General Joseph K. F., 11
Marston, Captain Daniel W., 16th
    Maine, 36, 37, 102
Maryland, feminine chivalry of, 45–
    46; youth of, 46
Maryland brigade, 131, 139
Masked batteries, 18, 19, 28
Massachusetts troops: artillery—*1st
    Regiment,* Heavy, 41; infantry—*6th
    Regiment,* 11, 11 n.; *12th Regiment,*
    44, 54 n., 66, 72, 91; *13th Regiment,*
    47, 82, 82 n., 91, 93, 99–101 n.; *39th
    Regiment,* 121
Mathews, Lieutenant Thomas L., ad-
    jutant, 2d Maryland, 111, 295
Mattocks, Major Charles P., 17th Maine,
    commanding 1st United States
    Sharpshooters, 280, 280 n.
Maxfield, Dwight, adjutant's clerk, 16th
    Maine, 50, 50 n., 76, 77; sergeant-
    major, 16th Maine, 198

Meade, Captain George, aide-de-camp to General Meade, 118, 118 n.
Meade, General George G., 97, 99–101 n., 103 n., 116, 125, 130, 131
Meade's division, 62, 64, 65
Meridian Hill, Washington, 12, 12 n., 14
Middleburg, Virginia, 111, 111 n.
Militia muster of the 'forties, 1 ff.
Mine exploded at Petersburg, 154
Mine Run campaign, 117–119, 119 n.
Mitchell's Station, camp of 16th Maine at, 123 ff.
Morrill, Lot M., 9 n., 37, 37 n., 277
Mosby, Captain John S., Partisan Rangers, 117, 117 n.
Mose, servant, 124
Mount Vernon, Maine, 1, 1 n., 2, 35
Mount Vernon, plantation, 28–29, 29 n.
Mower, Wilbur F., 16th Maine, 152
"Mud March," 77–78
"Muggers," 165, 258
Mulford, Lieutenant-Colonel John E., United States agent of exchange, 283, 284

Negroes' singing, 95–96
New Jersey troops: infantry—22d Regiment, 91–92; 29th Regiment, 91–92
New York, 11
New York Herald, 153; quoted, 249 n.
New York troops: infantry—38th Regiment, 30; 40th Regiment, 30; 83d Regiment, 44; 94th Regiment, 58, 72, 86, 93, 97, 147; 97th Regiment, 66, 72; 104th Regiment, 58, 87, 91; 105th Regiment, 58
Newton, Captain Henry C., 93d New York, 279, 282, 284, 290, 292
Newton, General John, 103, 103 n., 111 n.; quoted, 126
Nordquist, Surgeon Charles J., medical director, 2d Division, 1st Corps, 55, 55 n.
North Anna River, fighting near the, 144–146
Nye, Joshua, 4, 4 n.

Oakland, Maine. See West Waterville
"Old Hundredth," 145, 145 n., 153
O'Neal's brigade, 101 n.
Ord's corps, 257 n.
Otis, Benjamin F., 254, 256, 290
Ould, Robert, Confederate States agent of exchange, 254, 254 n., 255, 276, 283

Palmer, Charles F., 16th Maine, 136
Palmer, Surgeon Gideon S., 3d Maine, 26
Parker, Governor Joel, of New Jersey, 83
Partridge, Charles K., chief clerk, adjutant-general's office, Maine, 35
Patriotism and practicality, 199–200
Paul, General Gabriel R., 94, 100
Paul's brigade, 91, 93, 99–101 n., 108
Peabody, George, 16th Maine, 110
Peace commission, 284, 284 n.
Peirson, Lieutenant-Colonel Charles L., 39th Massachusetts, 121
Pender's division, 107
Pendleton, George H., 175
Pennsylvania troops: artillery—Battery B (Cooper's), 1st Light, 99 n.; infantry—11th Regiment, 44, 93 n., 102; 88th Regiment, 66, 72, 99–101 n.; 90th Regiment, 140; 107th Regiment, 58, 91; 136th Regiment, 61
Petersburg, Virginia, 151, 152, 156, 157, 249, 249 n.
Petersburg, fighting near, 151–154
Pickett, General George E., 102 n.
Pickett's division, 107
Pierce, Frank, 8
"Pleyel's Hymn," 153, 153 n.
Plumer, General Arthur, 9, 9 n.
Plumer, Sedgwick, 277
Plummer, Lieutenant Lincoln K., 16th Maine, 109
Pope, General John, 42, 43
Pope's army, 42, 43
Porter, Captain Byron, assistant adjutant-general, 3d Division, 5th Corps, 285
Portland, Maine, 10, 112, 115, 116

Prescott, Lieutenant Royal B., 13th New Hampshire, quoted, 288 n.

Presidential election in Prison No. 3, Danville, Virginia, 175, 267

Prey, Colonel Gilbert G., 104th New York, 140, 285–286

Prisoners of war: experiences of, in Libby Prison, Richmond, Virginia, 157–161, 177–178, 249–258; on the way from Richmond to Salisbury, North Carolina, 162–164, 258; in Salisbury stockade, 164–168, 258–261; in Prison No. 3, Danville, Virginia, 168–177, 169 n., 261–287; reflections on Confederate soldiers' thoughts of, 201

Pullen, Frank D., 3d Maine, 4, 26–27, 27 n.

Putnam, Lieutenant George H., adjutant, 176th New York, quoted, 266 n.

Raid for sheep at Mine Run, 119, 119 n.

Randall, Emma Jane, 286

Rapidan River, night search for, 89–90

Raulston, Colonel William C., 24th New York Cavalry, 176, 280, 281

Readfield Corner, Maine, 1, 1 n., 36

Recruits, 4–8, 38–39, 147–148

Red Badge of Courage, The, 185

Regimental character, 199

Reminiscences of the Civil War [General John B. Gordon's], 201

Reynolds, General John F., 50, 51, 89, 91, 97, 98

Reynolds' corps, 60, 61, 62, 84, 86, 93 n., 98; under Doubleday, 102

Richards, Lieutenant Lewis G., 16th Maine, 136

Richardson, Albert D., New York *Tribune* correspondent, 202

Richardson, Frank, 123

Richmond, Virginia, 157, 159–160, 161, 178, 180, 287

Richmond *Dispatch,* 161

Richmond *Enquirer,* 153, 161, 251, 255, 269

Richmond *Examiner,* 254

Richmond *Whig,* 257, 280

Ricker, James F., 3d Maine, 4, 27–28

Ricketts' division, 41, 47 n.

Ridgeville, Maryland, 44–45; tea at, 45–46

Roath, Captain Emanuel D., 107th Pennsylvania, 290

Robert, servant, 124

Roberts, R. F., 16

Robinson, General John C., 80, 83, 85, 87, 88 n., 89, 91, 99–101 n., 100, 101, 126, 136, 199

Robinson's division, 85 n., 98, 99–101 n., 130, 135, 136

Root, Colonel Adrian R., 94th New York, 58, 60, 61, 64, 64 n., 65, 66, 67, 68, 69, 72, 80, 87, 89, 91, 93, 100; quoted, 72 n.

Root's brigade, 57–58, 63, 67, 85, 86, 92, 93

Rose, Colonel Thomas E., 77th Pennsylvania, 159

Rose's tunnel, 159, 159 n.

Rosengarten, Major Joseph G., aide-de-camp to General Reynolds, quoted, 47 n.

Ross, Erastus W., chief clerk, Libby Prison, 158

Ruggles, Major D. Colden, paymaster, 281, 286

Sage, Lieutenant Edward R., 144th Ohio, 161, 170, 251, 255 n., 256

Salisbury, North Carolina, military prison at, 164 ff., 169, 258, 258 n., 261, 264, 274, 275, 285, 285 n.

Sampson, Mrs. Charles A. L., nurse, 26, 26 n., 33

Savannah, fall of, 282, 282 n.

Scott, Mrs., 15

Scott, General Winfield, 17, 25, 28

Sedgwick, General John, 30–31, 33, 126, 137, 195

Sedgwick's brigade, 30; corps, 84, 137

Sellers, Major Alfred J., 90th Pennsylvania, 99–101 n.

Shaver, old, of Readfield, 3

Shea, John, principal musician, 16th Maine, 83, 122–123

Sheridan, General Philip H., 146, 195, 261, 261 n., 280 n.

Sherman, General William T., 253 n., 277, 277 n., 282 n.

Shooter's Hill, near Alexandria, 15

Sickles' corps, 84, 86

Sickness in the army, 186–189

Sinks, 198

Sloan, Captain Benjamin P., 2d Pennsylvania Cavalry, 254

Small, Abner, 1, 1 n., 254

Small, Mrs. Abner, 263, 273, 284

Small, Abner R.: born, Gardiner, Maine, 1 n.; recruit, Company G, 3d Maine, 4, 4 n.; corporal, 3d Maine, 7; sergeant, 3d Maine, 15, 16, 31; appointed sergeant-major, 13th Maine, 32; transfer to 13th Maine refused, 33; named on detail for recruiting service in Maine, 33; sergeant-major of post, headquarters, volunteer recruiting service, Maine, 34; authorized to raise a company for the 16th Maine, 35; 1st lieutenant, 35, 35 n.; appointed adjutant, 16th Maine, 36; busied in raising of the regiment, 36–37, 36 n., 38–40; acting aide-de-camp to brigade commander in the battle of Fredericksburg 60, 64 n.; mentioned for gallantry, 72 n.; on reconnaissance in the battle of Chancellorsville, 87–89, 88 n.; acting assistant adjutant-general of brigade in the battle of Gettysburg, 103; mentioned for services, 103 n.; named on detail for recruiting service in Maine, 110; apprehending deserters and taking arrested deserters to forts in Portland and Boston harbors, 112–116; taken prisoner in the battle of the Weldon Railroad, 155; major, 16th Maine, 179; in command of regiment, 180–181; in grand review, Washington, 181–182, 182 n.; quoted, 47 n., 50 n., 99–101 n., 102 n., 141 n., 173 n., 249 n.

Small, Emilus N. D., 35, 35 n.; first sergeant, Company A, 16th Maine, 75

Small, Emma Sedgwick, 284

Smith, Lieutenant-Colonel Robert C., commanding military prisons at Danville, Virginia, 169, 176, 177, 272, 273, 275, 276, 281

Smith, son of Governor William, of Virginia, 268, 268 n.

Smith's [William F.] corps, 60, 61, 62

Soldier: in battle, 184, 185; philosophy of, 186; loyalty and knowingness of, 186; and sickness, 187–188; as growler, 188–189; as grumbler, 189; portrait of, 192–193; a composite, 193; education of, 193–195; heroes of, 195; on the march, 196

Sons of Maine, 11

Southern noncombatant victims of war, 127–128, 200–201

Southern soldiers, humanity of, 202

Spotsylvania Court House, 135, 141, 149; fighting near, 135–143

Sprague, Lieutenant-Colonel Homer B., 13th Connecticut, 264, 285–286

Springfield musket, 190–191

Stanton, Edwin M., 278, 278 n.

Staples, Major Henry G., 3d Maine, 9, 15, 29 n.; colonel, 3d Maine, 31, 32, 33

Staples, Mrs. Henry G., 33

Stevens, Sergeant-Major Edwin C., 16th Maine, 127, 151

Stevens, John L., Maine politician, 37, 37 n.

Stevens, Captain William A., 16th Maine, 151

Stevens' [Greenleaf T.] battery, 99 n.

Stewart, Captain James, 146th Pennsylvania, 174, 266, 285, 291, 293

Stoneman's corps, 67

"Stovepipe artillery," 29–30, 29 n.

Stragglers, in the battle of the Wilderness, 133

Sumner's grand division, 60, 61, 69

"Superior officer be damned!" 195–196

Taliaferro, James, 73–74, 75

Taliaferro, the Misses Betty and Sally, 74, 75

Taylor, General Nelson, 51, 55, 66, 67, 72, 80

Taylor's brigade, 51, 57, 62, 63, 65, 66, 68

Thompson, Captain Isaac H., 16th Maine, 43, 78

Tibbetts, forager, 16th Maine, 52, 78

Tidd, Lieutenant Luke R., 39th Massachusetts, 161, 249 n.

Tilden, Lieutenant Charles W., 2d Maine, 7; lieutenant-colonel, 16th Maine, 40–41, 41, 43, 46, 50, 59, 60, 65, 72; colonel, 16th Maine, 80, 83, 99–101 n., 99, 101, 101 n., 102, 102 n., 108, 127, 139, 142, 149, 152, 159, 163, 180, 182, 200–201, 202, 249, 249 n., 254, 259, 259 n.; quoted, 102 n., 155 n.

Trull, Captain Ezra J., 39th Massachusetts, 293

Tucker, Lieutenant-Colonel Isaac N., 3d Maine, 9, 15; quartermaster, 16th Maine, 40

Turner, Corporal, Prison No. 3, Danville, Virginia, 282

Turner, Richard R., turnkey, Libby Prison, Richmond, Virginia, 160, 169, 257, 261, 261 n.

Turner, Major Thomas P., commanding military prisons at Richmond, Virginia, 157, 160, 169, 250, 250 n., 252, 264 n.

Turner, Lieutenant William T., Partisan Rangers, 117 n.

Tyler, General Robert C., 143

Tyler's [Daniel] division, 20

Vermont troops: infantry—*2d Regiment*, 15, 21

Vienna, Maine, 1, 1 n., 35

Visitors in camp, 76–77

Wadsworth's division, 84, 91, 131

Waldron, Captain William H., 16th Maine, 54, 73, 92, 99

War correspondents, 190, 202

Warren, General Gouverneur K., 126, 131, 139, 141, 147, 195, 195 n.

Warren's corps, 126, 130, 137, 141, 142, 144–145, 147, 148, 149, 154

Washburn, Captain Henry N., 13th Massachusetts, 149

Washburn, Governor Israel, Jr., of Maine, 4 n., 7 n., 9, 9 n., 32, 35, 36, 37, 37 n.

Washington, D.C., 11, 12; appearance of, 13, 13 n.; defenses of, 25, 26, 43

Washington, George, 28, 124

Waterville, Maine, 4, 4 n., 7

Watkins, scout, 249, 290

Weldon Railroad, battle of the, 154–155

West Waterville (now Oakland), Maine, 4, 4 n., 6, 7

Wheelock, Colonel Charles, 97th New York, 72

Whipple, General Amiel W., 41

White, Charles, 115–116

White Oak Bridge, 150

White Oak Church, 92, 93

Whitehouse, Captain Stephen C., 16th Maine, 98, 99

Whitman, Jones, 16th Maine, 110

Wiggin, Lieutenant Francis, 16th Maine, 136, 146; quoted, 36 n., 102 n.

Wilderness, the, 86 n., 92 n., 117, 119, 131, 143; battle of, 131–134

Wildes, Colonel Asa W., 16th Maine, 36, 40, 46, 49, 50, 75

Williams, Captain Charles A., 16th Maine, 53

Williams, General Seth, 47, 47 n.

Wilson, Major Thomas J., paymaster, 288

Winter quarters, 30, 75–76, 81, 119–120, 123

Wisconsin troops: artillery—*1st Regiment*, Heavy, 41

"Worm castles," 51

Worth, Benjamin F., 16th Maine, 108

Wounded soldiers: at Bull Run, 21; at Fredericksburg, 68; at Gettysburg, 107–108

Wyman, William W., 3d Maine, 4

Yeaton, William N., 16th Maine, 99